# THE IRISH PEARL

# The Irish pearl

## A cultural, social and economic history

John Lucey

First published in 2005
Wordwell Ltd
PO Box 69, Bray, Co. Wicklow
Copyright © The author

Cover design: Rachel Dunne, Alicia McAuley


ISBN-10: 1-905569-01-7
ISBN-13: 978-1-905569-01-4


British Library Cataloguing-in-Publication Data.
A catalogue record for this book is available from the British Library.


This publication has received support from the Heritage Council under the 2005 Publications Grant Scheme.


Typeset in Ireland by Wordwell Ltd.

Editor: Alicia McAuley.

Book design: Nick Maxwell, Alicia McAuley.

All photographs by the author unless otherwise stated.

Printed by Graficas Castuera, Pamplona.

Necklace of pearls collected from the rivers of County Tyrone *c.* 1890 (Welch Collection, Ulster Museum).

# Contents

# Preface

An interest in the biology and distribution of the pearl mussel in Ireland has spawned a project on the history of the gem it produces. Pearl fishing may have an exotic ring to it, but a number of rivers in the Emerald Isle were formerly celebrated for their pearls and some of these at one time supported a small industry. It is apparent that the exploitation of native pearls is a neglected aspect of Irish cultural, economic and social history, and that is what the book sets out to rectify. The study reveals that freshwater pearls have been taken at 46 locations in 21 counties. They have been exploited in all four provinces, but particularly in Ulster: they have been found in all the counties of Northern Ireland. Pearl fishing has survived as a tradition right down to the present, albeit at a low level of activity, and pearls have even become incorporated into the folklore and legend of some districts.

While references from before then have been used, it is the sources of literature, both primary and secondary, from the seventeenth century and onwards that were consulted in order to gain a useful understanding of the history of pearls in Ireland. It is from that century, when interest in their exploitation was greatest, that the most informative material is available on native pearls. From contemporary newspapers, magazines and journals it has been possible to give a chronological account of the fishing methods used throughout the country over four centuries.

It seems clear that pearl fishing was always a casual occupation over the summer months and that specimen pearls were sold up the social and economic chain. The trade would have been stimulated by the development of the cash economy which was so noticeable in Ulster in the seventeenth century. The holding of the assizes twice yearly at a venue in each county provided an ideal opportunity to offer specimens for sale to the gentry. Although overfishing would have damaged prospects in the short term, stocks would have regenerated over a period of years. Water pollution, however, would have posed a more dangerous threat.

It has to be admitted that it is difficult to take the industry seriously in strict economic terms. Based on the estimates that only about one mussel in a hundred contained a pearl, and that only one per cent of these was of any value as a jewel, it is easy to see that, like the marine pearl fisheries, success depended on large stocks of the raw material.

By tracing the position of the pearl in myth, history, commerce, science, the arts and literature of Ireland, as well as through communication with those previously or still involved in pearl fishing, a considerable body of information has been gathered. Thus, a wide range of sources has been used in this book to describe the history of pearls in Ireland and to develop the theme that the native trade, though it failed to become a significant national industry, was of local importance.

This book started life as a thesis (Lucey 1997), and special thanks are due to Mr J. McAllister and the late Mr D. Johnson of the Queen's University of Belfast for their faith in a project whose subject matter did not appear in standard historical textbooks. Mr J. Fairleigh of the Institute of Irish Studies gave initial advice for which he is thanked, and I am very grateful to Dr W. Crawford for his constructive criticism of the original manuscript.

The various libraries in Britain and Ireland visited during the study are acknowledged, with special thanks due to the Local Studies Department of the Western Education and Library Board in Omagh. Ms. D. O'Farrell, Dunmanway Library Service, Mr D.W. Riley, John Rylands Library, University of Manchester and Mr C. Hurst, Bodleian Library, University of Oxford, also provided useful information.

Thanks are also due to Ms. B. Flynn, Department of Irish Folklore, University College, Dublin, for her assistance in searching the archives, and to the late Prof. F.X. Martin for access to Brigid Pike's thesis. Mr P. Connolly, National Archives, Dublin, Dr L.R. Atherton, Public Record Office, London, and Ms. A. McClintock, Public Record Office of Northern Ireland, Belfast, are thanked for their helpful advice.

The following provided illustrations for which I am grateful for permission to reproduce: Mr N. McCormick; Revd Dr D. Murray; the Department of the Environment, Heritage and Local Government; the Office of Public Works; the National Museum of Ireland; the National Gallery of Ireland; the National Portrait Gallery, London; Banbridge District Council; Dr H. Chesney, Ulster Museum; the British Library; the Board and Trustees of Trinity College, Dublin; and a very gracious lady in County Wexford who wishes to remain anonymous, for allowing me to photograph her beautiful necklace of Slaney pearls.

Special thanks are due to two Scottish jewellers, Cairncross of Perth and Hamilton & Inches of Edinburgh, for generous information. It is a pity that the same cannot be said of some of their Irish counterparts, who were largely indifferent or unhelpful.

To the pearl fishermen, particularly Mr J. McGrath, Mr N. McCormick and Mr E. Chesters, who generously provided useful information based on their personal experiences, I am grateful. Special thanks are also due to the late Mgr P.J. Hamell and Fr John Chrysostom (O'Mahony) OFM Cap., for their translations of Latin texts, and to Ms. R. Shortall for help with German translations. Dr M.J. Costello, Dr E. Moorkens and Mr D.T. Quigley also provided information which was very helpful to the project.

Finally, I would like to thank Mr R. Ó Floinn for advice on publishing and, of course, the Heritage Council for providing a grant towards the cost of printing the book.

J.L.
Kilkenny
October 2004

# Introduction

…there are in this islande…such store of pearle & other rich stones…as nature seemed to have framed this countrey for the storehouse or jewelhouse of hir chiefest tresaure…

*Raphael Holinshed, The historie of Irelande* (1577, 72)

Freshwater pearls were known to the Chinese by the beginning of the first millennium BC (Clark 1986, 80) and were exploited from before Roman times in northern Britain. Indeed, if Suetonius (1692, 35) (a chronicler of affairs who wrote in the early part of the second century AD) is to be believed, pearls were one of the factors that helped to persuade Julius Caesar to invade Britain in 55 BC. It is said that the first river pearls from the United States were discovered in 1857 (Taburiaux 1985, 59) but Native Americans had long known of these and used them for personal adornment. For example, in the funeral mounds of Hopewell Indians in Ohio, dating from the early centuries AD, freshwater pearl necklaces have been found (Ward 1985, 221). The gemmologist Fred Ward (1995, 3), believes that the first pearls used as gems came from freshwater mussels as, without boats or equipment, primitive food gatherers must have found those molluscs much easier to obtain than oysters.

It has been intimated by Charles O'Conor (1814, xvii) that even in prehistory the Phoenicians traded with the ancient Irish, exchanging the secrets of producing purple (Tyrian) dye from the juice of shellfish for native Irish pearls. The earliest written reference to pearls in Ireland apparently comes from the ninth-century Welsh writer Nennius (831, 198) in his *Historia Britonum*. He refers to Loch Lein (Lough Leane) in Kerry, where he says they are found, and that kings wear them in their ears. They are also mentioned in passing in the commentary to the *Senchus mór*, the ancient law tracts which were revised and written down following the introduction of Christianity. But a poor translation of the passage into English (Anon. 1865, 2), by probably the most eminent historian of his time, did nothing to stimulate interest in native pearls by any other writer.

Pearls were used from an early time in decoration, particularly of religious ornaments, but many items were apparently lost in the marauding Viking raids of the eighth to tenth centuries. It has been said that Ireland had a flourishing 'golden age' while the rest of Europe was enveloped by the Dark Ages.

Whether there is any basis in fact for this has been questioned (e.g., Ó Cróinín 1995, 196) but certainly many artefacts were taken by the Norsemen. Earlier historians and poets have described the brief reign of Brian Boru (Brian Bóraime) as the 'golden age' of their country (e.g., Wright *c.* 1850, 51; Haverty 1867, 134). This period has been epitomized by the poet Thomas Moore, who wrote, 'rich and rare were the gems she wore', to signify that at that time a young woman bedecked with jewels could walk the land unmolested. Pearls were definitely in currency in the late eleventh or early twelfth century in Ireland, as will be seen from a record of the time, and in the following two centuries they were used to decorate the vestments of clergy and nobles. In the fifteenth and sixteenth centuries pearls were much used in ecclesiastical decorations such as missal bindings, rosaries and mitres, and there are surviving Irish examples from that period.

Pearls were apparently used lavishly in personal decoration by the Anglo-Norman women of Geraldine Ireland, as contemporary paintings show. We do not know what treasures, including pearls, were lost when the armies of Henry VIII and Edward VI looted the monasteries, but some which were hidden survived and were found by later generations. They are mentioned in the official correspondence of the late sixteenth century during the wars in Munster. The official and other state papers relating to Ireland, while initially prompting further investigation, have proved only fragmentary as a source of material relating to pearls. In some cases calendars and summaries were the only evidence from which to work, as the originals of those of interest had invariably been destroyed in the fire at the Four Courts in Dublin in 1922. Thus, in the present context the following lamentation, with its comparison between the loss of the actual treasures and that of the destroyed recorded information, is doubly apt (Macalister 1925, 23):

> We cannot tell what treasures, artistic or literary, were lost when the Scandinavian pirates raided our shores a thousand years ago. We cannot tell what we lost when the emissaries of Henry VIII and Edward VI looted the monasteries four hundred years ago. But we know that the wanton hand which fired the Record Office inflicted on the heart and soul of Ireland the heaviest blow that foe ever struck on her.

From the sixteenth century, there are some references to the occurrence of pearls in West Munster in the correspondence to London of the military campaigners. Similarly, in the following century visitors such as Thomas Dingley, or Dineley (Shirley 1860, 143), the English schoolmaster, traveller and antiquary who visited Ireland between 1675 and 1680, mention pearls in passing. In the eighteenth century their occurrence is noted in various topographical and chorographical works. It can be said that while references from before then do exist, one must turn to the literature sources, both primary and secondary, from the seventeenth century onwards in order to gain any useful idea of the history of pearls in Ireland. It is from that century, when interest in their exploitation was greatest, that the most informative material is available on native pearls.

Pearls have been used in Ireland for a very long period, for personal decoration and ornamentation as well as for medicinal and other purposes. The shells from which they came were also utilized, as spoons or scoops and as a dressing on base-poor soils. The uses of pearls in Ireland and in its main market, Britain, will be examined in this book to determine demand for them down through the ages. The study will, however, not only be from the utilitarian standpoint but will also have among its aims an examination of the history of pearls in Ireland from a sociological and cultural point of view.

There is a dearth of information regarding the numbers of people who fished for pearls either professionally or on a part-time basis, and no attempt has been made to quantify these; an estimate has, however, been made by others for the British Isles as a whole for a particular year in the first decade of the twentieth century. With regard to the price of pearls, the data are somewhat sketchy, but sufficient to estimate the general value to the finder as well as on the retail markets over some 350 years of trading. Unfortunately, a large archive of one jeweller's company papers, extending back some 200 years, which would have been an invaluable source of pearl prices, was destroyed during relocation of the firm's premises.

Because of what has come down to us in the way of source material, the nature of the topic does not immediately lend itself to systematic quantitative analyses and so will be treated in what might be called the older tradition of scholarship, based on literary evidence and unsystematic data in the main. But this, it is proposed, will nonetheless yield meaningful conclusions. Because the subject matter of the book has been poorly treated in the more formal documents on which historians usually rely, the inclusion of literary evidence is justified. In the context of social history, the extent to which pearls have entered into the mythology, folklore, superstition and religious symbolism of the culture will be explored. It will be proffered as a theory that, because of incorrect or poor translations from Latin and Gaelic, pearls may not have received the attention they deserve in the annals of history, nor indeed as a natural resource. What appears to be a bias against pearls by some nineteenth-century writers may in fact be attributed to the fact that they were sceptical that Ireland produced pearls at all, but this is no excuse for poor or (in one case deliberately) incorrect translations.

Contemporary newspapers, magazines and journals give accounts of pearl fishing, reporting on when and where good pearls were found. These deal largely with pearls as a curiosity and generally offer little regarding the economic significance of their exploitation as a commodity. There are, however, good contemporary accounts of the fishing methods that were used throughout the country and it has thus been possible to give a chronological account of these spanning a 300-year period in four centuries.

The older Irish literature, in Latin and Gaelic, as well as that written in English on the subject of pearls has been perused. By tracing the position of the pearl in myth, history, commerce, science, the arts and literature of Ireland, as well as through communication with those previously or still involved in pearl fishing, a considerable body of information has been gathered. Information was canvassed, with some little success, from those engaged in fishing for pearls and those involved in their sale on the retail market, both in Ireland and Scotland (where the largest market for freshwater pearls in these islands exists) and has been used to supplement historical data and to gauge the present level of exploitation.

Because Ireland and Britain are so closely linked, any discussion on Irish pearls would have to include reference to the neighbouring island. This book will make a comparison with the fisheries in Britain, particularly Scotland, and also with those of the rest of Europe in an effort to gauge the status and importance of the Irish pearl fisheries within a wider context. In the eastern rivers of North America the same species of mussel as occurs in Ireland furnished pearls, especially in the nineteenth century, and a brief overview of the fisheries in the United States and Canada will be included. The available information on freshwater pearls and pearl fishing in a third continent, Asia, will also be examined.

If pearl fishing in Ireland can be likened to any other activity or industry, then it must be to the exploitation of alluvial gold. The two have many similarities in terms of the methods of exploitation as well as in the source material describing them, and will be compared and contrasted. Pearl fishing, much like panning for gold, is still prosecuted in Irish rivers at a low level of activity and the tradition is likely to be passed on to future generations, although its survival may be seen in some quarters as being threatened by new licensing procedures. The most likely outcome of the imposition of a licensing system, however, is that, as in the eighteenth century, pearl fishing will again become more clandestine.

The above sources have been used to describe the history of pearls in Ireland, and to develop the argument that the native trade, while of little national economic significance, was of local importance. Thus pearls had, in the past, some contribution to make to the social conditions of the poorer classes and were used to make profits on transactions by the middle or richer classes prior to the twentieth century. Following the discussion, a conclusion will be drawn as to the reasons why the exploitation of pearls, like the inland fisheries generally, never developed into a significant national industry.

In the first chapter, the origin of pearls as well as their distribution in Ireland will be treated to set the scene, so that a full account of their exploitation can begin.

# 1. Pearl formation and distribution

And muscles are found that breede pearles…
*Roderick O'Flaherty, A chorographical description of West or H-Iar Connaught*
(1684, 53)

Pearls are found in the soft parts of aquatic animals known scientifically as molluscs, and popularly as shellfish (Dakin 1913, 11).

*Origin of pearls*
A variety of marine molluscs inhabiting the seas around the British Isles are known to bear pearls occasionally (Fisher 1927, 233) and the common edible sea mussel, *Mytilus edulis*,[i] readily forms small seed pearls (see Figure 1.1a) which can be a problem in its marketability as food (Fernandes and Seed 1983, 107). The pearls occasionally found in the two edible oyster species occurring in Ireland, the native flat oyster (*Ostrea edulis*) and the introduced rock oyster (*Crassostrea gigas*), generally lack lustre and iridescence and are usually of little or no commercial value.

It is, in fact, a freshwater mussel which is associated with pearls of gem quality in Irish waters. As its vernacular and Latin names indicate, the freshwater pearl mussel, *Margaritifera margaritifera* (see Figure 1.1b), is a prolific pearl producer. In the Gaelic language, various names have also been used to describe the mussel including *sligane* (Dingley 1675–80, 262), *closhen* (Smith 1750, 269), *fiascán* (O'Hanlon and O'Leary 1907, 42), *sliogán néamainn* (Scharff 1916, 148), *sliogán néamhannach*, (de Bhaldraithe 1959, 517) and *diúilicín fionnuisce* (An Roinn Oideachais 1978, 94).

This mussel has an extensive range worldwide, spreading from Iceland and Lapland to Portugal and Russia, and across Siberia to Kamchatka and Japan, while in North America it reaches from Labrador and Newfoundland to Pennsylvania and from Alaska to California (Ellis 1978, 12). In Britain it is absent from the Midland Plain and the south-eastern parts of England, while in Ireland it is also largely absent from the Central Plain (Jackson 1925, 195). It is considered to be a declining species throughout its natural range in Europe and has become extinct in some areas where it was previously common, such as Lower Silesia and Poland (Collins and Wells 1987, 148). In Ireland it has declined in many parts, especially in Northern Ireland (Mackie 1992, 90) but is still widely spread in southern areas, showing greatest expression in the south-west (Lucey 1993, 308).

The pearl mussel has an interesting and complicated life cycle that includes a parasitic larval stage on salmonid fish in Irish waters (Ross 1992, 43). After a period the young mussel drops off its host and settles into a suitable substratum where it remains half buried; it is capable of movement, by means of a 'foot', but is rather sedentary. It belongs to a very ancient Cretaceous family (from *c.* 120 million years ago) and probably recolonized Irish rivers and lakes after the last glaciation, within the past 14,000 years (Chesney *et al.* 1993, 287). Generally it is the largest and longest-lived invertebrate species in its habitat; in low temperature regions it can attain a maximum lifespan of more than 130 years (Bauer 1992, 425).

*Natural pearls* Many theories on the causes of pearl formation have prevailed throughout the ages, including: flashes of lightning; the mollusc taking in dew; grains of sand; parasites; eggs of the mollusc; and shell-repair substances (Dakin 1913, 93). We shall see in chapter five that according to ancient Irish folklore, showers caused by a blacksmith's anvil being thrown through the air were responsible for pearls being sown in a lake. The theory of dew-formed pearls, believed by the ancient Chinese and Hindus, was current even among some British writers down to the close of the sixteenth century. William Camden (1551–1623), author of *Britannia*, for example, accepted that river pearls were thus formed.

The Irish poet Thomas Moore (1779–1852) was aware of the theory when, in the nineteenth century, he penned the following lines (Herbert 1876, 121):

> And precious their tears as that rain from the sky
> Which turns into pearls as it falls in the sea.

In the seventeenth century, Christopher Sandius (1674, 11) gave an account of the theory of pearl formation in the mussels of 'sweet waters' (freshwaters) in Norway and elsewhere which believed it to be due to eggs which remained in the mussel when the others had been expelled:

> But sometimes it happens, that one or two of those Eggs stick fast to the sides of the matrix, and are not voided with the rest…and they do grow, according to the length of time, into pearls of different bignesses, and imprint a mark both in the fish and the shell, by the scituation conform to its figure.

Sir Robert Redding (1693, 662), of Dublin, who had visited the pearl fishery near Omagh in 1688, believed that 'the Pearl answereth to the stone in other Animals, and certainly like that encreaseth by several Crusts growing over one another'. Oliver Goldsmith (1774, 54), in his foray into natural history, dismissed the concept of pearl formation by declaring that 'whether pearls be a disease or an accident in the animal is scarce worth enquiry. The common opinion is, that they are a kind of calculous concretion in the body of the animal, somewhat resembling a stone in the bladder, and are consequently to be considered as a disorder.' Tom Mullin (1947, 5), an experienced Ulster pearl fisherman who had collected mussels for their pearls between the two World Wars, wrote of his theory thus:

> The origin of the pearl in the shell appears to be some grit or other foreign body which irritates the mussel. In its efforts to free itself of this irritation, the mussel moves the object to the side of the shell, at the same time coating it with mother of pearl. Having got it to one side, the fish cannot get it any further and the object, now a pearl, remains there and grows larger. All good pearls come from the hinge of the shell. I cannot agree with those who hold the pearl is the result of a grain of sand getting inside the double skin, as I fail to see how even so small an object could get inside the skin.

Since at least the beginning of the twentieth century it has been known in the West that 'pearls are formed as a pathological secretion of the mineral arragonite, combined with a certain amount of organic material, formed by the oyster or other mollusc around some foreign body, whose presence forms the irritant which stimulates the secretion' (Shipley 1908, 1).

Natural pearls are globular cysts composed of numerous thin, concentric layers around a nucleus of sand or small parasite. They consist (Taburiaux 1985, 109) largely of calcium carbonate as aragonite crystals (91.72%), as well as organic material called conchiolin (5.94%), a small amount of water (2.23%) and other substances (0.11%).

Irregularly shaped pearls are known as 'baroques' and are usually formed when a grain of sand or some other hard foreign substance is accidentally forced into the mantle cavity of the mollusc, whereupon the bivalve walls off the intruded matter against the inside of the shell and adds to the wall, layer after layer, the smooth coating which reduces the irritation (Bartsch 1968, 26).

*Cultured pearls* Attempts at copying the process of natural pearl formation have long exercised the minds of men. The first serious attempts apparently date from the twelfth century, when the Chinese devised a method wherein various shaped objects—mostly images of Buddha—were placed in the mussel. It was not until the twentieth century (*c.* 1920), however, that the technique was perfected, in Japan, using pearl oysters (Cipriani and Borelli 1986, 276).

Linnaeus (Carl von Linné (1707–78), the Swedish naturalist and progenitor of modern biological nomenclature) has been credited with developing a method to induce river mussels to produce pearls, apparently by drilling a hole in the shells. For this he was said to have been ennobled[ii] and received a pension from the state (Brown 1836, 78). Frank Buckland (1875, 395), who was Inspector of Salmon Fisheries for England and Wales, related how experiments were tried by one John Hunter in 1787 to force 'Scotch river mussels to form pearls after the manner of the Chinese experiment' by putting an extraneous body in the shell of live mussels.

Experiments by Irish pearlers to cultivate pearls resulted in failure. Tom Mullin (1947, 8), who had fished the Strule in County Tyrone for 30 years, explained how objects, including small pearls, were inserted into living mussels and left in the river. On opening the shells again after two years, however, it would be found that the pearls were only coated on one side.

*Pearl improvement* A process called skinning was sometimes employed by the fishers, whereby pearls of poor lustre can be much improved by removing outer layers or skins. Tom Mullin (1947, 5) once found a large pearl of 22 grains which appeared to be of no value, but when he had carefully removed a layer he had a fine pearl of 18 grains which sold for £25. In the seventeenth century at the Bann pearl fishery, those of a darker hue were immersed in a vat of hot lime, which was alleged to bleach out the colour a little (Robb 1939, 6).

In the nineteenth century, Robert Garner (1873, 426–28) carried out various experiments with British pearls. He had hoped to introduce the small pearls of the edible sea mussel into live river mussels, but was unable to carry out the trials. He did, however, make attempts at improving such pearls:

> We have made a few experiments in the last direction; and though we have not made our fortune or taken out a patent, we have found that they really may be improved by chemical means, some made quite ornamental. The method we have tried is boiling the pearls for a short time in a dilute solution of potash and afterwards letting them remain in it for a few days, noting that a very strong solution destroys their lustre instead of increasing it. These inferior pearls have been collected for sale for many years in the Lower Conway [Wales]; and we think it possible that they are afterwards submitted to some such process.

Some more fanciful ways of improving pearls had reportedly been used in earlier times. French pearl specialist Jean Taburiaux (1985, 62), whose work has been translated into English, says that a chronicler of the sixteenth century, Francis Reues, explained how when dull pearls taken from a river near the Vosges mountains were forcibly fed to pigeons, they emerged pure and shining. Thomas Moore was aware of the similar notion that doves could polish pearls, which he attributed to *De rerum varietate* by the Italian philosopher Cardanus (1501–76), as can be seen in Moore's own writing (Herbert 1876, 312):

Where Epicurus taught the Loves
To polish Virtue's native brightness,
Just as the beak of playful doves
Can give to pearls a smoother whiteness!

Francis Bacon (1561–1626), the English philosopher and statesman, says that there was a tradition that pearls, as well as other precious stones, which had lost their colour could be recovered if they were buried in the ground for a time (Bacon 1626, 380).

*Imitation or artificial pearls* Artificial pearls were made in Europe as early as the seventeenth century by coating the inside of hollow glass beads with a glistening white pigment obtained from fish scales and filling the beads with wax (Harry 1990, 580). They are mentioned by Charles Smith (1750, 269), the eighteenth-century Irish writer and apothecary, who quotes from *Savary's dictionary de commerce* on how they were made. The son of the Earl of Cork, Robert Boyle (1665, ii), the physicist/chemist who became famous for Boyle's Law, gave the composition of the artificial pearls made in Venice in the seventeenth century as consisting of mercury and glass.[iii]

An artificial-pearl industry was set up in Belfast after the Second World War (see Box I), in which this was the manufacturing process (Anon. 1971, 65):

All artificial pearls commence life as glass —a special glass made up in rod form and in varying colours and thickness. The first of a long series of skilled manual processes concerns the heating of the glass and the conversion of the liquid into a bead.

The next process is the complicated one of dipping. There are different mixtures according to the desired finish but the main ingredient is nitro-cellulose lacquer in which is suspended a solution of guanin. This is a material extracted from the scales of the bonito, a fish found off the shores of North America, Scandinavia and other countries. It is the blend of guanin and lacquer which gives depth and lustre to the glass bead.

Dipping varies according to quality. There are five or six dips for the lowest-priced commodity and seventeen to twenty for the more expensive pearl. Pearls are dried between dips. For tinting, colours are added to some of the dips. The making of a pearl for a necklace may take as long as seven days during which the pearl will have grown with each acquired skin. Iridising, one of the new finishes developed in the laboratory, has gained greatly in popularity because of the extra warmth and sheen it gives to the pearl.

9

---

*Box I*
## Ulster Pearls Ltd., Dunmurray

This artificial-pearl industry was established in 1946 as an offshoot of Harriman's London firm of Pompadour Products Ltd., jewellery manufacturers. The owner of the parent company and the manager, later a director, of the Belfast factory were both refugees from Nazism and the latter, Frank Kafka, had fought with the Free Czech Army.

Thousands of tiny pearls which decorated the wedding dress of Princess Elizabeth—now Queen Elizabeth—were made there, as were the many small pearls on her matching shoes. Similarly, those used to decorate the costumes of the leading players in the Bristol Old Vic's production of *Hamlet* in March 1965 came from Ulster Pearls Ltd.

It was a small industry and a large percentage of its output was exported. The produce went all over the world. New Zealand and Australia were the firm's best customers, while the United States, Canada and Portugal were also steady buyers of these Ulster-made pearls.

Ulster Pearls Ltd. filed its last accounts (to 4 April 1993) in April 1994 and applied to the Registry of Companies to be struck off the register in October 1994.

(Sources: Anon 1965a, 3; Anon 1971, 65; McCrum 1996, *in litt.* [iv])

---

Imitation or artificial pearls are cheap substitutes for the natural ones, whereas cultured varieties are naturally formed, but under controlled conditions. Today the cultured pearl has superseded the natural, although the latter is still fished for in both salt and fresh waters.

*Distribution of pearls in Ireland*
Freshwater pearls will be found wherever the pearl mussel occurs, although the quality can vary from river to river and even within the same river. Apparently the colour of the pearl depends upon the minerals in the host river and its position within the shell of the mussel (Green 1985/86, 29). We will see in chapter four that of the pearls produced in northern rivers, those from the Bann were regarded as superior to those from the Strule and Lagan. The locations where pearls have been found in Ireland are delineated in Figure 1.2 and details of these, together with the reference sources, are listed as an index to the Figure. Although it is obvious that the occurrence of pearls will be the same as that of the pearl-producing mussel, the distribution of where pearls have been found is only plotted where a reference source exists for a record.

Because the mussel principally occurs in rivers, it was from such waterbodies that the pearls were mostly taken. Lakes, because of their depth, were more difficult to fish, but there are also many records for lake pearls, for example Lough Eske (Thompson 1856, 341), Lough Fern (Milne 1907, 1), Lough Gal (Colgan 1914, 60), Lough Allua (von Hessling 1859, 188), Lough Leane (Nennius 831, 198), Lough Ree (Pike 1976, 90) and Lough Corrib (Maxwell 1832, 80).

Brigid Pike, when discussing the source of pearls sent by Bishop Gillebert of Limerick to Anselm, Archbishop of Canterbury in the twelfth century, says she saw one of 'a good three centimetres in diameter', which had been taken from Lough Ree in the 1920s (Pike 1976, 90). As she refers to a seed pearl it is likely that she meant millimetres and not centimetres—the latter would be an extraordinary size for a freshwater pearl. It is also likely that it was from the species *Anodonta cygnea*, found in the lakes of the Shannon system, rather than the usual pearl producer *Margaritifera margaritifera*, which is largely absent from the catchment,[v] that the pearl was taken.

The information with regard to the occurrence of pearls in Ulster is from a variety of sources dating from the seventeenth century to the present, while that for the other three provinces is more sketchy. Most of the information for Counties Cork and Kerry comes from two sources, Charles Smith and Friar O'Sullivan, written in the middle of the eighteenth century, although the latter was not published until 1900. The first half of the eighteenth century is almost totally lacking in information regarding Irish pearls: this point will be examined more fully later. Curiously, pearls in the lake at Killarney are mentioned in dispatches (Hamilton 1867, 232; Hamilton 1885, 124) during the Desmond Wars in the 1580s and they may have been exploited by the soldiers cantoned there.

Pearls have been found at 46 locations within the following 21 counties: Antrim, Armagh, Cavan, Clare, Cork, Donegal, Down, Fermanagh, Galway, Kerry, Kilkenny/Laois, Londonderry, Louth, Mayo, Roscommon/Westmeath, Tyrone, Waterford, Wexford and Wicklow. They have been taken in all four provinces but were more common in Ulster, having been exploited from all the counties of Northern Ireland.

The occurrence of pearls in Ireland, with few exceptions, shows a general correspondence with the maritime counties, though a concentration is found in particular areas. While occasional occurrences are reported from the east and west of the country and more inland, the regions of Ireland with the most pearl-bearing areas are, in descending order, the south-west, north-west, north-east and then the south-east. It is, however, from two northern counties in general, Down and Tyrone, and two rivers in particular, the Bann and Strule, that most pearls have been taken. Both rivers have supported pearl fisheries, but the latter has been the most enduring in Ireland. Even now pearl fishing is carried on there as a pastime or on a part-time basis.

Sometimes more than one pearl may be found in a shell. Tom Mullin (1947, 5), the Omagh pearler, found up to eight pearls in a single shell and remarked that some were good and others brown, while Thomas Pennant (1812, 163) reported that up to 16 have been found within another freshwater shell. The fishing techniques used and the methods for extracting the pearls from mussels will be outlined in the next chapter.

*Notes*

[i]Pearls collected by a lady from shoreline specimens of the common mussel (*Mytilus edulis*) in the west of Ireland in the 1930s were made into a necklace but were estimated to be of little commercial value (Quidnunc 1931, 4).

[ii]Streeter (1886, 246), however, questions whether Linnaeus was in fact raised to nobility or ever rewarded for his discovery.

[iii]Glass beads, of various colours, were manufactured in Ireland as early as the fifth or sixth century.

[iv]J. McCrum (1996) Registry of Companies, Department of Economic Development (Northern Ireland). *In litt.*, 11 April.

[v]Theodor von Hessling (1859, 188) does mention *Margaritifera margaritifera* as occurring in the Shannon in the middle of the nineteenth century.

# 2. Pearl fishing and extraction methods

> …also in some of its largest rivers, pearls of a considerable size and fine
> colour are found…
> *Caesar Otway, Sketches in Ireland* (1827, 128)

As pointed out in the introduction, pearls have been exploited in Ireland for at least eleven and a half centuries, but we do not find references to fishing methods until relatively recently. In the examples given here to describe pearl fishing in Ireland, which have been set out in a chronological order, no attempt has been made to modernize the older texts, and syntax and orthography remain unaltered.

*Fishing methods*
The earliest reference comes from a letter written in 1688 by Sir Robert Redding of Dublin to Dr Martin Lister, leading conchologist of the day and later physician to Queen Anne, on pearl fishing in the north of Ireland which he had witnessed on a visit in August of that year. Part of the letter was communicated to the Royal Society by Lister and later published. Enclosing some pearls and the shells from which they came, he described the method by which these were retrieved from the river, most probably the Strule, near Omagh in County Tyrone (Redding 1693, 660, 662–63):

> The manner of their fishing is not extraordinary, the poor People in the warm Months before harvest is ripe, whilst the Rivers are low and clear, go into the Water, some with their Toes, some with wooden Tongs, and some by putting a sharpened Stick into the opening of the Shell take them up: And although by common Estimate not above one Shell in a Hundred may have a Pearl, and of those Pearls not above one in a Hundred be tolerably clear, yet a vast number of fair Merchantable Pearls, and too good for the Apothecary, are offered to Sale by those People every Summer Assize. Some Gentlemen of the Country make good Advantage thereof, and my self whilst there, saw one Pearl bought for 50 Shillings that weighed 36 Carrats, and was valued at 40*l.* and had it been as clear as some others produced therewith, would certainly have been very valuable…I was informed that in the course of the River of

about Sixteen Miles, there were many deep Pools, which could never have been searched by these unmechanical People, for whom I made a Dredge with some Teeth in the Knife of it to rake them out of the Sand...The shells that have the best Pearls are wrinkled, twisted or bunched, and not smooth and equal as those that have none, as you may observe by one of the Shells herewith sent, of a lighter Colour than the rest; this shell yielded a Pearl sold for 12*l*. And the crafty Fellows will guess so well by the shell, that though you watch them never so carefully, they will open such shells under the Water, and put the Pearls in their Mouths, or otherwise conceal them...Upon Discourse with an old Man that had been long at this Trade, he advised me to seek not only when the Waters are low, but in a dusky gloomy day also Lest, said he, the Fish see you, for then he will shed his Pearl in the sand: of which I believed no more, than that some Muscles had voided their Pearls, and such are often found in the Sands.

A copy of this letter is preserved, in manuscript form (see Figure 2.1), among the *Molyneux papers* (Trinity College Dublin, MS 888/2, 63 *et seq.*), appended to which is a questionnaire on pearls in the same hand. Walter Harris (1744, 148) gave an account of the Bann pearl fishery in which the method of fishing was taken practically verbatim from the above and will therefore not be repeated here.

The following picture of pearl fishing in the 1670s has been recreated by Meagher (1928, 385):

At the end of the summer months, when the lakes and rivers were at their lowest, the toilers collected the pearls. The workers, wading to the waist, bending under water, tore the shells from the stones to which they clung in clusters, and dropped them into baskets slung across their shoulders.

This writer gives no sources for the material and falls into the error of assuming that the freshwater mussels were found, like their marine counterparts, attached to rocks or stones. In fact, they have no mechanism for attachment and live, mostly half buried, in the substratum.

Pearl fishing was pursued in some rivers in the south of the country and Smith (1750, 362) describes how it was carried out in the stretch of the River Lee near Carrigrohane Castle:

In the river Lee, near this castle, are the fresh water muscle; they lie in the deepest part of the river, sticking in the gravel, on the small end of the shell; the fisherman is naked when he goes to take them, having a small osier in his hand, and in fair sun-shine weather, otherwise they cannot be taken; for then only they open their shells, which being observed, he gently guides the end of his small stick between the shells; the fish feeling the stick, shuts them so close, that he easily draws them up.

Holmes (1801, 175) plagiarized this account of pearl fishing in one of his letters which made up an account of a tour, in August and September 1797, of some southern counties. As it adds nothing further regarding the methodology of pearl fishing in Ireland at that time, it is not worth including here.

The pearl fishery of the River Bann was one of the most celebrated of those in Ireland and many authorities refer to it—for example, Payne (1794, 174) in his *Universal geography*, where the river was called Band.[i] The fishery was in decline by the end of the eighteenth century when 'The common method of fishing for these muscles, was by wading into the water in summer, and thrusting sticks into the opening of the shells to take them up' (Dubourdieu 1802, 315). That pearl fishing was still prosecuted there in the middle of the nineteenth century is evidenced by J.B. Doyle (1854, 133) in the following:

> The pearls are not sought after as much as formerly, although very frequently valuable ones have been found. Those of the brilliant rose tint are the most esteemed. They are found in a species of muscle (the *Unio atratus*), of an oval shape, about four inches long, by two or two and a half broad. It is generally in the deep pools with loamy bottoms that the fish are found. In the shallower pools or still waters they are taken by wading in and collecting them by the foot, and throwing them up upon the bank. In the deep waters they are taken by thrusting a long stick between the valves when the shell is open; the white substance of the fish directs the eye to the mark. It is most generally in diseased shells that the best pearls are to be had. These are known by their wrinkled and branded appearance.

A description of pearl fishing, apparently in County Donegal rivers, was given by Dr John Barker (1862–65, 113) which was based on the observations of the aforementioned J.B. Doyle:

> The favourite season for taking them is during the summer months, when the rivers are low. Selecting a calm bright day, the fisherman sallies forth, armed with a sharp-pointed wattle and a large wooden scoop. Having stationed himself upon the brink of the pool, he waits until he sees some of the Mussels move, but which they do with great rapidity by the aid of their strong muscular foot. Sometimes they lie basking, as it were, in the sunshine, the foot extended, and mantle visible. They thus

form a conspicuous object at the bottom of the pool, and a convenient mark for the fisherman, who instantly thrusts his pointed stick between the valves, and thus lifts the shell cautiously out of the water, repeating the process as long as he finds an open shell. Having thus discovered the situation of the bed, he wades into the pool and shovels them out by wholesale on the bank. The heap is then carefully examined, and all the deformed and wrinkled shells are selected, as likely to contain the best pearls. The residue, or healthy Mussels, are also carefully examined, although, generally speaking, with little success.

An instance of diving for pearls in the west of Ireland was recounted by Frank Buckland (1864, 400), author, journalist, naturalist and public servant in *The Field* following a visit to this country and again in his *Curiosities of natural history* (1878, 336–37). At Oughterard, in County Galway, he met with a character known as 'Jemmy the pearl-catcher', whose activities he portrays thus:

Jemmy gets his living by collecting pearls…He is like the 'medicine man' among the Red Indians, very mysterious in his movements when he goes out to look for pearls, his principal enemies being the small boys, who, could they find out where Jemmys mussel-preserves were, would come and poach upon what he considers his own rightful property, and, taking his pearls, would injure his business in the pearl trade. He told me that he knew without opening it, when a mussel had a pearl in her, because 'she sits upright with her mouth in the mud, and her back is crooked, that is, it is corrugated like a cow's horn,' a fact he demonstrated to me from a number of mussels which he had in the basket. He opened one of these crooked-backed mussels, and sure enough Jemmy was right in his diagnosis, for there was a pearl in it a little larger than a turnip seed. He then mysteriously produced from the lining of his very old shabby hat, a very dirty bit of rag, and in this rag were two of the most beautiful pearls I ever beheld, which, if properly set, would form ornaments fit for the locket of any lady of her Gracious Majesty Queen Victoria's court. Such pearls as these Jemmy said he did not get every day. It was a very rare piece of luck to find them, and they were generally found in mussels which lived in such deep water at the edge of Lough Corrib, that, having no boat or dredging apparatus, he is obliged to go into the water, swim over to the place where the pearls are, and then keep on diving down for them like a cormorant fishing among a shoal of herrings. Sometimes poor Jemmy has a run of bad luck. Last winter he was nearly starving, and he did not know what to do, for none of the mussels he opened had any pearls in them…When matters were at their worst, he saw four mussels with their noses out in the mud, a sort of family group; he went into the water and brought them out. When he opened them, to his great delight, one of them had two large pearls in it: he sold them at once, and they fetched him 2*l*.8*s*. No wonder, therefore, that Jemmy does not like the boys to know where his favourite hunting grounds for mussels are situated.

In the south-east, the Slaney was noted for its pearls and Colonel Solomon Richards (Hoare 1862, 91), an ex-Cromwellian soldier, remarked that it 'oaught to preeceede all the Rivers in Ireland for itts pearle fishing'. Two centuries later, Streeter (1886, 244–45) gave an account of the method by which the pearls were taken:

> In the river Slaney, Co. Wexford, during the summer months when the water is low, some ten or fifteen men are (or were) in the habit of fishing for Pearls. They take the mussels from the bed of the river by a net, or slit at the end of a pole…

At the turn of the twentieth century, Synnott (1899–1902, 193) observed that 'Though there is not anything like a systematic fishing industry, pearls are still found in the Slaney.' Pearls continued to be taken from the Slaney in the twentieth century and evidence of this can be seen in a necklace of more than 100 fine pearls which has been passed down through three generations of a County Wexford family (see Figure 5.2).

A letter, apparently written to G.F. Kunz, co-author of the then-unpublished *The book of the pearl*, giving information on pearls and pearl fishing in the north of the country in the early years of the twentieth century, was compiled by James Milne (1907, 1–2) at the request of Robert Welch (1859–1936) the pioneering photographer and naturalist. The information in the letter, which may have arrived too late to be included in the book,[ii] mentions the following fishing methods used in County Tyrone rivers and a County Donegal lake:

> The pearlers are young people as a rule who spend part of their idle time searching for the shells which they always open on the spot. Very few give much of their time to the search. The time to search is after a spell of fine weather when the water is low. The only apparatus used is what is called a water telescope which is simply a tube with a bit of plain window glass in one end. By immersing the glass end in the water the bottom of the river is clearly seen in spite of the ripples that may be on the surface. At Lough Fern, Milford, Co Donegal a sort of rake with long curved teeth is used to work among the mud to where mussels are known to lie.

Peadar MacDomhaill (1937, 88), who collected material for the Irish Folklore Commission, learned how pearl fishing in the River Doirín (the Derreen) in County Carlow was carried on:

> The shells are removed from the bed of the river with a cleft-stick. They are afterwards opened and examined at leisure.

Also in the late 1930s, Owen Quinn (1939, 38), who wrote for the *Irish Press* newspaper, saw how pearl fishing was carried out in the River Blackwater, near Mallow in County Cork:

> Pearl fishing calls for patience and perseverance. What implements are necessary can be easily improvised. A long tapering hazel rod spliced at the narrow end serves to fork out the shells from amongst the pebbles and limestone slabs of the river bed. To enable the searcher to see the bed clearly a glass bottom is put in a can or bucket, and the vessel then pressed into the water. In this way the surface of the stream is broken and the stones, fishes, eel—and mussels—appear as through a thick pane of glass. The 'hunting' is carried on either from a flat punt or by wading. Using the 'butt end' of the hazel rod, the searcher pokes amongst the deposits on the river bed, and when he sees a likely shell he reverses his rod and grasps the shell in the slotted end. There is an art in lifting the mussel through the water, which practice will master.

One of the most experienced pearl fishermen of the twentieth century, Tom Mullin from Omagh, has given the following first-hand account of the materials and methods he used in the 1920s, 1930s and 1940s to search for mussels in the rivers of County Tyrone (Mullin 1947, 5):

> The equipment is very simple. A box about nine inches square with a glass bottom, a stick about five feet long with a fork at one end to lift the shell, and a pair of waders. In calm water it is possible to see the shells without the box, but in rough or streamy water the box is essential. When placed on the surface with the glass under the water, it gives a clear view of the bottom in the roughest stream…Nowadays the usual method of fishing is by wading with the box, or with a boat for the deeper water. A square flat-bottomed boat is best as there is less danger of overturning. It is very tiring work lying across the boat with the box examining the bottom, and at the same time trying to keep the boat in its place. It is much more convenient to anchor the boat while searching a small area.

In the 1940s, the fishermen on the Strule sometimes used 'a specially made small square boat for the work and a long cleft stick with which they lift the mussel shells from the river bed' (Loudan 1943, 2). An article entitled 'Pearl fishing in Ulster' by A.E.J. Went is listed in *A bibliography of Irish ethnology and folk tradition* (Ó Danachair 1978, 93) as appearing in the *Ulster digest* of 1949 (vol. iii, 16–17), but could not be traced.

Pearl fishing in more modern times does not go unrecorded, as the following example (Moore n.d. *c.* 1980, 89), of a pearl-fishing postman in the 1960s, shows:

> Pearl fishing as an occupation may have an exotic ring to it in this part of the world, yet it is a pursuit still followed in some parts of Ireland. In Donegal town I have been shown a handful of pearls culled from the bed of the River Eske, one of which by present-day rates would be worth close on £200. It was part of a haul made by a local postman in his spare time, and as many as 200 shells might have to be spotted and opened, he told me, before discovering one with a pearl in it. 'The shells in which the pearls come are longer and flatter than mussel shells, and have ridges raised on their surfaces', he said. 'They're found on sandy patches of the river bottom, and a glass-bottomed box about the size of a biscuit tin is used for spotting. This is pushed down into the river and you can see the sandy bed clearly. In deep water and pools a split hazel stick is used for grasping the shells and bringing them to the surface.'

The apparel and apparatus used in County Wicklow was described by Brosnan (1985/86, 47) as told to her by the son of a deceased pearl fisherman:

> Fishing for mussels meant standing for long periods in the river so they wore 'donkey suits'—waterproof suits that protected them fully. In order to look down to the river bed to see the mussels they used a 'water glass'. This was simply a wooden frame containing glass about a foot square…The 'water glass' was placed on the surface of the water to define more clearly what was on the river bed. When a mussel was located, a 'claw' was used to pick it up. The claw was a steel hand on a long shaft. A lever at the other end of the shaft was used to operate the fingers of the claw. The open claw was lowered over the mussel and then closed to grip it. It was slow tedious work. After a day's fishing the mussels were opened—not for their meat, but for their pearls.

Jean Taburiaux (1985, 61–62), informs us that it is likely that individual prospectors still fish in the lakes and rivers of Ireland, because a Parisian dealer bought a small collection of pearls in 1980 which, from the colour, had been fished only recently. Taburiaux gives the following short account of the fishing technique employed here:

Fishing for the *Unio* is only carried out when the water is low. The fisherman's equipment is very simple; apart from waders, he has a stick about two metres (6.5 ft) in length, pointed at one end, and a tube about 5 cm (2 in) across with a glass end which allows him to scrutinise the river-bed and direct the movement of his stick in order to catch the mulette. This sort of fishing is sometimes carried out from a barge. The stick is then longer, but the technique is identical.

As can be seen from the foregoing examples, the depth of the water dictated the technique employed in collecting pearl mussels. In shallows the mussels could be simply picked by hand, while in deeper waters a net, tongs, wooden scoop, cleft stick or even the toes of the fisher were employed. Only rarely, it appears, did the Irish pearler dive for the shells, though in lakes it would have been necessary, as shown in the account given by Buckland (1864). Henry Hart (1884, 220), while botanizing in Kerry in 1883, was told how the local people got pearl mussels from a lake under Mount Brandon. His guide said that 'three or four men went there lately with oilskins and dived for them'. Also, pearlers occasionally dived in rivers and lakes in the twentieth century (e.g., Mullin 1947, 5).

Sometimes a boat (Mullin 1947, 8)—a flat punt (Quinn 1939, 36), a small square boat (Loudan 1943, 2) or a barge (Taburiaux 1985)—was also employed for deeper waters by the Irish pearlers. The use of a simple stick (osier) seems to have been universal, not only throughout Ireland but across Europe. We see that three of the sources, Redding (1693), Doyle (1854) and Mullin (1947), cite the use of the foot or toes to retrieve the mussels from the river bed, and in this there is a parallel with the pearl divers of Ceylon (now Sri Lanka), who were adroit at picking oysters from the sea bed in the same manner (Percival 1803, 59–61; Smith 1854, 41). The feet or toes were used in deep fresh water in other countries also. For example, Geiger (1637, 43), quoting Boethius,[iii] describes a Scottish technique called 'pedum digitis', and the same method of using the toes to dislodge the mussels from the river substratum was used by German fishermen in the province of Hanover (Möbius 1846, 47). We are told by Linnaeus (1811, 104) that in the deeper pools the pearlers in Lapland hung from rafts and seized the mussels with their toes. One of the Irish sources (Robb 1939, 6) says that the mussels were sometimes retrieved by thrusting the big toe into the opening in the shells. While this may be possible with some of the larger mussels, it could also be uncomfortable or even painful, as the mussel closes its shells with some force.

Depth seems to have been a difficulty not easily overcome by the early Irish pearlers, who apparently did not employ any sophisticated apparatus to retrieve the mussels of deeper waters. In other European countries, special devices were used in the lower, deeper, reaches of large rivers. For example, in the deeper waters of the River Charente in western France, the mussels were collected with a dredge towed behind a boat. Also, in the same river in the late nineteenth century, the scaphander or diving apparatus, which required seven men for its operation, was introduced (Kunz and Stevenson 1908, 171).

Edward Chesters of Omagh, an experienced pearl fisherman, gave his equipment as 'a glass bottomed box (9"x9"), a forked stick about 5 ft long and of course a pair of waders' (Anon. 1984, 12). He added that some used a metal mechanical grab instead of the forked stick, but 'that the serious Sligger man[iv] sticks to traditional methods'.

Although attempts to devise more mechanical methods of exploitation such as raking or dredging were made in Ireland, the forked stick has endured and is still the most popular instrument for collecting mussels today. The only item of equipment carried by the pearler of the twentieth century which was not apparently among the apparatus of his predecessors was a tube or box (more recent varieties being glass bottomed) for viewing the river or lake substratum. It is said that this idea was first introduced to the County Tyrone rivers by Scottish fishers (Mullin 1947, 8). In the pearl fishery at Banbridge, which operated in the late seventeenth and early eighteenth centuries, the pearl-fishing season apparently commenced after the May floods and usually extended to September (Robb 1939, 6). However, it is likely that where river flow and visibility allowed, pearl fishing was carried on also in the winter and spring. Certainly the latter-day pearlers, such as Bill Abernethy, fished throughout the colder months (e.g., Pilkington 1991, 26).

*Methods used to extract the pearls*
Once the mussels had been collected, various methods, which were invariably crude, were employed in examining the mussels for pearls, as the following brief chronology will show.

At the pearl fishery in Banbridge, which was operated on a systematic basis in the late seventeenth and early eighteenth centuries, the mussels were put into basketware skips when picked from the water, and taken to a curing house for examination. After this, the pearls were extracted and graded (Robb 1939, 6).

A description of how the mussels were left to decompose on the riverside in the seventeenth century to facilitate the examination was given by Meagher (1928, 385):

> The mussels were then conveyed to the bank and spread broadcast upon the sands and left to dry. They were then easily opened and the contents extracted. Pearls found inside were husbanded in a linen bag, tied with a leather thong, until the end of the season.

The method of extracting the pearls from the mussels fished from the Bann in the nineteenth century was described by Doyle (1854, 133) thus:

> When a large quantity has been fished up they are left in heaps to
> decompose, after which they are carefully washed, and the pearls
> collected from the residuum.

At the extensive pearl fishery at Portglenone, also on the River Bann, the
following (Barker 1862–65, 113) was the method for extracting the pearls:

> At this place it was customary to throw the Mussels into a large heap to
> decompose, which they do very rapidly. They were then taken and
> washed in large tubs, the mass of the shells and pulp being stirred with
> a stick. After repeated washings the shells and grosser parts were
> removed, and the pearls sought for at the bottom.

Having described how the mussels were fished from the River Slaney in the
late nineteenth century, Edwin Streeter (1886, 244–45) goes on to say:

> ...the shells are then opened, and are subsequently either left on the
> banks or returned to the river. Sometimes from two to three hundred
> may be opened and no Pearl found. It is in the large deformed shells
> that the Pearls generally occur, and these are mostly buried in deep
> water, the Pearls being worth from £4 to £10 each.

The journalist Owen Quinn (1939, 38) saw at first hand how the pearls
were extracted from mussels taken in the River Blackwater in County Cork in
the 1930s:

> When sufficient shells have been taken the searcher retires to his punt
> or to the river bank and proceeds to sort and examine his haul. Unlikely
> shells, coarse or dull, receive only a cursory glance and are cast back into
> the river. The others are deftly opened with an empty half-shell, and by
> running his thumb along the inside the experienced man soon discloses
> any evidence of a pearl.

Throughout the years, the usual method of examining the mussels was to
prise open the shells (see Figure 2.2 for how the mussels were leisurely opened
by County Tyrone fishers in the 1940s). This was achieved using an old shell
or, alternatively, 'the bivalves are split open on the bank with a knife' (Deane
1965, 6).

As long as the mollusc lives, the pearl remains hidden within the shell.
Therefore, pearls are not found casually and can usually only be collected by
killing the mussel and opening the shell (Moriarty 1994, 19). If the two shells

of the mussel can be opened a little, however, without severing the abductor and adductor muscles or the hinge ligament, and the inside seen or felt for a pearl, then those not containing a pearl can be returned to the water and can live perhaps to produce a pearl in the future. As will be seen in a later chapter, there is some evidence that methods for conserving the mussel stocks were employed in a fishery on the Bann in the eighteenth century, and we know that techniques were in use in Germany at that time which did not destroy all the mussels examined. The few remaining Scottish semi-professional pearlers, who still come to Ireland to fish, employ a method using specially adapted pliers. Those mussels not containing a pearl are marked, to show on subsequent visits that they have previously been examined, and returned to the river bed (McCormick 1996, *in litt.*[v]).

Just as with the fishing methods employed, the techniques to examine the mussel for the hidden pearl were crude and, as will be related, invariably led to mass destruction of mussel stocks.

Having found a pearl, the finder must then sell it on the market. How much the pearlers could expect for their pearls, where they disposed of their treasure, and to whom they sold them will be investigated in the next chapter.

*Notes*

[i]According to Joyce (1875, 14) the letter d 'is often added to the end of words, sometimes with a collective meaning, sometimes with scarcely any meaning at all'.

[ii]Prof. James N. Milne of Belfast is, however, included among those acknowledged in the introduction to the book for providing information.

[iii]i.e., Hector Boece (*c.* 1465–1536).

[iv]i.e., pearl fisher.

[v]N. McCormick, Scottish pearl fisherman. *In litt.*, 12 January (1996).

# 3. Pearl prices and markets

> It is not that pearls fetch a high price because men have dived for them; but on the contrary, men dive for them because they fetch a high price…
>
> *Richard Whately* (1787–1863), Archbishop of Dublin, *Introductory lectures on political economy* (1832, 253)

Natural pearls are very valuable because each one has had to be fished or dived for separately. As opposed to the cultured varieties introduced in the early twentieth century, these occur randomly, and therefore the supply is limited.

The unit of weight for pearls is the pearl grain, which is one quarter of a carat, the carat in turn being fixed at one fifth of a gramme. The value of a pearl is computed by squaring the weight in grains and multiplying the result by a 'base' figure assessed according to the quality of the pearl. The most valuable pearls are those which are most nearly spherical in shape, of fine orient (lustre) and unblemished skin (R.W.A. 1967, 528). While the carat is the usual modern way of expressing the weight of a pearl, the pearl fishers often use diameter (in millimetres) as a measure of size.

Freshwater pearls are not as well known as their saltwater counterparts, but comparable ones from both sources are similarly priced (Ward 1995, 19). They occur in a wide range of colours including light, medium and dark orange, lavender, purple, violet, blue, rose and grey, and the larger ones in unusual colours are usually very expensive (Matlins 1996, 42).

It has been suggested that the Phoenicians traded with the ancient Irish for the native pearls occurring here (O'Conor 1814, xvii) but there is no positive evidence for this. Similarly, it has been postulated that Phoenician mariners probably obtained the pearls of the Scottish rivers in the course of their commerce with these islands (Kunz and Stevenson 1908, 319). Although Irish pearls were utilized and traded for a very long period, it is not until the seventeenth century that information on their prices and on where and to whom they were sold becomes available.

*Seventeenth century*
Pearls found during the seventeenth century in Ireland were usually sold locally to jewellers or to merchants who sometimes exported them to London.

The value of a good pearl to the seller can, as is the case with any other commodity, change as it passes through various hands, and such enterprise and exploitation was as much a part of business in the seventeenth century as it is today. A good example is given by Richard Boyle, Earl of Cork, who writes in his diary on 3 January 1634 (Grosart 1886, 66):

> Sir Randall Cleyton & his Lady, with my 2 daughters, came to Lismoor, and he brought me a veary Large Rownde faier Pearle, taken in the River of Bandon, which the poor woman that found it sowld in Corke for ii$^s$ in money and iiii$^d$ in beer & Tobackoe; that partie sowld it againe for 2 Cows, who sowld it the third tyme for xii$^{li}$ ster: to a Merchant of Corke, and then my Cozen Bardsey counseled Sir Randall Cleyton to buy yt for me, who paid for it in ready gold xxx$^{li}$ ster:, And I bestowed it for a new years guifte on my daughter Dongarvan: it is worth a C$^{th}$ marckes, and weighs xviii graynes: 75$^{li}$. I have paid for perles which I have given my daughter Dongarvan.

So we see that the pearl which was originally sold by the pearl fisherwoman for two shillings and four pence (equivalent to 12p) eventually fetches £30, having in the meantime been traded for two cows, and subsequently for £12. Boyle's own estimation was that it was worth 100 marks, which, as a mark was worth 13s 4d (Longfield 1929, 234), would convert to a value of about £66. This pearl, as Sir Richard says, weighed 18 grains and so can be compared with one of exactly the same weight taken in the 1940s, some 300 years later, which sold for £25 (Mullin 1947, 5). According to *A discourse of coin and coinage*, which was published in London in 1675 (Kunz and Stevenson 1908, 338), a pearl of 18 grains was then valued at £35, and so the price cited by Boyle for a pearl of that weight on the Irish market is in line with international prices for that time. Sir Robert Redding (1693, 660), while visiting the pearl fishery near Omagh in 1688, had seen a pearl which was valued at £40[i] being sold by the pearler for 50s (£2.50). He also tells of a pearl sold for £4 10s (£4.50) eventually fetching £30, having in the meantime been resold for £10:

> A Miller took out a Pearl which he sold for 4*l*.10*s*. to a Man that sold it for 10*l*. who sold it to the late Lady Glenanly for 30*l*. with whom I saw it in a Necklace; she refused 80*l*. for it from the late Dutchess of Ormond.

The same Robert Redding (1688, 159) mentions that pearls were taken 'in a small river…in the County of Fermanagh, commonly known in the County by the name of the River of Maguires Bridge'. One of these was apparently estimated to be worth £50, and others £10, £20 and £30. That river also produced a pearl 'as big as a pistoll bullett & worth £80', which was sold to a

Lady Berisfords (Dublin Philosophical Society 1683–87, 193). These examples serve to illustrate just how highly prized freshwater pearls were in Ireland in the seventeenth century.[ii]

It appears that in some instances pearls were sold directly by the pearlers or merchants to the occupants of the 'big house' in northern counties in the seventeenth century, and the same was practised in some of the south-eastern counties (e.g., Carlow and Kilkenny), as shall be seen in a later chapter.

It has been suggested that in the economic recession of the 1670s, searching for pearls was a proud alternative to begging for survival, and that it may even have enabled the dispossessed[iii] to rebuild their lives (Meagher 1928, 385):

> Two hundred and fifty years ago many peasants, driven from the soil by economic pressure, and unwilling to become mendicants, found in the pearl-fishing industry a ready means of prolonging existence. Some few indeed, were fortunate in finding good-class pearls, and thus they were enabled to purchase land and re-establish themselves as farmers.

In the seventeenth century the pearls were apparently sold largely to Dublin and Cork merchants, who exported them to the English capital (Meagher 1928, 385). We know from the visit of Sir Robert Redding (1693, 662) to a pearl fishery in 1688 that 'middlemen' bought pearls from the fishers in County Tyrone, and the same practice was in operation in the south of Ireland. Speaking of the pearls taken from the River Slaney in County Wexford, Sir Solomon Richards (Hoare 1862, 91), writing in 1682, says:

> They have lately been sold by a Merchant that dined this day with me, for 20$^s$, 30$^s$, 40$^s$, and three pounds a pearle to the Goldsmiths or Jewellers in London. He sould twenty lately for twenty broad pieces of gold, and a parcel of small ones for 40 pounds.

Therefore any evaluation of the fisheries in Ireland would, in addition to what was paid to the pearler, have to take account of possible subsequent transactions to arrive at a figure for the value of the fisheries to the local economy.

In the late seventeenth century, pearls were sold during the assizes, particularly on the northern circuit. For example, Redding (1693, 662), speaking of the pearls taken from the rivers in County Tyrone, noted that 'a vast number of fair Merchantable Pearls…are offered to Sale by those People every Summer Assize'. At that time also, in East Ulster, there was a thriving pearl fishery at what is now known as Banbridge, but the settlement had no market and consisted of only a few houses on the banks of the river. Prior to Banbridge becoming a town, Loughbrickland and Dromore, on either side of it, absorbed the trade and commerce of the entire district (Linn 1910, 317).

Pearls from there were probably sold locally as well as in Belfast, Dublin and London.

*Eighteenth century*

Some 70 years later, in the eighteenth century, Edward Willes (1762, 125), the Chief Baron, mentions the pearl fishery at Omagh while on legal business at the assizes. Thus it would appear that the periodical sessions were still among the main markets for the local pearls in County Tyrone in the middle of that century.

Sometimes in the eighteenth century, Irish pearls were advertised for sale. John and James Majore, who then had a lease for the pearl fishery at Banbridge, advertised in the press in 1732 that they had 'a choice selection of Bann pearls, specimens of which could be seen at the Fighting Cock in Dublin or at the Bear and Harrow Tavern in London' (Robb 1939, 6). We find that in the same period it is said that the pearls taken by the people from the River Lee in County Cork were 'sometimes as large as a pea and of a good water, which they sell in Cork for a trifle' (Smith 1750, 362). Obviously there was a great disparity between what those who controlled a fishery and sold direct to the nobility received for their pearls, and the price pocketed by the poor individuals who sold to 'middlemen' or direct to jewellers.

Very little information appears to be available for the early part of the century. Pearls were subject to taxes, probably first levied during the reign of Charles II, which were in operation in the early part of the eighteenth century. These duties were abolished in England, however, by the parliament of 1727–32 (Kunz and Stevenson 1908, 367) following the accession of George II. During the period of the levy on pearls[iv] very few finds of pearls in Ireland appear to come to notice. This point will be discussed in a later chapter, in relation to the Penal Laws of the time and the possibility of pearl fishing becoming an underground activity. In 1709, some official letters regarding a large pearl, reputed to weigh 62 carats and be worth £400, passed between Secretary Dawson in Dublin and a Mr Thomas Putland in London. These letters apparently refer to efforts made at recovering the pearl and may relate to its having been smuggled out of Ireland. Unfortunately, they have not survived—the originals were destroyed in the fire at the Four Courts in 1922—and the sketchy information is based on summaries (Burke 1882, 141–42).

The whole question of duty on the import, export or sale of Irish pearls must, if it ever was levied, have been fraught with difficulty. With goods such as pearls—lacking in bulk and easily concealed—there were bound to be many attempts to avoid paying; in disaffected regions like Ireland, the inclination to evade the duties must have been strong.

Because both the Ceylon and Red Sea fisheries were unproductive during the whole of the eighteenth century, pearls were scarce and most supplies came from the Persian Gulf and freshwater sources (Dakin 1913, 10). In that century, diamonds became very fashionable following the discovery of new methods of cutting and preparing them. At that time, according to Jeffries (1751, 130), the general price of pearls, good and bad blended together, was eight shillings per carat, whereas diamonds cost eight pounds. This would give an average price of £2 16s (£2.80) for a 'good' pearl (say 18 grains) on the main markets in the middle of the eighteenth century.

Despite this competition, however, pearls continued in favour and by the end of the nineteenth century would be more sought after and valuable than ever.

*Nineteenth century*

In Donegal in the 1830s, low prices were paid for pearls by merchants who probably in turn made big profits on them. For example, a businessman, the proprietor of quarries near the Rosses, 'bought, for a few shillings from a poor boy, one of such size and beauty, that Messrs. Rundle and Bridge, London, offered him forty guineas for it' (R.Y. 1833, 389). Similar meagre prices were paid to the pearlers in the neighbouring county of Tyrone during the same period, on which merchants made handsome profits. In a statistical report compiled in 1834 by Lieutenant William Lancey, on the parish of Drumragh, County Tyrone, it is said that pearls could always be obtained in Omagh during the summer season with 'the finest, about the size of a pea, for 4 or 5 shillings' (Day and McWilliams 1990, 104).

Such prices are only a fraction of those paid by a Dublin jeweller in the 1850s. The jeweller, West of Dublin, bought £500 worth of Irish pearls in a few years of the 1850s, of which £5 to £7 was paid for each of 20 specimens and £2 to £4 for 100 others (von Hessling 1859, 189). One of the suppliers of pearls to this jeweller was apparently a farmer in County Galway (von Hessling 1859, 188). Some years ago, when the firm moved its premises on Grafton Street, all the old records were destroyed. Had these been available for the present study, they might have been a valuable source of information on prices of native pearls throughout some 200 years of trading.

In the 1860s in County Galway, two pearls, found in the same shell, were sold for £2 8s (£2.40) by the man known locally as 'Jemmy the pearl-catcher' (Buckland 1878, 337), which at the time was considered a good price.

Good prices appear to have been paid for pearls in the late nineteenth century in general, as we find that in 1894 several varying in value from £10 to £20 were sold in County Tyrone (Anon. 1894, 138). Professor J.N. Milne (1907, 3), of Belfast, also gives £10 as the value for a good pearl in the late nineteenth century. At the opposite end of the country, a pearl taken from the River Blackwater in County Cork some ten years previously was, according to a report in the *Cork Constitution* newspaper of 23 October 1884, valued at £5 (A.M. 1892, 211). At this time we see that in County Wexford those taken from the River Slaney were worth from £4 to £10 each (Streeter 1886, 245).

Thus, in this period, contemporary sources from three different areas of the country can be seen to be consistent at least to some degree, and it may be computed that the average price of a good pearl in Ireland in the late nineteenth century was just under £10, within a range of £4 to £20.

*Twentieth century*

In the year of the outbreak of the First World War, a pearl taken from the River Moy in County Mayo purchased a horse and cart for its finder, a Scottish pearl fisherman (whose son-in-law with his sons still carry on the tradition and come regularly to fish the Irish rivers) (McCormick 1996, *in litt.*). Some seven years previously, a pearl of 21 grains had sold for £80 in Scotland (Kunz and Stevenson 1908, 167). One taken in a County Tyrone river in the early part of the twentieth century, which was seen by the pioneering Ulster photographer Robert Welch, was apparently worth £50 (W[elch] 1908, 90). We also find, however, that in the same year as Welch was writing one was sold (again in Tyrone) for £8 and others for £1 or less (Anon. 1908, 5).

In the first half of the twentieth century, pearls fished from the rivers of County Tyrone were sold in Omagh, Belfast, Edinburgh, London and Dublin (Anon. 1965b, 1; Loudan 1943, 2). At one time there was a market with tourists, especially Americans, for pearls in Omagh (Anon. 1984, 13)—particularly among those whose families had originally come from the area and who would seek to buy the famous 'Strule pearls'. Bryans (1964, 157), writing in the 1960s, remembered when the shops in Omagh sold pearls taken from the Strule. Pearls taken in rivers of County Wicklow and County Wexford by one pearler in the early part of the twentieth century were first sold in Dublin, but later on he found a buyer in England who paid a better price (Brosnan 1985/86, 47).

In some areas we find comparatively low prices, even for what were called 'good' pearls—for example, 7s 6d (38p) in County Carlow in the 1930s (MacDomhaill 1937, 88). Yet we see that a good pearl in Ulster fetched £25 in the 1920s (McCrea 1973a, b, 10, 13) and up to £50 in the late 1930s (Loudan 1943, 2). In the 1940s, pearls from the River Strule in County Tyrone were valued from 20s to 30s a grain, which meant that the average pearl was worth about £6 (Loudan 1943, 2). This average price is less than a quarter of that paid to Tom Mullin (1947, 5) for his best pearl taken in the same period. Thus, large confidence limits (the range within which the true mean lies) would have to be applied to get a meaningful typical value for pearls; from the information available in this period, it appears that the average price would be £6, within a range of £1 to £25.

By the 1940s, the market for pearls in Belfast had apparently declined and the best demand for County Tyrone pearls, according to one local pearl fisherman, was in Edinburgh (Loudan 1943, 2). This is probably due to higher prices being paid at the time, when supplies of the Japanese cultured pearl were unavailable.

During the Second World War, in fact, pearls from Omagh were very much in demand, and one was sold for £50 in Dublin (Loudan 1943, 2):

> Unlike some other industries Omagh pearl fishing has improved since the outbreak of war. Some 20 to 30 years ago it was possible to make a living at this trade alone, but a slump came when the Japanese began to flood the world market with artificially produced pearls. People were unable to distinguish between them and the Strule pearl, with the result that the latter decreased rapidly in price. Now, however, when the Oriental pearl is no longer available, Omagh is coming back into its own, and a pearl from the River Strule was sold not long ago in Dublin for £50.

During the 1960s, a Scottish professional pearl fisher came to Ulster regularly and bought the pearls collected by the local fishers (McCrea 1973a, b, 10, 13), which were then resold on the Scottish market.

Irish pearls occasionally ended up on the Paris market, and as late as 1980 a small collection was bought there by a dealer (Taburiaux 1985, 62). Pearls to the value of £250 were purchased by the Ulster Museum in 1982 from John McGrath, a part-time pearl fisherman from Sion Mills in County Tyrone. McGrath sold his best pearl, a fine specimen of approximately nine millimetres in diameter, through Christie's of London, where it fetched £200 in an auction in 1984 (McGrath 1996, *in litt.*[v]). In another auction, also in 1984, Christie's offered for sale 'A collection of vari-coloured Irish freshwater pearls, all undrilled' (Item 144, *Christie's of South Kensington catalogue*—Sale No. JJW 0304/84—for 3 April 1984, 14) which may also have come via the same pearler.

In the Edwardian period, pearls were rare and more expensive than diamonds (Scarisbrick 1989, 142), and we have seen above how this was reflected in prices in Scotland and Ulster in 1907 and 1908. Since the 1920s the importance of freshwater pearls has continued to decline because depleted mussel populations have reduced their availability, and because of the competition they have faced from the cultured Japanese varieties.

In the 1990s, however, prices rose again and it has been estimated that a very good specimen is nowadays worth £250 to £300 sterling, which is about the same as or a little more expensive than saltwater pearls (Woodward 1994, 65).

It is difficult to gain an accurate valuation for Irish pearls down through the years. This stems largely from the fact that each pearl is individually valued according to certain criteria, which were outlined at the beginning of the chapter. From a review of the literature it can be gleaned that the value of a

---

*Box II*

## Pearl prices in perspective

In order that the price of pearls be put in perspective, it is instructive that the price of other commodities as well as land valuation and wages be given for comparison.

We know, from William Petty's survey, that an acre of land was priced at 40s (£2) in the 1680s. In the late seventeenth century many of the inhabitants of the countryside lived in poverty; wages from agricultural employment for labourers were about 4d (1–2p) a day when available. Pearlers received at that time prices of from £2.50 to £4.50, the equivalent to a year's wages, for a single good-quality pearl; if they sold direct to nobility they could get as much as ten times these amounts.

In 1777, farm labourers' wages were 3s 6d (18p) per week, and we read of pearls from the River Lee in County Cork being sold for a 'trifle' some years previously. They probably sold for the equivalent of the weekly wage.

In the first years of the nineteenth century, the wages of farm labourers in County Tyrone ranged from 6d to 1s (5p) per day, with the higher rate paid at harvest time. At this time, cottiers were part-time weavers as well as agricultural labourers. In the early 1820s, Belfast's cotton weavers were the best paid among the poor in Ireland, earning from 9s to 21s (£1.05) a week.

In the 1830s, pearls could be purchased for 4s or 5s (25p) each in Tyrone which was about the same as the weekly wage. The daily wage for the time was from 8d to 12d (5p); men and women engaged in the manufacture of hats and shoes in Omagh received from 50s to 63s (£3.15) and 24s (£2.20) to 50s (£2.50) respectively every half year. At the beginning of the nineteenth century, a cabin which was reckoned 'a respectable and comfortable mansion for a cottager' could be built for under £7.

Later in the nineteenth century, just before the Great Famine, the annual income of landless labourers was apparently £11. This is an average and would have been supplemented in some areas by income from spinning and weaving, fishing, or seasonal migration to Britain. The finding of a couple of fairly good

---

'good' native pearl to the finder at various times over the past 300 years in Ireland has been given as follows: £4 in the 1680s (Redding 1693, 662); £30 in the 1740s (Willes 1760, 125); £7 in the 1850s (von Hessling 1859, 189); £10 in the 1880s (Streeter 1886, 245); £10 in the 1890s (Anon. 1894, 138; Milne 1907, 3); £8 in the 1900s (Anon. 1908, 5); £25 in the 1920s (McCrea 1973b, 13); £50 in the 1930s (Loudan 1943, 2); £25 in the 1940s (Mullin 1947, 5); £35 in the 1960s (Anon. 1965b, 1); £200 in the 1980s (McGrath 1996, *in litt.*).

These prices, however, are those which have come to notice and cannot be taken as representing average values. Each represents a figure around which

pearls could thus earn as much again in income for a part-time fisher as the annual wage from farm labouring.

In 1852, the average price of land was £6 10s (£6.50) per acre in the depressed state of affairs after the Famine.[vi] At the same time, a Dublin jeweller paid between £5 and £7 for some pearls to suppliers including a County Galway farmer. The average weekly wages of farm labourers in Ulster in the 1860s, when a pearl could fetch £1 4s (£1.20) for its finder, were about 7s to 7s 6d (35–38p), but varied across the province by as much as 2s (10p), with the highest rates paid in County Antrim and lowest in County Fermanagh. Wages more than doubled, however, between 1850 and 1894.

In the late nineteenth and early twentieth centuries, when good pearls fetched £1 to £20, farm labourers earned 10s 8d (53p) per week.

In the 1920s, the annual agricultural wage was about £25—the same as could be earned by the sale of a good pearl. In the 1930s, farm labourers were still poorly paid, with a half-yearly wage of about £16, when a pearl could fetch as much as £50. In the same period, however, away from the main centres—in County Carlow, for example—good pearls apparently sold for as little as 7s 6d (38p).

In the middle of the 1990s, prices for freshwater pearls were in the range Ir£250–£300 for good-quality specimens, within which the average industrial wage in the Republic of Ireland (Ir£270 or €342 for a 40-hour week) fell. Thus, the modern value of a good-quality native pearl is to the finder, as it has been at various other periods in history, approximately equivalent to a week's wages. By 2004 the average industrial wage in the Republic of Ireland had risen to €576 or Ir£453.

(Sources: Smith 1750, 362; McEvoy 1802, 144, 149; de Lavergne 1855, 385; von Hessling 1859, 188–89; Anon. 1894, 138; Anon. 1908, 5; Adams 1932, 58; MacDomhaill 1937, 88; Cullen 1987, 20, 23; Kennedy 1987, 62, 87; Day and McWilliams 1990, 104; Ó Gráda 1995, 95, 236, 237; Central Statistics Office data.)

large confidence limits would have to be applied. Where data are available, the mean price within a price range has been derived for some periods over the past 350 years, and these are shown together with the prevailing market retail price in Table 3.1.

The table serves to show just how deficient the sources are in data regarding prices of pearls. What it also shows, however, is that since the 1920s the difference in the price of a pearl to the finder and on the retail market has narrowed considerably, and it would appear that before that time, large profits were made on pearls purchased cheaply from the fishers.

To view these prices in perspective, it is necessary to have regard to the cost

Table 3.1
Estimated range in value (with computed average in parentheses where available) of Irish pearls taken at various periods over 350 years, and the price for the same period of a 'good' pearl on the retail market. Prices are expressed as modern denominations.

| Period | Value to finder | Market value |
|--------|-----------------|--------------|
| 1630s | £0.12 | £30 |
| 1680s | £2.50–£4.50 (£3.50) | £30–£40 |
| 1750s | £0.05–£2.80 | £30 |
| 1830s | £0.20–£0.25 | £40 |
| 1850s | £2–£7 (£4.50) | £10 |
| 1890s | £4–£20 (£10) | £20 |
| 1900s | £1–£8 (£4.50) | £50 |
| 1920s | £14–£25 (£20) | £25 |
| 1940s | £1–£25 (£6) | £50 |
| 1960s | £35 | £35 |
| 1980s | £200 | £200–£300 |

(Sources: Redding 1693, 660; R.Y. 1833, 389; Grosart 1886, 66; Anon. 1894, 138; W[elch] 1908, 90; McCrea 1973b, 13; Woodward 1994, 65; McGrath 1996, *in litt.*)

of living for the various periods. Such data, however, are rather meagre for Ireland, particularly regarding commodity prices in the seventeenth and eighteenth centuries. Price indices, as well as cost-of-living indices, have been compiled for some commodities over time in England[vii] but not apparently for luxury items such as pearls. Recently Ó Gráda (1995, 237) has compiled estimates, from two sources in particular, of nominal wages in Ireland for some years between 1777 and 1911. These, together with other wage estimates and commodity prices as well as land valuation from various sources, have been used in Box II to place pearl prices in a proper context over some 300 years of trading.

From Box II it is apparent that, even allowing for differences in quality, there was some quite large regional variation in pearl prices obtained by the fishers during the same periods. For some of these periods, including the present time, the price of a good-quality freshwater pearl is approximately equivalent to a week's wages for an average worker. In other periods, however, particularly the seventeenth century, it could equal a full year's income. Perhaps the best conclusion to be drawn regarding pearl prices is that they varied not only according to individual quality but also depending on to whom and where they were sold.

Today, most of the world's wild pearl-producing molluscs, both freshwater and saltwater varieties, have been decimated by overfishing and pollution, and natural pearls are thus rarer than ever before. Some jewellers still obtain them occasionally, mainly from the pearlers and through auctions, for special clients who can appreciate and afford them (Matlins 1996, 25). In Scotland, recent years have seen a continuous downward trend in the number of freshwater pearls coming on the market. While the information for some periods is deficient with regard to markets and prices, the best information available appears to be for the seventeenth and twentieth centuries. It is apparent that in the former, unless sold direct to jewellers or to nobility, the price received by the pearl finder was generally only a fraction of that for which it sold on the retail market.

In the next chapter, the pearl fishers and the pearl fisheries will be profiled to gain a picture of the activities involved in the business.

*Notes*

[i] In the same year the estimated income of soldiers and labourers in England and Wales was £14 and £15 respectively (Mathias 1969, 24).

[ii] We also find that other commodities were highly prized and so highly priced in the seventeenth century. For example, Lord Ossory paid £6 for a setter in 1685 (MacLysaght 1939, 142). It is interesting that such a dog with good pedigree would fetch about £300 today, about the same as a good freshwater pearl. Yet £6 then would have a far higher modern equivalent than £300 and some pearls, as we have seen, were purchased by nobility for ten times that amount. To put this in perspective, we know from William Petty's survey that an acre of land was priced at 40 shillings (£2) in the 1680s (Cullen 1987, 20).

[iii] Tenants fared badly from 1665 onwards, owing mainly to livestock losses caused by weather conditions and disease. This was compounded by the outbreak of war in early 1672, and some did indeed abandon their farms (Cullen 1987, 13–14).

[iv] In the previous century, following the rebellion of 1641, most commodities were subject to import excise duty, but jewels (which presumably included pearls) among other items were exempt (O'Brien 1919, 198).

[v] J. McGrath (1996) Ulster pearl fisherman. *In litt.*, 16 May.

[vi] Irish estates worth some £20 million changed hands in the 1850s. However, it was not the native tenants but local speculators, as well as members of the landlord class, who were the purchasers (Foster 1988, 336).

[vii] For example, the Schumpeter-Gilboy cost-of-living index is a useful broad guide to secular price trends in England between 1696 and 1823 (Mitchell and Deane 1962, 466).

# 4. Pearl fisher and fishery profiles

There be also some store of good pearls upon the coast, especially within the river of Loughfoile…
*Calender of the patent and close rolls of chancery in Ireland, of the reign of Charles the First* (1609)[i]

The prospect of pearls was listed among the motives and reasons to induce the City of London to undertake the plantation in the north of Ireland (later known as the Plantation of Derry) in May 1609 (Morrin 1863, 620). It is clear that there was a pearl-fishing culture among the native Irish and we will see that this pre-dates the beginning of the seventeenth century by a long while. With very few exceptions, however, it is not until that century that information on the fishers and the fisheries first comes to notice.

*Fishers*
In County Donegal, the River Eske was fished in the seventeenth century by the local people 'in a dry summer' (Anon. 1683b, 213), and in County Tyrone the same was observed for the River Strule (Redding 1688, 141). There are also observations in the same period for pearls taken from the rivers in the south-east: Thomas Dingley (1675–80, 88), writing about Ballynunery in County Carlow, says that pearls were found in the local river (the Burren) 'which ye Lady of the Castle hath to shew', and Robert Redding (1688, 160) tells that a lady had a necklace of two rows of pearls gathered in the River Nore within nine miles of the town of Kilkenny. It is most probable that in both of these instances the pearls were collected by the locals and sold to the lady of the 'big house'. In another river in the south-east, the Slaney, the pearls collected in the seventeenth century were sold to merchants who disposed of them to jewellers in London (Hoare 1862, 91).

William Majore of Banbridge, who died in 1710, is described in his will as a pearl fisher and curer (Robb 1939, 6). The trade was passed to his sons, James and John Majore, who, according to a press advertisement dated 1732, informed the nobility and gentry that they had a choice selection of Bann pearls, specimens of which could be seen in Dublin and London. This family was probably not typical of the social status of the average pearl fisher of the time.

*Box III*
**Pearl fisher profiles**

*Tom Mullin* (see Figure. 4.1) from Omagh fished the rivers of County Tyrone and others in Ulster for some 30 years until at least the late 1940s. As a small boy he was stirred into trying pearl fishing after having heard many stories from old fishers of their experiences. He appears to have been a part-time pearler, but he and his companions seem to have fished for extended periods, as they often camped by the side of the rivers being searched. He got three good pearls in one day's fishing, and on another expedition took a pearl of 18 grains which fetched £25. He once found a shell that contained eight small pearls.
(Source: Mullin 1947, 5,8.)

*Tom Hamilton* was still fishing into his eightieth year in 1973, having spent most of his life as a part-time pearler on the rivers of Counties Donegal, Londonderry and Tyrone. He found his first pearl at age six, in 1900, and his last 73 years later—both having come from the River Foyle. His biggest price for a pearl was £25, obtained in 1923, and he had many other good ones, some of which he had mounted in jewellery for his wife. He tells of a Scottish professional pearl fisher who came each year to Northern Ireland, staying for five or six weeks, and bought all the Ulster pearls he could from the local pearlers. Tom Hamilton's ambition was to find a priceless ebony-black pearl; his brother had found one but lost it in the river whence it came.
(Source: McCrea 1973b, 13.)

*John McGrath* from Sion Mills fished the rivers of Counties Tyrone and Donegal and has featured in radio programmes on the topic of pearl fishing, for example on BBC Radio Foyle in 1979 and BBC Radio 4 in 1993. Pearl fishing has been a hobby in his family for five generations and he has passed on the skills of the trade to his sons. A collection of his pearls was purchased by the Ulster Museum

It is difficult to paint a picture of the typical pearl fisher in Ireland. Undoubtedly he would have been very poor in the seventeenth and eighteenth centuries. There is a similarity in this with the description of the pearl divers of the same period in the Persian Gulf, of whom Oliver Goldsmith (1744, 58) says, 'The wretched people that are destined to fish for pearls, are either negroes or some of the poorest of the natives of Persia.'[ii]

Pearl fishing in Ireland, though largely a male preserve, was not exclusively so, as we have seen (in chapter three) from an entry in the seventeenth–century diary of the Earl of Cork. Some 250 years later, in 1885, a young girl found a pearl in the River Blackwater, near Lismore, which was afterwards sold by her father (A.M. 1892, 211). In the 1940s an Omagh woman found a beautiful pearl in the River Strule (Loudan 1943, 2) and there is little doubt that a very

in 1982 for £250, and his best pearl fetched £200 in a Christie's auction in 1984. (Source: McGrath 1996, *in litt.*)

*Joseph Brogan*, a confectioner from Omagh, was still pearl fishing in 1965 at 70 years of age. In 50 years of pearl fishing as a hobby he had found hundreds of fine specimens, some of which were worth up to £35. Joe Brogan sold his pearls in Belfast, Edinburgh, London and Dublin. In one day's fishing in 1964 he collected 11 pearls. He could remember a time when as many as 30 men and women from the town would be seeking their fortunes on the River Strule. Among the other rivers he had fished were the Coagh, Maguiresbridge, Swanlinbar, Camowen, Drumragh and Finn. Pearl fishing was obviously carried on by his family for many generations, and an ancestor of his, James Brogan, is mentioned in the diary of the noted conchologist and photographer Robert John Welch.
(Sources: Anon. 1965b, 1; Ross 1988, 42.)

*Edward Chesters* from Omagh started pearl fishing with some friends as a 16- or 17-year-old. He became a keen and knowledgeable conventional angler and was for many years a water bailiff for the Strule area. He fished regularly for pearls with Tom Mullin (see above), from whom he learned the skill and who was then the acknowledged expert on pearl fishing. Eddie, together with Tom Mullin's brother Sammy and three other local men, Walter Megahy, Joe Brogan (see above) and Dan McBride, made up an unmatched band of what were known as 'sligger men'. He found many pearls of all sizes and has given some as presents or tokens of friendship, to family and acquaintances, who have usually sent them to jewellers to be mounted as rings, tie-pins and earrings. He has, however, kept some of his finds. He says that although the art of pearl fishing is not lost, he would like to see more people getting involved, especially the young, in order that it may be passed on to future generations.
(Sources: Anon. 1984, 12; Chesters 1995, *in litt.*)

many women fished for pearls in that river over the years, and particularly in the seventeenth century.

In parts of Europe, too, women were sometimes employed in the pearling business. In the province of Olonetz in northern Russia, for example, it was the young girls who did the pearl collecting in the local rivers (von Hessling 1859, 196). Female pearl divers or *ama* have traditionally worked the oyster beds in Japan's offshore waters since the pearl industry started to grow there in the middle of the twentieth century (Joyce and Addison 1992, 136), and in some parts such women were the acknowledged heads of their families (Hunter 1957, 760).

In the 1850s, the professional pearlers on the Strule were mostly army pensioners, whereas for the only four devotees—a doctor, an architect, a parson and a journalist—of a century later, it was an amusing pastime (A.N.N. 1960, 3).

Scottish pearlers have traditionally come to Ireland to fish, and the one remaining professional still does, as did his father and grandfather before him (Meagher 1928, 385; Taylor 1928, 36). A group from Scotland fished the rivers in the west of Ireland in the summer of 1995, when the water levels were lower than they had been for many years (Viney 1995, 15). In the early part of the twentieth century it was possible for some to make a living from pearl fishing alone on the Strule, and Omagh was the centre for this minor industry (Loudan 1943, 2).

Since the Second World War, the pearl fishers in Ulster appear to have been part-time or hobbyists (see Box III and Figure 4.1). There are instances from the nineteenth century also of part-time pearlers. About the middle of the nineteenth century, for example, J.B. Doyle observed on his travels in County Donegal that 'at that time there was a revenue officer at Ramelton, who realized more by the sale of pearls than by his situation' (Barker 1862–65, 113). It is interesting to note that a century later, in Donegal town, a local postman was carrying on the pearl-fishing tradition in his spare time (Moore n.d. *c.* 1980, 89).

In County Tyrone and parts of Counties Cavan and Fermanagh the pearl fishermen were known as 'sligger men' (Anon. 1984, 12; Oscar II 1977, 5), a name most probably derived from the Gaelic word *sliogán,* signifying a shell; Thompson (1856, 340) says that in the north, the freshwater mussel was known as *sliggaun* [*sic*].

Pearl fishing was probably self-limiting in that the mussels were easily overfished. Populations would then recover as fishing pressure lessened. One fisherman remembers that before the Second World War, in the upper River Bann, 'The density of the bed was such that mussels were crushed underfoot while wading out to fish for salmon' (Mackie 1992, 22).

Pearl fishing is still carried out at a low level in some of the rivers. Because of the decline in mussel numbers from overfishing and pollution, a licence is now required to fish for pearls both in the Republic of Ireland and in Northern Ireland (see final chapter).

*Fisheries*

There are few recorded examples of instances where pearl fisheries were carried on in a systematic way.

An account of a survey of the revenues of the Earl of Desmond and others, taken after his lands in Munster were forfeited in 1584, refers to a productive salmon and pearl fishery at Killorglin in County Kerry (de Dodd 1945, 160):

> And a most excellent fishery in the river flowing near the walls of the said castle as far as the lands of the aforesaid castle and town extend. In

which river many salmon and pearls are taken and found with industry and labour—valued per annum at £10.

The original account of the survey was destroyed in the Record Office fire of 1922, but fortunately a copy of portions had been made and survived. In a further division of the Earl's forfeitures, 42,000 acres in Counties Cork and Waterford were granted to Walter Raleigh confirmed by letters patent, bearing date 16 October, 29 Elizabeth, 1586 (Hayman 1856–57, 25). When Raleigh first came to Ireland, in 1579, he was a mere soldier of fortune, but in a few years had risen to the highest honours after helping to put down the Desmond revolt. His lands were purchased in 1602 by Richard Boyle (Hayman 1856–57, 18).

In the 1630s, the same Richard Boyle, who had since been made Earl of Cork, bought 140 pearls taken in the River Bandon, County Cork, where there was obviously a productive fishery. We do not know if this enterprising adventurer, who had other fishery interests such as those at Crookhaven (Townsend 1904, 67), did become involved in the pearl fishery of 'my River of the Bandon' (Grosart 1886, 56).

The pearl fishery of the River Bann was managed in a systematic way in the seventeenth century and the pearl-producing mussels were stocked from other areas to particular stretches near Banbridge for ease of fishing. The first mention of Bann mussels and pearls is apparently in an inventory of goods stolen and destroyed in the Rebellion of 1641 belonging to John Ware, or Weir, of Lenaderg in the parish of Seapatrick near Banbridge (Robb 1939, 6). The inventory states that the Irish destroyed, among other things, a barrel of Bann oysters (or pearl mussels) and a small bag of pearls valued at £10.

In the late seventeenth century, efforts were made by the Dublin Philosophical Society to investigate the existing pearl fisheries, presumably with a view to gauging their worth and to effecting their improvement. The minutes of the Society's meeting for 10 May 1693 show (see Figure 4.2) that some papers were read relating to the pearl fisheries in County Antrim and it was decided that inquiries should be made into these as well as about the fisheries in Counties Kerry, Laois/Kilkenny and Tyrone (Dublin Philosophical Society 1683–87, 183):

S[r]. Ric[d]. Cox proceeded in his description of Ireland; & read what he had putt together for ye County of Antrim, after w[ch] some papers were read relating to ye Pearl fishings in yt County, & particular Queries ordered to be drawn up by D[r]. Mullineux in order to a full Enquiry of what may be observable from Each of them. The like Enquiries ordered to be also made from ye Pearl fisheries in ye other parts following viz. County of Kerry, in the River Lean yt comes from Lough Lean, Countys of Kilkenny & Queens County, in ye River yt runs through

Kilkenny & by Coll[ll]. Wheelers house. County of Tyrone, by Macguire's bridge, where a pearl was taken (now my Lady Berisfords) as big as a pistoll bullett & worth £80.

Apparently Dr Molyneux[iii] or another did draw up a questionnaire made under various headings to inquire into the fisheries (see Figure 4.3).

A Charles Balfour made a petition (see Figure 4.4) to the Crown in October 1693 to establish a pearl fishery in the rivers of County Fermanagh (State Papers 1693, 40):

Upon the Petition of Charles Balfour Esq in the behalfe of himselfe & others Shewing that he hath a lawfull Right & Interest of Fishing in the Rivers of Macquare in the County Farmanagh in Ireland & other Waters in the said Kingdom, and is willing to erect at his owne Cost & Charge a Fishery, in the s[d] Rivers by which the Poor will be set at worke in fishing for Shell Fishes commonly called Horse Muscles or Mother of Pearle, and whereas the Same cannot be brought to perfection without a Joint Stock. Prays for Letters Patents to be incorporated for the managem[t] of y[e] said Fishery during y[e] Terme of 14 yeares

At y[e] Court at Whitehall 9 Octob. 1693 Her Maj[ty] is graciously pleased to referr this Pet[on] to the Right Hon[ble] the Lords Justices of Ireland to consider thereof, and report what her Maj[ty] may fitly do therein, whereupon her Maj[ty] will declare her further pleasure Nottingham

The content of the petition has been paraphrased into a more modern idiom by Hardy (1903, 359) as follows:

1693.
Oct.9
Whitehall.
Proceedings upon the petition of Charles Balfour, esq., on behalf of himself and others. Shows that he has a lawful right to fish in the rivers of Maquare in the County Fermanagh, and other waters in Ireland, and that he is willing to erect a fishery at his own expense in the said rivers, by which the poor will be 'set at work' in fishing for shell fish called horse muscles or mother of pearl. As this work cannot be brought to perfection without a joint-stock, he prays for letters patent of incorporation. Referred to the Lord Justices of Ireland.

We see that the intention was to set the poor at work collecting pearl mussels. We do not, however, learn whether or not the application was successful. A similar application for a patent for a pearl fishery was granted for the rivers of Cumberland in England, wherein the poor people collected pearls for a gentleman of that county (see chapter seven). It is probable that the fishery in Fermanagh proceeded, as it seems that a gentleman by the name of Charles Balfour collected pearls from the River Maguiresbridge (now known as the River Coolebrooke).

Some years prior to the application. Robert Redding (1688, 159), in a letter dated 23 October 1688, mentions that 'pearls are also found in a small river…in the County of Fermanagh, commonly known in the County by the name of the River of Maguires Bridge; between the towns of Lisnaskea and Enniskilling', and that a 'Mr. Ballfour that lives in the town of Lisnaskea…has…a very numerous collection of pearls gathered in the river; and some of them of a very considerable value; one among them was so estimated at 50 pound, and has several others of 10, 20 and 30 pounds price'. Thus it would appear that it was a profitable pearl-producing river and he sought, through his petition to the Crown, legally to establish a right to the fishery.

Together with the Bann in County Down, the river which has always attracted most attention is the Strule in Tyrone, where at one time as many as 50 fishermen, some of them making it a full-time employment, plied the trade (see Box IV).

The Custom House in Dublin, built in the 1780s, has 14 carved heads, representing 13 of Ireland's most important rivers and the Atlantic Ocean, on the keystones of the arches of the main doorways and windows. The heads show representations of the produce of the catchments of the rivers, and the Bann, as well as a turban of linen representing the important flax-growing and linen-weaving industries of the upper reaches, wears a string of pearls (see Figure 4.5). This indicates that it was well known as a pearl fishery down to the late eighteenth century.

The tributaries of the Foyle were fished by both amateurs and professionals in the first decade of the twentieth century, as this shows (Anon. 1908, 5):

> During the past week some very valuable finds of pearls are reported to have been made in the rivers round Strabane, county Tyrone. Pearl fishing is a regular employment in these streams, which are all tributaries of the Foyle, and for a considerable time past business in this line has been dull. A day or two ago, however, one man after half an hours fishing found a pearl which he is said to have sold to a local jeweller for £8. Several other smaller ones found by the same person fetched from 10s. to 20s. Some amateurs have been successful in getting very fine pearls.

According to Alexander Knox (1875, 674), most of the pearls found in the Bann in the nineteenth century were of a diminutive size, but he had in his

*Box IV*

**Pearl fishery profiles**

*Omagh* This fishery on the River Strule was first described in the 1680s in a good contemporary first-hand account. The writer, Sir Robert Redding of Dublin, who visited the area in 1688, gives a description of the fishing method (see chapter two) and says that the pearls 'are offered to Sale by those People every Summer Assize'. In the eighteenth and nineteenth centuries the pearls fished from the rivers of County Tyrone were sold locally in Omagh and in Belfast, Dublin, Edinburgh and London.

Pearls from the Strule were exhibited at the Great Exhibition of 1851 at Crystal Palace by John Nelis and later in Cork at the National Exhibition of 1852.

Pearl fishing in the Strule was a hobby for many people at one time and in 1965, one man who had fished for 50 years could remember a time when as many as 30 men and women from the town would be seeking their fortunes on the River.

An article in the *News letter* in June 1894 reported that in a week, County Tyrone fishermen had collected 14 top-quality pearls. The anonymous writer continued that 'The Strule, without exception is the best river in Ulster for pearls.'

When pearls from Japan were unavailable during the Second World War, those from Omagh were much in demand (see chapter three). Pearls continue to be fished from the Strule but, in common with the rest of the tributaries of the Foyle, the mussel is now scarce, with an estimated total population of less than 1,000 for the catchment.

(Sources: Redding 1688, 140; Report by the juries 1852, 164; Maguire 1853, 349; Loudan 1943, 2; Mullin, 1947, 5, 8; Anon. 1965b, 1; Ross 1988, 44; Mackie 1992, 65; Chesney 1996, 146.)

*Banbridge* One of the best pearl-fishing stretches in Ireland was that portion of the upper Bann between Katesbridge and Gilford. In the latter half of the

possession two or three as large as very small peas, procured from the County Tyrone rivers. Good pearls were still being fished from the Strule towards the end of that century (Anon. 1894, 138).

There is no evidence that any systematic pearl–fishing industry on the scale of some in Central Europe existed in Ireland. At least two attempts at organizing a pearling business were made however, in County Fermanagh in the seventeenth century and in County Down in the eighteenth. Charles Balfour made the attempt in Fermanagh in 1693 (see above); Walter Harris (1744, 149), speaking of the fishery near Banbridge, says that in about 1721 'a Scotch Pedler bought a few Pearls from the People about that place, which were pretty valuable, and from thence proposed to himself some Advantage in carrying on that Branch of Commerce; but at his Return, finding it not worth

seventeenth and first decade of the eighteenth century, pearls to the value of many thousands of pounds were taken from the Bann in the neighbourhood of Banbridge.

In 1726, Solomon Whyte of Dublin renewed a lease to James and John Majore of Ballinvalley, where the present town of Banbridge stands, for a stretch of the Bann (435 perches, Irish measure) to fish for mussels and pearls. In a deed dated March 1736, the Majores sold their interest in the pearl fishery to Hugh McClaine of Greenock, Scotland, including a curing house on the left bank of the river.

Although Payne's *Universal geography* (1794) refers to it, it appears that even by the middle of the eighteenth century the pearl fishery on the Bann was in decline, probably owing to overfishing. A contemporary source says that the pearl industry at Banbridge seemed to fall into decay about the year 1740. In that account, the demise of the fishery was attributed to the advent of the linen industry, when bleach works were erected on the river. The pearl mussel's decrease was due to the chemicals used in the bleaching process. It was said that at the beginning of the nineteenth century the value and chances of finding a pearl were not sufficient to tempt people away from their more regular and profitable occupations.

A coat of arms of Banbridge dating from about 1870 has the pearl mussel as one of its emblems, indicating its importance in the history of the town (see Figure 10.1). Pearls continued to be found occasionally in the eighteenth and nineteenth centuries, and in 1892 'the Bann yielded one of the choicest pearls that ever came from Ireland'.

Nowadays the mussel has almost totally disappeared from the River Bann. (Sources: Harris 1744, 146–49; Camden 1789, 165; Payne 1794, 174); Doyle 1854, 133–34; Dubourdieu 1802, 315; Kunz and Stevenson 1908, 165; Linn 1935, 193; Robb 1939, 6; Weatherup 1974, 54; Ross 1988, 42; Chesney 1996, 146.)

while, he gave it over'.

By 1740 the Bann fishery was in decline, as we learn from a letter apparently sent to Hans Sloane[iv] by John Copping (1740, 198), Dean of Clogher, in which it is stated that pearls were then rarely taken, 'the people being better employed in the Linen manufacture'.

We know that the Bann was still producing fine pearls in 1768, as in November of that year 'at a numerous meeting of the inhabitants of Bannbridge, James Law being in the chair, a gift of 50 Bann pearls was presented to the Countess of Hillsborough, per Mr John Bateman' (Robb 1939, 6). A century later, according to Barker (1862–65, 113), the travel writer J.B. Doyle saw an extensive pearl fishery at Portglenone, on the River Bann. Up until the close of the nineteenth century, the Bann was still occasionally producing fine pearls. For example, Kunz and Stevenson (1908, 165) report that 'In 1892 the Bann yielded one of the choicest pearls that ever came out of Ireland.'

That pearl fishing was largely opportunistic in Ireland by the middle of the eighteenth century can be gleaned from a manuscript copy of a letter dated 20 September 1762, sent by Edward Willes to the Earl of Warwick. Having said that the greatest curiosity in the town of Omagh was the pearl fishery (see Figure 4.6), the Chief Baron goes on to relate the following (Willes 1762, 125):

> I heard of a pearl which had been found about 20 years ago, which is reported to have been sold for £30 in London. When a prize of that value is discovered, it sets the people all at work to put into the pearl lottery; and they are as Busy as the Brokers in Change Alley, when a large prize is just Drawn in the State Lottery, by Degrees the adventurers, not meeting with the same Success, the Humour of pearl Fishing subsides, and is neglected, 'till some lucky person by accident meets with a good pearl, and this set's them all at work again.

Referring to the pearl fishery of the River Lagan in former times, in which 'the common method of fishing for these mussels was by wading into the water in Summer, and thrusting sticks into the opening of the shells to take them up', Mulligan (1886, 21) informs us that 'This business has long since been given up. The pearls found were not of sufficient value to induce people to continue the occupation, and were generally of a muddy colour, and sometimes full of specks, which very much diminished their value.' Of the pearls found in northern rivers, he says, those from the Bann were superior to those from the Lagan and Foyle. According to Welch (W[elch] 1908, 90), however, it was the formation of the Lagan Canal which destroyed the pearl-fishing industry of the Lagan.

Although active beforehand and afterwards, it appears that the pearl-fishing industry in Ireland was at its zenith in the seventeenth century. While there is some information on aspects of the fisheries, it is generally lacking with regard to specific points such as numbers of fishers and revenues. Unlike in parts of Europe, but consistently with the rest of the British Isles, the pearl fisheries in Ireland did not attract serious royal or government interest.

This aspect will be developed further in chapter eight, where a comparison with the exploitation of the alluvial deposits of gold will be made. In the next chapter, however, the extent to which pearls and pearl fishing have entered into Irish culture will be explored.

*Notes*
[i]The year 1609 was, in fact, during the reign of James I.
[ii]While his decription of the pearl divers may have been accurate, Goldsmith was

certainly ill informed on the duration for which they could remain under water. He declares, 'It is amazing how very long they are seen to continue at the bottom. Some, as we are assured, have been known to continue three quarters of an hour under water without breathing; and to one unused to diving, ten minutes would suffocate the strongest.' In fact, investigations made more than a century after Goldsmith was writing, by Prof. Galbraith of the Royal Dublin Society, established that pearl divers remained under water for 50 seconds on average and a maximum of 90 (Gillman 1859, 289).

[iii]Thomas and William Molyneux were founders of the Dublin Philosophical Society, and the latter was its first secretary in 1683. William Molyneux left Ireland in 1689 because of political unrest, but returned in 1691 and is remembered for his pamphlet, *Case of Ireland...stated* (1698), which was condemned by the Westminster parliament.

[iv]The celebrated County Down-born naturalist, baronet and physician to George II, whose collection of books and manuscripts formed the nucleus of the British Museum Library.

# 5. Pearls in mythology, folklore, literature and symbology

> Mar a raibh cantáin na n-éan ar ghéagaibh crainn ghlais,
> Lacháin is éisc ag scéitheadh ón dtaoide,
> An eala go glé ag téacht ar tuinn ann,
> 'S an péarla i n-íochtar trath as cómhair…
> *Eoghan Rua Ó Súilleabháin* (1748–84), *Do rinneadh aisling bheag aereach*
> (Ua Duinnín 1902, 120)

To what extent pearls have entered into the Irish culture through mythology, folklore, superstition, literature and the other arts of poetry and music as well as religious symbolism will, *inter alia*, be examined in the present chapter. Aspects of the etymology of pearls and their usage in the names of places will also be included for discussion.

*Myth and saga*

What is known as euhemerism—the reference of myths to historical basis, such as where divine beings are treated as if they were men of a far-off age—has long been a favourite method of manufacturing early history in Ireland, as elsewhere. The Irish pseudo-historians and inventors of the pre-Christian genealogies were apparently euhemerists. By humanizing and mortalizing the divinities of pagan Ireland, they hoped to eradicate the pagan beliefs that still lingered on among many of their countrymen (O'Rahilly 1946, 260–61).

The tradition of the early stories, encompassing both impacted myth and corrupted history, originated with the Celts, an Indo-European group who are the ancestors of the Irish people and from whom the Gaelic language came. The myths and sagas were probably first written down around the eighth or ninth century and represent the oral tradition of the Iron-Age Celts who flourished in Europe during the seven centuries before Christ. With the growth of the Roman and Viking Empires, their influence died out, except in Ireland which was less exposed to new tradition. Thus the original culture of the Celts is preserved in these stories.

In Celtic society there were apparently three classes: a warrior class headed by a king; a priestly class, the druids (who are magicians in the mythological tales); and a class of farmers and free men (Gantz 1981, 8).

The two main sources for the stories are *Lebor na huidre* and the *Book of*

*Leinster*, and there are a few instances in these texts where pearls are mentioned. In a tale of historical romance from *Lebor na huidre*, a manuscript transcribed in AD 1100, apparently from a ninth-century text (Best and Bergin 1929, xiii), they are used as an epithet of teeth. The writer, in describing the hero Cu Chulaind (or Cúchulainn) sitting in his chariot, says, 'Ata lim-sa ba frass do nemannaib rolad in a chend,' which means, 'I should think it was a shower of pearls that was flung into his head' (O'Beirne Crowe 1870, 377). Similarly, in the *Book of Leinster*, compiled about AD 1150, pearls are mentioned in some of the stories, for example in *Imallam in da thuarad*: 'Némain i fothud .i. is glidir némaind ani fhothaigim' (Best and O'Brien 1965, 822).

The homilies and legends of the childhood of Christ contained in the *Leabhar breac* (Speckled book), a work compiled from earlier manuscripts at the close of the fourteenth century, give an insight into the religious stories then current. One of the stories regarding the magi, who are called druids in the language of the time, includes the gifts given to the infant Jesus. Having told of the gold, frankincense and myrrh, the writer goes on to say that a pearl was also given (Anon. 1876a, 138):

> Atbert didiu Iacop gluinech .i. brathair Crist fesin, co tucsat na drúdi ascada imda ele do Crist .i. corcair derscaigtech co sollsi némdibaide margrent thaitneamach. [7]

This has been translated as follows (Hogan 1895, 66):

> Then James of the Knees, i.e. the brother of Christ himself, said that the magi gave many other presents to Christ, i.e. remarkable purple of imperishable light and a bright pearl.

The magi (or druids) in pagan times in Ireland are said by Lady Wilde (1890, 255), alias Speranza, to have swallowed an Irish pearl to attain eternal youth, and she also credits the mythical Tuatha Dé Danann with having this power:

> The magi had the power of prolonging life, and for this purpose an Irish pearl was swallowed, which rendered the swallower as youthful as when in his prime. The *Tuatha-de-Danans* possessed this secret, hence the tradition of their long existence secreted in caves, after their defeat by the Milesians.

We do not know the source for this information as she cites none. But while such practices may sound fabulous, there might be some basis in fact, such as the consumption of pearls for medicinal purposes or to counter the effects of poisons. Pearls of poor quality were used in medicinal potions in

Ireland down to the end of the seventeenth century and are still used for such purposes elsewhere (see chapter six).

*Folklore, legend and superstition*

The *Dinnshenchas* is a collection of legends in prose and verse about the names of noteworthy places in Ireland, whose date has been variously given as the eighth and twelfth centuries (Stokes 1892, 467). One copy (MS Rawlinson B.506 in the Bodleian Library) was written in Middle Irish on parchment at the end of the fourteenth or beginning of the fifteenth century. Regarding the origin of the pearls in Lough Leane in Kerry it contains the following:

> Ni ansa .i. Loch .i. Lein Linnfiacclach maic Bain Bolgaig maic Bannaig, cerd sen Side buidb. Is e romboi fo loch ic denam niamlesstair Foltlibre ingine Flidaise. Iar scur a opri cach n-aidhce a hindeoin uad cosin feirt, & na frasa foecerded iarsin din muin it eat na nemanna rosilat ann di. Nithnemannach dorigni a cetna oc slaidi cuich Concobair maic Nessa a uaid. Is do sin ata Lein & indin na nDeissi. Unde Loch Len.

The translation of this has been given by Whitley Stokes (1892, 485) as follows:

> The lake, that is, of Lén Linnfiaclach, son of Ban Bolgach, son of Bannach. He was the craftsman of Síd Buibd. It is he that was under the lake making the bright vessel of Fann the Long-haired, daughter of Flidais. Every night, after quitting his work, he used to fling his anvil away to the Indeoin na nDése, to the mound; and the showers which, thereafter, it used to cast forth from the back, they are the pearls which were sown by it. Nithnemannach did the same in beating out the cup of Conor mac Nessa in the north. Hence is Loch Léin and the Anvil of the Dési.

So the origin of pearls in Lough Leane[i] in the south-west as well as in the north of Ireland was attributed to the showers generated by these blacksmiths' anvils. It may be noted that the name of the craftsman in the north, Nithnemannach, is the same as that by which the River Dee in County Louth was known in the old annals of Ireland. In the *Annals of the Four Masters*, the eruption of various rivers, including the River Dee (Nith), is said to have taken place in the Age of the World 4169 (O'Donovan 1856a, 53). The *Annals of Inisfallen* mention 'Tomaidm nemnach hi Maig Muirthimne', which may be translated as, 'The eruption of [Nith] Némannach [i.e., abounding in pearls] in Mag Muirthemne' (MacAirt 1977, 48). We will see later that this river, with its connection with pearls, will feature again as one of the places where part of the ancient laws of Ireland, the *Senchus mór*, was compiled.

Even down to the late part of the nineteenth century, folklore regarding where pearls came from was current. Nathanial Colgan (1914, 60), who had visited Kerry in 1888, met a man who told him that the local pearls came from an animal called the Carrabuncle. Colgan was informed that 'it was a kind of snake that lived in Lough Geal [now called Lough Gal] and made the lake shine, and threw off shells with precious stones in them'. This was confirmed by another informant, the local postman, who said that 'It lit up the whole lake…and the pearls found in the river that flowed out from Lough Geal came off the Carrabuncle.' Incidentally, there is also a gem called the carbuncle.[ii]

At the beginning of the twentieth century, Daniel Deeney published the 'peasant lore' he had collected, which included a story in absurd language of how, when two men were collecting seaweed, one saw the 'Queen o the Sea an her beautiful daughter…covered over with pearls an diamonds' (Deeney 1900, 28). When he relates his vision, his companion tells him that 'Twis only wanst afore I heard tell o them bein seen, an the wan that seen them didn't do a day's good after it till he died.' Obviously it was unlucky to catch sight of the 'Queen o the Sea', and apparently the same fate befell this poor man as had the only other previous observer of the phenomenon in the district.

In folklore, pearls have a dubious reputation and are generally considered unlucky (Pickering 1995, 201). While giving a baby the gift of a pearl—the birthstone for June—may be said by some to guarantee the infant a long life, to others pearls symbolize tears and are therefore unlucky, especially when worn by brides.[iii]

The river above Omagh in County Tyrone is known as the Drumragh and there is a legend connected with pearl fishing in the district. It is said that a great pearl which will buy out the seven townlands of Drumragh will be found there by a red-haired son of a widow. According to the prophecy, however, this pearl will bring misfortune and death to its owner (Mullin 1947, 8).

Also in the same area there was, and still may be, a superstition that pearls faded when worn by men; Jack Loudan (1943, 2), who visited Omagh during the Second World War, was told by a pearl fisherman:

> That a pearl will lose its appearance if worn by a man? And there's only one way to restore its beauty. It must be given to a woman, and she must wear it for a time next her skin. If this is done, the lustre will come back again—and thats no lie, for I've seen it happen many a time myself.

It would appear that the wearing of pearls by men in Ireland was anathema, since the nineteenth century at least, and perhaps this superstition has its origin in the attitude that they are regarded as non-masculine items of jewellery (see chapter six).

*Literature*

Pearls feature in many forms of Irish fictitious writing, with examples to be found in comic tales, historical novels and political satires as well as in romantic tales and even in the Anglo-Irish literature of the first part of the twentieth century.

Some stories have come down to us in which pearls are weaved into the politics of the day and the following, as related by George Kunz (1917, 50), is an example:

> About 1830, when popular feeling was roused to the highest pitch by the agitation for the repeal of the Corn Laws, many rings were set with the following stones, the initial letters forming the word 'repeal':
> Ruby
> Emerald
> Pearl
> Emerald
> Amethyst
> Lapis lazuli
> An Irishman, who owned such a ring, noted one day that the lapis lazuli had fallen out, and took the ring to a jeweller in Cork, to have the missing stone replaced. When the work was completed, the owner, seeing that the jeweller had set a topaz in place of a lapis lazuli, protested against the substitution; but the jeweller induced him to accept the ring as it was, by the witty explanation that it now read 'repeat', and that if agitation were often enough repeated, the repeal would come of itself.

Gerald Griffin (1803–40) apparently wrote *The invasion*, an historical novel, in 1832. It was reprinted in 1862 by James Duffy, with the eminent historian Eugene O'Curry contributing notes and 'corrections' in an appendix to the later edition. Why it was necessary to provide such a critique of a work of fiction indicates the seriousness with which some sought to ensure that the 'correct' version of aspects of the ancient history of Ireland was portrayed. Griffin (1862, 385) describes the dress of a chieftain as including pearls worn behind the ears:

> Two pearls, the purest that had ever left Loch Lene, hung gracefully behind (not from) his ears, and marked the wearer's rank, while they adorned his person.

In a Romantic tale with political overtones set in the eighteenth century, Samuel Lover (1844, 366) describes how the hero, on the run from government forces in the west of Ireland, would go up into the hills with his female companion to look for pearls:

Among many haunts, the most favourite was a small river, which, having its origin in the hills, bounded wildly from crag to crag, and made its precipitous road to the sea by a succession of picturesque falls, one more beautiful than another. This stream was remarkable for abounding in a species of mussel, frequently containing pearls, which, though inferior in lustre to the oriental, were still of great beauty, and in search of these Ned and Ellen passed much of their time. He, as well as his 'lady love', had assumed the peasant guise, (a practice rather common to the refugees,) as thus they might appear with less chance of observation from evil eyes, when they ventured from the security of their mountain retreats, and trusted themselves towards the plains. In these loose habiliments, Ned was more free to wade and search in the shoals of the pearl river for the shelly treasures which were destained for a necklace for his loved one, who, seated on some jutting rock, smiled on the labours of her lover, as she received from his hand the produce of his search.

The illustration accompanying the piece is shown in Figure 5.1, where it may be noticed that the mussels collected resemble more the type found in salt water than the pearl-producing variety of fresh water.

In Anglo-Irish literature, too, mention is made of pearls and pearl fishing. Molly Keane (1904–96), who was born in County Kildare, grew up in an Anglo-Irish hunting, fishing and church-going family, concealing her literary interests from her sporting friends (Jeffares 1982, 251). The theme of her novels is that of the 'big house' and its proud occupants in decline, painfully involved with yet separated from the rest of Ireland (Vance 1990, 216). She wrote 11 novels under the pseudonym M.J. Farrell (a name adopted for fear of ridicule from the Anglo-Irish hunting set), the first—*Young entry*—in 1928.

In the story, the heroine, Prudence, who is 19 years old, goes pearl fishing in the local stream with her friend (Farrell 1928, 139):

They had come out pearl-fishing; and she, personally, was going to wade for mussels. It was chilly work, even with James' waders…Staring absorbed through her glass-bottomed bucket into the golden, dark water, Prudence would plunge down an arm and pick up stone after stone, in mistake for the dark, elusive mussel shells…Prudence dived her arm in again, cursing when the sleeve of her jumper unrolled itself in the water; but this time she did pull out an ancient and hoary shell-fish…she prised the shells apart and with an eager forefinger explored the mucous consistency of the unhappy fish within.

The author obviously had first-hand knowledge of the art of pearl fishing and knew of the most valuable colours of freshwater pearls—our heroine finds a pink one to match others she had acquired.

There was a tradition among the Ascendancy since the seventeenth century of collecting, or having collected for them, pearls from the local rivers (see chapter four). An example of a beautiful necklace of pearls from the River Slaney collected by one such family in the early part of the twentieth century is shown in Figure 5.2. Its emerald clasp gives the necklace a particularly Irish finish.

*Poetry and music*

Some examples of pearls in Irish poetry, both in Gaelic and English, can be found spanning more than a millennium. Pearls are mentioned in early Irish poetry and in one ninth-century poem they are Latinized as *margarét* (Meyer 1910a, 14) rather than given the Old Irish designation *némann*:

> Leath a forine ó buidhe,
> alaile is fiondruine,
> a hindech do margarét,
> brecht le certa cíarét.

In *Párliament na mban* (Parliament of women), a work of poetry and prose composed by Domhnall Ó Colmáin in the late seventeenth century (during the period between the Restoration of Charles II and the Penal Laws of Anne and George I), the phrase 'péarla na glóire' (Ó Cuív 1952, 63) is used in passing. In 'Cúirt an mheadhon oidhche' (The midnight court), which is a satirical *aisling* (or vision) poem written by Brian Merriman (*c.* 1747–1805) in the late eighteenth century, the presiding queen is referred to as the 'Pearl of Majesty' (Corkery 1924, 226).

The line, ''S an péarla i n-íochtar trath as cómhair', from a poem by Eoghan Rua Ó Súilleabháin (1748–84), which is the final line of the epigraph at the beginning of this chapter, has been said to be a perfect example of lyric verse in the Irish language, to which the literal translation ('The pearl in the water's depth, sometimes visible') does no justice (Corkery 1924, 215); Ó Súilleabháin's versions of the *aisling*, apparently because of their structure, are recognized as masterpieces of atmospheric euphony (Welch 1996, 459).

It is said that when Donal na Rasca, or Donal the Outlaw (Daniel O'Keefe), who was on the run from the law in the south of the country in the eighteenth century, found that his lover (Margaret Kelly) had betrayed him for a large reward, he composed a lament, of which the following is part (O'Flanagan, 1844, 157):

> With strings of rich pearls
> Thy white neck was laden,

And thy fingers with spoils
Of the Sassanach maiden…

Favourite poems and other literary writings are often referred to as pearls. For example, *The casket of Irish pearls* is, as its subtitle informs, 'a selection of prose and verse from the best Irish writers' (MacMahon 1846).

Thomas Moore used pearls in his poetry (see chapter one for an example) and at least six references to them can be counted among his works. In his music he also alluded to pearls. He knew of native pearls and in his *Irish melodies* they are mentioned twice; in 'Fairest! Put on a while', which is really a description of Ireland, his knowledge that pearls were found in Lough Leane was used in framing the following quatrain (Herbert 1876, 461):

Lakes where the pearl lies hid
And caves where the diamond's sleeping
Bright as the gems that lid
Of thine lets fall in weeping…

In 'Desmond's song' he uses the pearl and the violet as examples to illustrate how things can grow into things of beauty despite their origins (Herbert 1876, 463):

Hath the pearl less whiteness
Because of its birth?
Hath the violet less brightness
For growing near earth?

George Petrie (1790–1866) collected old Irish music and songs. Among these is an old love-song known as 'Péarla an bhrollaigh bhain' (The Snowy-breasted pearl), the final verse of which goes as follows:

A's mara dam-sa taoise indan
A phéarla an bhrollaigh bhain
Nar thi mise slan ó'n Aonach.

Petrie translated this as (Healy 1962, 126):

For if not mine, dear girl,
Oh, snowy-breasted pearl,
May I never from the fair
With life return.

In *Hardiman's Irish minstrelsy* there are many references to pearls describing attributes of beauty in women and they are used, as in the early Irish sagas, as an epithet of teeth in one instance (Anon. 1834, 540):

> Mild Mable Ni Kelly, bright coolun of curls!
> All stately and pure as the swan on the lake,
> Her mouth of white teeth is a palace of pearls,
> And the youth of the land are love-sick for her sake.

Turlogh Carolan (1670–1738), the harpist and composer who lost his sight from smallpox at the age of 14, used pearls in some of his compositions, as the following example shows (Ó Máille 1916, 147):

> Is dearbtha an gníomh gurab agam a bhéar rí,
> Ó a maireann fáluíhe na gréine,
> Agus nach peacadh dhuit, a naoí, ler chuiris fá shlighe,
> Í, an taithneamh thas mílte péarla.

Even in the present time they are sometimes mentioned, as in the 1980s music of the rock group U2. For example, 'she brings me white golden pearls, stolen from the sea' ('Running to stand still').

*Symbolism*

The pearl has been used to represent spiritual or religious concepts, such as Christian salvation, the chaste soul, or heaven, as well as to signify more secular ideals like innocence, virginity and beauty (Joyce and Addison 1992, 219) and some examples of the latter were given above. In fact, the pearl is used in a symbolic way in most religions.[iv]

An indication of the status of pearls in Christendom is their use in iconography as symbols of regeneration (Clark 1986, 81), and we will see Irish examples of their use in religious ornamentation in chapter six. For the present, the symbolic role of pearls, gleaned from Irish writings, will be addressed.

In the *Book of Lismore*, compiled in the latter half of the fifteenth century, Saint Patrick is described in the lives of saints as 'in margreit ₇ in leg loghmhar isa lithlaithe so .i. Sanctus Patricius', which has been translated as 'the pearl and the precious stone whose festival day this is, to wit, Sanctus Patricius' (Stokes 1890, 150).

In Penal times, James O'Gallagher (1681–1751), who was Bishop of Raphoe (1725–37), preached sermons in Gaelic to the peasants while on the run from the authorities. In his sermons he, like the early Christian writers of the Gospels, makes many references to pearls to signify purity and precious things in the scriptures (Bourke 1877, 168, 384)—for example, 'n peurla neamhda, mór-luachmher, Mac Dé' ('that heavenly pearl of immense value, the

Box V
## The Irish pearl

This anonymous work, though the style cannot hide the true identity of its author, opens with a group of people from Ireland being introduced to Queen Anne by the Duke and Duchess of Ormond, one of whom, a young lady, has an ornament—a chaplet of pearls—in her hair. This woman, Lady Florence Glenleary, is told afterwards by her friend Lady Ormond that the Queen was so taken with the pearls that she wanted to purchase them. This is despite the fact, says Lady Ormond, that 'it was an old family relic; in fact, part and parcel of yourself—the more precious, as it was the only hereditary possession the civil war had left you'. Florence then asks Lady Ormond to 'spare me one short hour, while I relate how those pearls came into my possession and why they surpass earth's richest treasures in my heart'.

The pearls were 'collected by our tenantry' from the lake of Gougane Barra near the source of the River Lee, and presented to her mother to welcome home the foreign bride. Her mother had had it made into a rosary and had entrusted it to her priest before her premature death.

The story is interwoven with the historical events of the time and has as its background the disappearance of the old Irish aristocratic order: the heroine's father is depicted as one of those who sailed for Europe after the fall of Limerick. The pearls come into her possession when she meets the priest—now a hermit—while undertaking a religious pilgrimage to the lake from which the pearls came 'for immersion into the waters on St. John's day—midsummer's day'. The pearls are fixed to her bridal veil when she and Lord Glenleary 'were united by Protestant rites', which indicates a changing of religion accompanying the change in order.

Having related the story of the pearls, the heroine is kept in suspense while the Queen has them. However, the sovereign eventually returns them with the words, 'receive these jewels then again from our hand, as the title deeds of that romantic region where first they were discovered'.

She returns to Ireland and is reunited with her father, who had fallen at the Siege of Barcelona but survived, and who had obtained a royal consent for repatriation. The heroine's father regains his family property and their friend Lord Ormond is created lord lieutenant. Throughout the tale the pearls remain as the central motif, linking all aspects and used particularly to symbolize religious salvation. The story is essentially a parable and ends with the moral lament, 'If a love for the souls of their fellow-countrymen, if tenderness for their feelings had actuated those who enjoyed such superior privileges, then indeed might righteousness have exalted our nation.'

(Source: Anon. 1855, 7, 11, 32, 95.)

Son of God'); 'peurla na glóire' ('pearl of eternal glory').

Luke Waddinge (1600–91), who became Bishop of Ferns in Wexford, wrote a poem, 'For Saint Stephen's day', in which all three stanzas end with the symbolic refrain of the stones that were used to stone him to death being replaced by pearls in heaven. The final stanza is as follows (Murray 1986, 66):

> The most sweet saint with his last breath
> Doth pray for those who seek his death,
> And leaves not off while life doth last,
> As thick as hail their stones to cast;
> And for those stones in Heaven he found
> Of precious pearls a glorious crown.

An historical novel, *The Irish pearl*, set in the time of Queen Anne (1702–14), first appeared in the *Christian ladies' magazine* of 1847 and was published in book form in 1850 with a reprint in 1855. It is replete with symbolically-charged references, both religious and otherwise, to native pearls (see Box V). The pearls in that story have been used as the central motif to signify various things. They appear as fashion accessories for the hair and later bridal ornaments, respectively to accent or frame female beauty and to signify purity. They are also used, among other things, to romanticize the country from which they came and to symbolize religious salvation.

*Etymology and place names*

Most civilizations have words in their languages to describe pearls[v] and in the Irish language specific as well as general terms have been used to describe the pearl.

In the ninth century *margarét*, which is apparently a corruption of the Latin word for pearl, was used in some instances (e.g., Meyer 1910a, 14). The Old- and Middle-Irish texts appear to use *némann* and *pérla* respectively (Royal Irish Academy 1983, 476, 495), while *péarla* has been used in the late seventeenth century (Ó Cuív 1952, 63), in the eighteenth century (Bourke 1877, 420) and in the twentieth century (de Bhaldraithe 1959, 517).

Charles O'Conor (1826, 365) noted, in his translation of the *Annals of Ulster* from the Irish into Latin, that the word *seoda* signifies gems, or pearls, and in general things that are very precious, when he says, 'Vox Hibernica *Seoda* gemmas significat, vel margaritas, et in genere res valde pretiosas.' According to Joyce (1903a, 227), in ancient Ireland a pearl was usually designated by the word *séd*, old form *sét*, but adds that it was often used to designate a gem or jewel of any kind.

It would appear that a number of words, but particularly three, or their variants, have been used specifically to describe a pearl since the written word was first used in Ireland in the fifth century. The earliest to be used was apparently from the Latin *margarita*, and a variation of it, namely *margréit* (Stokes 1890, 396; Joynt 1939, 64), was used down to the latter half of the fifteenth century. Variations on the Old Irish word *némann* have been used from an early date. For example, in the *Senchus mór*, part of the ancient laws of Ireland, the genitive case *nemunn* was used (Anon. 1865, 2); in a fifteenth-century text of Early Modern Irish, *nemanna* as well as *clocha nemuinda* have been used (Wulff 1929, 108). Similarly, Philip O'Sullivan Beare (*c.* 1630, 39), in the seventeenth century, used *piarla* rather than *péarla*, which was then also in use[vi] and which continues to be the modern designation.

John O'Donovan, with the help of others, had before his death in 1861 almost completed the translation of the ancient laws of Ireland. According to W. Neilson Hancock, the *Senchus mór* maintained, after its modification from pagan origins in the fifth century, its authority amongst the native Irish for a period of some 1,200 years (Anon. 1865, v). In the 'commentary' to the *Senchus mór*, the compilers give three possible explanations as to why one of the places where it was composed, 'Nith nemonnach', on the banks of the river named 'Nith', was so called. One of these is given as, '.i. mill nemunn fo gabtair ina traig', which O'Donovan has translated wrongly as, 'i.e. onyx stones they used to find in its strand' (Anon. 1865, 2). A more accurate rendering of the phrase would be, 'i.e., balls of [or round] pearls they used to find in its strand'. O'Donovan, who elsewhere has censured others such as Charles O'Conor for incorrectly translating passages from Irish manuscripts (see Box VI) is clearly guilty of the same here.

Sir James Ware, the most eminent of Ireland's antiquarians (who had been imprisoned by the Parliamentarians during the English Civil War and expelled from Dublin in 1649, but returned upon the Restoration in 1660), said of Irish pearls, 'Ibi etiam inveniuntur Margaritae, sed pleraeque vel pallidae vel subfuscae' (Waraeo 1654, 35), which a poor translation has rendered as, 'There are also Margarites, but of a pale colour' (Ware 1705, 20).

Pearls have also been referred to as 'margarites' by other writers who, apparently, have been unable correctly to translate *margaritae*. For example, in a translation of O'Flaherty's *Ogygia*, by James Hely (1793, 178), pearls are called margarites, and Dalton (1828, 159) calls them 'margaritas' when attempting to translate a passage from O'Conor's *Rerum Hibernicarum scriptores*.

Thus, perhaps, Irish pearls may have been overlooked to some extent, as these four examples over three centuries would attest, because earlier material, particularly in Latin but also in the Irish language, was poorly or incorrectly translated.

In present-day Ireland there are apparently very few place names associated, either directly or allusively, with pearls. It is apparent also, from the old annals and other sources, that in former times very few places were named for their connection with pearls.

It is annotated in the *Lismore papers* 'that a tributary of the Blackwater at

Lismore, the Ownashade (*Abhainn-na-sed* in Irish), is when translated into English, its native appellation, The river of the jewel=pearl' (Grosart 1886, 239). Sometimes *séd* was indeed synonymous with pearl but, as shown earlier, it could refer to a gem or jewel of any kind. The word is often found forming a part of local names (Joyce 1875, 357)—for example, as in *Dun-na-séd* (castle of the jewels), the old name for Baltimore in County Cork; Cloghnashade (stone of the jewels), the name of a townland as well as a lake in County Roscommon; Loughnashade (lake of the jewels) the name of a lake in each of the Counties Armagh, Leitrim and Offaly.

Two lakes, Lough Namona in County Kerry and Lough Naminn in County Donegal, are in areas where pearls have been found and their names are possibly associated with, or derived from, the specific Old Irish word for pearl, *némann*. Also, we have seen earlier in the chapter that in the *Annals of Inisfallen* (MacAirt 1977, 48), as well as in the *Senchus mór* (Anon. 1865, 2), the River Dee in County Louth was called Nith Némannach, which literally means 'abounding with or of the pearls'.

The name Pearl Valley was apparently used for an area, Clountiquick or Cloontiquick, near Dunmanway in County Cork in the 1800s (D. O'Farrell, T. O'Mahony, pers. comm.), although its provenance has been lost. We know the nearby River Bandon furnished pearls in the sixteenth century, and the name may well have been to do with that fact. Trawnferla (Strand of the pearl) in County Cork apparently received its name from a ship, the *Pearl*, having foundered there (O'Brien 1991, 123) rather than for having any association with pearls. In fact, depositions taken in the seventeenth century show that a ship of this name, which incidentally had pearls listed among its cargo, was *en route* for Calais and subsequently went aground at Dursey in 1614 (Appleby 1992, 120, 140).

While many used in ancient Ireland may not have survived to the present day (see chapter six) pearls have, to some extent, been enduring symbols in the literature of the country. Thus, albeit in a small way, it is evident that pearls have entered into Irish culture.

It has been said, by E. Estyn Evans (1957, xiv), that the outstanding interest of Ireland to the student of European origins lies in the fact that in its historic literature, language and social organization, as well as in its folklore and folk customs, it illustrates the marginal survival of archaic elements of the Indo-European world. From the exploration given here on pearls it could be said that these too form part of those elements.

Parallels with other cultures can also be drawn, as between the Irish legend and folklore regarding the mythic origins of pearls and that found, for example, in Polynesia and in China (Mackenzie 1994a, 51). Generally there are many interesting points of resemblance between certain of the Irish and Indian legends (Mackenzie 1994b, 111).

From the extensive literature search carried out it is evident that pearls have been mentioned in Irish writings from an early time. They have been incorporated into almost all aspects of the arts and literature of the people, including myth, folklore, legend, superstition and even place names, right down to the Anglo-Irish literature of the twentieth century. As would be expected, the legends and folklore regarding pearls appear to have survived longest in the more remote rural parts of the country, for example in Counties Kerry and Tyrone.

The present chapter dealt mainly with literary, allegorical and symbolic usage of pearls, and the following one will deal with the actual uses to which they have been put in Irish society down through the ages. By so doing it is proposed to determine their demand as a commodity in Ireland.

*Notes*

[i]Eugene O'Curry, the distinguished historian who, it seems, had an aversion to Irish pearls, mentions this passage from the *Dinnshenchas* on Lough Leane but avoids any reference to the pearls (O'Curry 1873, 203). Unlike with other passages, he does not give the original in Gaelic and calls them 'gems'.

[ii]The carbuncle is the name given to a red precious stone, a garnet, which could formerly refer to a number of gems including rubies. Carbuncles were used in ornamentation in early Ireland (Joyce 1903b, 230). There may have been some cross-fertilization of stories regarding pearls and carbuncles. Down to the middle of the eighteenth century, the local people believed that in fine weather what they called a carbuncle could be seen at the bottom of a particular part of the lake in Killarney (Smith 1750, 125). In the lore of Eastern countries the carbuncle was similarly believed to have luminous properties and was also associated with serpents (Kunz 1913, 62, 174). There is an obvious parallel with the folklore regarding Lough Gal, perhaps indicating a common Indo-European origin.

[iii]In Western countries the ill omen of pearls as bridal ornaments has been widely recognized, these determining the tears that will be shed in married life (Kunz and Stevenson 1908, 207).

[iv]References to pearls are made in the Bible, the Talmud and the Koran as well as in Hindu and Buddhist literature, while in Shinto, the ancient religion of the Japanese, they are also given prominence (Mackenzie 1994a, 335). They are mentioned in the Book of Job (28:18), one of the most ancient books of the Bible, and in the New Testament in several places. They were chosen by Christ as a symbol of that which was most precious, to be compared with the kingdom of heaven (Matthew 13:45). The parable of the man who sold all that he had in order that he might possess 'one pearl of great price' is an illustration of the high esteem in which pearls were held in Christ's time. In latter-day religions, pearls are also used symbolically. For example, one of the doctrinal works of the Mormons is called *The pearl of great price*.

[v]In Persia pearls were *margan* which means 'life-giver' (Mackenzie 1994a, 219) while in Greek and Arabic they were *margarítai* (or *margaríths*) and *lulu* respectively (Hastings 1900, 734). In Hebrew, pearls apparently were associated with the words *gabísh* and

*peninim* (Kunz and Stevenson 1908, 6). To the Romans *unio* distinguished a large pearl from the smaller ones which were called *margaritae*. In Sanskrit literature of the first century AD pearls are generally called *mukta* which means 'pure' (Kunz and Stevenson 1908, 4).

In these islands, as well as the modern English appellation, other words have been applied. The Anglo-Saxon, or Old English, word was *pærl* (Toller and Cambell 1980, 51) and the Anglo-Normans used *perle* (Rothwell *et al.* 1992, 518), the Middle English word (Gollancz 1936, 2). In Welsh it is *perl* (Anmyl 1922, 230; Evans and Thomas 1989, 359) while in Scots Gaelic *neamhnaid* and *neamhnuid* have been used (Armstrong 1825, 101; Highland Society of Scotland 1828, 684; Macbain 1896, 261).

The modern word to describe a pearl is similar in many European languages. For example, in Dutch and Swedish it is *paarl*; in Irish, *péarla*; in Portuguese, *pérola*; in Italian and Spanish, *perla*; in French, Danish and German, *perle*, and in English, pearl.
[vi]For example, in an Irish–English dictionary (*Focloir Gaoidheilge–Shagsonach*) contained in his *Archæologia Britannica*, Edward Lhuyd (1707) gives 'Pearla' for a pearl.

# 6. Uses of pearls

My draught-board, no mean treasure! is thine;
take it with thee…
Its woof is of pearls; it is the wonder of smiths
how it was wrought…
*The Tryst after Death* (ninth century) (Meyer 1911, 12)

Unlike other gems, which require at least some working or polishing, pearls come ready-made for use and were probably the first gems to be used by man. Unlike a gemstone, however, the pearl is an organic product of nature, and must be treated with great care if it is to retain its full beauty. The pearls that hang from the arches of the British State Crown have retained their lustre (Fisher 1966, 113) after more than 400 years. In order that the demand for pearls over time can be established, the uses to which they have been put must be examined. Moreover, because many were sold in London as well as in other markets, their use outside of Ireland must also be considered.

It has been suggested, though not established, that the ancient Irish traded native pearls with the Phoenicians in exchange for the secrets of producing purple (Tyrian) dye from the juice of shellfish (O'Conor 1814, xvii). It is known, however, that the uses to which pearls have been put through the ages are many and include personal adornment (as jewellery and on clothing), decoration and medicine, as well as others, and there are surviving examples of some of these uses in Ireland dating from an early time.

The shells from which the pearls came have also had various uses in Irish society, particularly as spoons by the poorer people and as lime on the poorer soils. The flesh of the mussel, unlike its marine counterpart, is largely inedible and has only been used as an article of food in desperate times such as during the Great Famine (Lucey 1998, 55).

*Personal adornment*
Pearls were probably used for personal adornment in Ireland from an early time, but there is apparently no evidence from the archaeological record. They are less durable than other precious stones, although, as will be seen later, some which were hidden in airtight conditions in County Waterford for almost 200 years survived intact.

Describing the dress and personal adornment of the ancient Irish, P.W. Joyce (1903b, 228) mentions in passing that Harris's Ware (1745, 178) 'quotes a record of Nennius that the kings of the Irish wore pearls in their ears: but he gives no reference, and I have not been able to find the original passage in Nennius'. Joyce had consulted one of the Irish versions of the *Historia Britonum* by Nennius[i] but the reference does not appear in any of the Irish texts of the work.

The passage appears at the end of the Latin work (see Figure 6.1) among the 'wonders of Ireland' (Nennius 831, 197–98):

> Est ibi stagnum quod vocatur Luch lein. Quatuor circulis ambitur. Primo circulo gronna stagni ambitur, secundo circulo gronna plumbi ambitur. Tertio gronna circulo ferri, quarto circulo gronna aeris ambitur, et in eo stagno multae margaritae inveniuntur, quae ponunt reges in auribus suis.

This may be translated as follows:

> There is a lake there called Loch lein. Four circles are around it. In the first circle it is surrounded by tin, in the second by lead. In the third by iron, in the fourth by copper, and in that lake are found many pearls, which kings wear in their ears.

It is of interest to note that there were kings of Lough Leane (*Eóganacht Locha Léin*) whose dynasty was dying out at the time when Nennius was writing; the last one with the title *Rí Locha Léin*, Cobthach, apparently died in 833 (Byrne 1987, 218). While the last line in the verse of Nennius above, could be interpreted as, 'and in that lake are found many pearls of the kind that kings wear in their ears', it does imply that it was kings in Ireland who used the pearls. The testimony of Nennius must therefore stand.

The much-maligned O'Conor (1814, *prolegomena pars* ii, xcvii) puts it well, though somewhat apologetically, when he writes:

> Reges Hiberniae Margaritis in auribus suis usos, aperte confirmantur. Neque prorsus despicienda est ista antiquiorum Hiberniae Regum series, ante saeculum nonum scripta, ab immemorabili tradita, et longa saeculorum veneratione consecrata, cum alia posthac in lucem prodire poterunt, quibus, quae nunc male cohaerentia, et mutilata apparent, veluti vetusti Aedificii rudera, Doctorum industria ad pristinam integritatem restituantur.

It is a great pity that, despite its imperfections, this large work in four volumes by O'Conor has never been rendered into English. A translation of this passage (J.C. O'Mahony 1991, *in litt.*[ii]) reads:

> That the kings of Ireland used pearls on their ears is clearly confirmed.
> We should not totally despise this series of the ancient kings of Ireland,
> which was written before the ninth century, handed down from time
> immemorial, and consecrated by the long veneration of the centuries,
> because other things may yet come to light through, which, those things
> which now fit together badly, and appear mutilated, like the ruins of an
> old building can, through the work of experts be restored to their
> original integrity.

This interpretation would suggest that though the impression given by
Nennius is that contemporary kings of Ireland wore the pearls, it was kings
from a more remote time who actually did so. Indeed, Nennius himself says
that the 'wonders' were existing documents which he copied (Morris 1980, 6).

So far as the present writer can ascertain, this particular 'wonder' does not
appear anywhere except in the MSS of *Historia Britonum* attributed to Nennius
(e.g., Stevenson 1838, 61; Mommsen 1898, 219; Morris 1980, 6). Yet Roderick
O'Flaherty (1685, 292) gave this verse as the tenth 'wonder' in his metrical list,
translated from Irish into Latin. He says it is the third of the 'wonders' of
Nennius, whereas it is the first in all other versions; the only textual difference
is that instead of *inveniuntur*, for 'found', O'Flaherty uses *reperiuntur*.

The extant Irish versions of that work do not, however, contain it (e.g.,
Todd 1848; Hogan 1895; van Hamel 1932) and the *Duan Eireannach*, an
historical poem by Maelmura of Fathain (*c.* 820–86), gives the same verse in
Gaelic—'ceathra chircilla uime .i. chircall sdain, 7 chircall luaghi, 7 chircall
iarind, 7 chircall uma', but no reference to the pearls (Todd 1848, 220).
Giraldus Cambrensis, who visited Ireland in 1185 with Prince John, does not
include it among his 'Wonders and Miracles of Ireland' (O'Meara 1951,
57–91); nor is it mentioned among the Irish wonders in the *Speculum regale*,
written in the Norse language about 1250, which is based upon oral
information obtained in Ireland (Meyer 1910b, 16).

Very few references to kings associated with pearls were found during the
study (see Box VI). In the historical novel, *The invasion*, originally published in
1832, Gerald Griffin (1862, 385) mentions an Irish chieftain wearing pearls
behind his ears, but in notes added by the publishers in posthumous editions,
Eugene O'Curry, the eminent Professor of Irish History and Archaeology in
the Catholic University of Ireland, dismisses this as follows (Griffin 1862, 407):

> In one instance in the text, pearls are represented as having been worn
> as part of the ornaments of a chieftain's dress; this, however, is incorrect;
> there is no case mentioned of pearls being worn save by women, though
> by them they were frequently used.

---

*Box VI*
## Irish kings and pearls

Apart from Nennius there are very few references to Irish kings associated with pearls, but O'Conor mentions 'Conchubair na Siudaine' (whose death he gives as 1267) which he renders into Latin as 'Concobari Margaritarum' and which may be translated as Concobar of the Pearls. O'Donovan says that 'Under the year 1267, the Dublin copy of the Annals of Innisfallen contains an account of the revolt of the tribes of Thomond against 'Conor na Siudaine O'Brien', of which the Four Masters have collected no account.' MacAirt, in his translation of the Bodleian *Annals of Inisfallen*, where Concobar is called 'king of Tuadmumu and head of the Gaedil of Ireland', gives 1268 as the year when Conchobar na Siudaine was slain; Holinshed says that 'In the yeere 1268 Conhur Obren was slaine by Dermote Mack Monerd.'

Elsewhere, O'Donovan says that O'Conor incorrectly translates 'Ruaidhri na Soigh buidhe' as 'Rodericus Margaritarum flavarum' and which he says is accurately rendered as 'Rodericus de flava cane' by O'Flaherty. While criticism levelled at some of his interpretations may be justified, the present writer could not find this error. In fact, it may be that O'Donovan confused this with the above reference to 'Concobari Margaritarum', as 'Ruaidri na Saige buidhe' is translated as 'Rodericum pennulorum flavium' in O'Conor's *Annals of Tigernach*. It appears, however, that O'Conor did translate what is generally termed 'jewels' as 'pearls'.

According to Wright, the King of Munster, Murkertach, invaded Ulster in 1103, but was defeated at Cobha in County Tyrone and 'The victorious O'Neils carried away among their booty the royal pavilion and standards of the king of Munster, rich stores of pearls.' Ó Cróinín has it that Muirchertach O'Brien was defeated by Domnall O'Loughlin, King of the northern Uí Néill, who made off with his tent and royal standard amidst other spoils. It would appear that, like O'Conor above, Wright took some liberties in specifying pearls, as these are not mentioned in the *Annals of Ulster* nor the *Annals of the Four Masters* and should be translated as 'treasures' or 'precious jewels'. It may well be that Wright's source did specify pearls, but it is probably more likely that he was simply copying what had been written some 15–20 years previously by Moore, who specifies pearls as among the spoils and who curiously gives his sources as the abovementioned annals.

In a portrait (in the possession of the MacCarthy Mór) the last King of Munster, Donal McCarthy (d. 1596), wears a cross with three pearls hanging from it; it is known as a Niadh Nask cross which symbolized a Gaelic form of knighthood.

(Sources: Holinshed 1577, 197; O'Flaherty 1685, 440; O'Conor 1825, viii, 313; Moore 1837, 385; Wright c. 1850, 65; O'Donovan 1856b, 403; O'Donovan 1856c, 958–59, 976–77; MacCarthy 1893, 72–73; MacAirt 1951, 367; Ó Cróinín 1995, 280; MacCarthy 1996, 1.)

It would appear that early Irish historians as well as more recent ones regarded the wearing of pearls by men too effeminate to be considered. In the north of Ireland, around Omagh, there is a superstition that pearls fade when worn by men (see chapter five), which may well have its origin in this deep-rooted antipathy to what is perceived as non-masculine adornment.

Not all historians of the nineteenth century, however, ignored or dismissed the idea of men wearing pearls. For example in his *History of Ireland*, which was dedicated to the Irish Brigade, the Abbé MacGeoghegan (1844, 24) quotes Nennius's verse on Lough Leane from O'Flaherty's *Ogygia*, which he renders as, 'pearls are found in it, which kings wear for ear-rings'.

Describing the jewellery of the Irish Celts from the second century BC to the twelfth century AD, Norris (1947, 24) includes the following:

> Personal ornaments worn by the wealthy comprised necklaces, ear-rings, bracelets, torques, fibulæ, brooches, rings, buckles and pins. They were of elaborate design and set with precious stones and polished pebbles. Ornamental pins or bodkins were used for fastening garments, as well as for ladies' hair. It was the custom for men of position to wear in their ears not only rings of gold, but frequently a large single pearl.

We see that the fashion for men wearing a single pearl in the ear was again in vogue in the sixteenth and seventeenth centuries. James I and his second son Charles I wore a pearl in one ear (see Figure 6.2). The pearl Charles wore at his execution in 1649 was bequeathed to his daughter Mary and apparently survives to this day; from a miniature by Isaac Oliver in the National Museum in Stockholm it can be seen that, even as a teenager, Charles wore a drop pearl earring.

Sir Walter Raleigh (1552–1618), like many other gentlemen of the sixteenth century, used pearls in personal adornment. For example, he commissioned a portrait (see Figure 6.3) of himself in 1588, aged 34, in which he wore a double-pearl earring (Lacey 1973, 147); he was in Ireland in September 1588, after the defeat of the Armada (Winton 1975, 88). While in London before he sailed for America in April 1584 he had a hatband of pearls worth £30 stolen from him, among other items (Williams 1988, 58). There is little doubt that Raleigh was aware of pearls in the rivers of his lands in Munster; these pearls were to be exploited a few years later in Richard Boyle's time. Raleigh sold his lands in Ireland for £1,000 in 1602 (Williams 1988, 163) but we do not know if any of the pearls he wore were from Ireland or from his adventures further afield. They may even have been bought from London merchants.

In seventeenth-century England there was disquiet in some quarters regarding men wearing earrings (Anon. 1683a, 132):

> Not content with this, we come to Fishes and
> do beg from them their Pearles to hang about us…

Harrison in his *Description of England* is horrified at the fact that 'some lustie courtiers and gentlemen of courage wore ear-rings, of gold, pearls and other precious stones' (Ribeiro 1986, 175).

The pearl was a favourite jewel in the sixteenth century. It was worn in the coiffure or sewn to women's gowns, and a single drop pearl earring was worn by gentlemen (Wilcox 1970, 262). Pearls were used by Irish ladies in the sixteenth and seventeenth centuries in the hair, as necklaces, and on the front and sleeves of dresses; a portrait of 'The fair Geraldine' (Elizabeth, daughter of Garret Óg Fitzgerald and sister of Silken Thomas) in the National Gallery of Ireland shows her costume and hat adorned with pearls. In a portrait, Katherine Fenton, wife of the Earl of Cork, is seen bedecked with pearls (see Figure 6.4); in his diary, the Earl tells that he gave a jeweller 'thirty Orient pearls to be holed and six Irish pearls, which she wears in a necklace' (Townsend 1904, 50). Thus it appears that native pearls were used with those from the East in Ireland in the seventeenth century. Pearl buttons were worn by gentlemen in the sixteenth century and the same Earl of Cork, Richard Boyle, had used some of his to bribe a messenger to tear up letters brought from England in 1594 regarding a dispute about a grant of land, and conceal the matter (Townsend 1904, 10).

A string of pearls, worn tightly around the neck such as that worn by 'Catherine Plunkett of Ardmagh' as depicted on her effigal slab, was extremely fashionable in the seventeenth century and could apparently cost as much as £80 (Rynne 1987, 288). We know from contemporary sources that ladies in Counties Carlow (Dingley 1675–80, 88) and Kilkenny (Redding 1688, 160) had necklaces made of pearls from the local rivers, and it is likely that this fashion was widespread throughout Ireland in the seventeenth century. Writing in 1777, Lady Templeton (wife of Baron Templeton of Templepatrick, County Antrim) who was a lady-in-waiting to Queen Charlotte, tells us that the Queen was possessed of a necklet of pearls taken from the River Bann (Robb 1939, 6).

Irish pearls were in vogue in Georgian jewellery and were sometimes specified by ladies when ordering earrings. For example, in 1769, 'Lady Isabella Monck ordered rose diamond tops hung with Irish pearls' (Scarisbrick 1994, 280). From paintings of the eighteenth century it is evident that pearls were much used by some Irish ladies in the same way as they had been a century earlier. In an oil painting attributed to Nathaniel Hone (1718–84), for example, the Countess of Glandore is seen with small pearls in her hair, and her dress is embroidered with large pearls on the sleeves, breast and waist (Crookshank and Glin 1969, 49).

In Victorian times, pearls were very popular, and there is a reference in the

*Irish journals of Elizabeth Smith* to a pearl ornament being fastened to the bridal gown on the morning of a wedding (Thomson and McGusty 1980, 262), probably to symbolize purity.

An example of a necklace made of pearls fished from the rivers of County Tyrone in the late nineteenth century is shown as the frontispiece to this book.

In the Edwardian period, pearls were still very much in fashion. Queen Alexandra (1844–1925) initiated a vogue for wearing a choker of jewels, and her famous 'dog collar', as it was sometimes known, consisted of rows of pearls from the neck to low on the bodice (O'Hara 1986, 17). In their classic work, *The book of the pearl*, Kunz and Stevenson (1908, 165) report the following:

> …within the last twelve months Lady Dudley,[iii] wife of the Viceroy of Ireland, presented to Queen Alexandra a number of pearls from the Connemara. These were mounted in a green enameled brooch, and excited so much admiration that an active demand for similar gems quickly developed in County Galway.

Thus we see that royalty could stimulate the wearing of pearls and increase demand for them, and we have seen above that some English ladies stipulated Irish pearls when ordering jewellery.

Many of the Ulster pearl fishermen in the twentieth century sold their pearls to jewellers, and some had them mounted in jewellery for their wives and friends. As an item of personal adornment, the pearl has endured, and since the sixteenth century has been established as among the most popular of jewellery items—albeit that the cultured variety has succeeded the natural in the twentieth century.

*Ornamentation and decoration*

As decorations for temples and jewellery for statues of deities, and as assets in the imperial treasury, pearls were an important component of the Roman Empire's political and economic structure (Joyce and Addison 1992, 85). Pearls were assigned such tremendous value that entire military campaigns could apparently be financed by the sale of a single pearl. For example, Vitellius, the Roman general and later Emperor, pawned one of his mother's pearls taken from a pendant to defray the expenses of a military expedition (Suetonius 1692, 467).

The epigraph at the beginning of this chapter would indicate that pearls were used in Ireland to decorate draughtboards or chessboards in the ninth century or beforehand, but it would be unwise to read too much into what is essentially mythic poetry and to surmise that just because something is mentioned that it was in use.

In the register of Edward, Prince of Wales (1330–76), who was known as the Black Prince, it is entered that 20,000 seed pearls, which cost £80, were ordered in November 1353, probably to be embroidered onto garments (Ribeiro 1986, 175); these small pearls were likely to have come from within the British Isles.

It will be seen in chapter eight, where two examples are illustrated, that gold and pearls were used together in Ireland from at least the ninth century down to the end of the nineteenth. Pearls were probably used extensively in ornamentation in Ireland from an early period, but surviving examples are few. In many cases the pearls just fell out of their settings, while in other instances they perished over time: because of their organic nature, pearls will lose their lustre and eventually decay unless they are looked after properly.

In the late sixteenth and early seventeenth centuries, London goldsmiths used pearls in the various decorative fashions of that 'exquisite' period, for example on earrings, cravat-pins and brooches. The seed pearl was largely used to decorate frames of the beautiful miniature oil paintings of the era, being mounted thereon in silver and gold settings (Meagher 1928, 385). Such paintings were copied two centuries later and one such example, in which the artist has depicted himself in Elizabethan costume (see Figure 6.5), may be seen in the National Gallery of Ireland.

It was suggested, by the sender, that a small pearl sent from County Kerry to Secretary Dawson at Dublin Castle in 1702 should be put at the top of his official seal to decorate it (see chapter eight for the text of the accompanying letter). Small pearls had a number of such uses as well as personal adornment for both men and women. It is not for some centuries after the introduction of Christianity that we find pearls being used in ecclesiastical ornamentation and decoration in Ireland. The likelihood, however, is that, just as they were used by the Irish kings and chieftains of the early Christian era, they were also used by the Church.

*Ecclesiastical*
The use of pearls as religious symbols, particularly of regeneration, was outlined in chapter five. Here, the use of pearls in ecclesiastical decoration and ornamentation will be summarized.

In the early years of the twelfth century, most probably 1107, Gillebert, Bishop of Limerick, wrote to Anselm, Archbishop of Canterbury, congratulating him on the successful outcome of his controversy with King Henry I and enclosing a gift of 25 pearls.[iv] A copy of the letter is shown in Figure 6.6. Another copy, textually slightly different from the one shown in the Figure, which was also in the possession of the English collector of literary relics, Robert Cotton (1571–1631), was reproduced by James Ussher (1632, 88):

> Anselmo Dei gratia Anglorum archi-præsuli, Gillebertus Dei quoque misericordia Lumnicensis episcopus fidele servitium et orationes.
> Audiens, pater, certaminis vestri laborem et laboris victoriam; subditas

esse videlicet indomitas Normannorum mentes regularibus sanctorum patrum decretis, ut legaliter fiat abbatum et præsulum electio et consecratio: immensas divinæ clementiæ refero gratias, et quas possum Deo preces effundo, ut perseverantiam vobis et tanti laboris præmium largiatur. Munusculum paupertatis meæ et devotionis transmitto, XXV. margaritulas inter optimas et viliores; et rogo ne sitis immemor mei in orationibus vestris, in quibus post divinam largitatem confido.

A translation of the Latin text reads as follows (Hamell 1991, *in litt.*[v]):

Gilbert, by God's mercy Bishop of Limerick, to Anselm, by the grace of God, Primate of England, with pledge of faithful service and prayers.

Father, I have learned what a hard struggle you have had and how successful you have been in securing the obedience of the ungovernable Normans to the decrees of the holy fathers regulating the lawful election of abbots and bishops. I give unbounded thanks to God for his mercy and spend myself in prayer to him that he may grant you perseverance and reward such great labour. From my small means and my devotion I send you a modest gift, 25 small pearls, some precious, some inferior; and beg remembrance in your prayers in which, after God's generosity, I place my trust.

Pearls were much used in Irish religious ornaments in the fifteenth and sixteenth centuries. In a letter to a Mr Hanna, who had sent him details of an old rosary, George Petrie gave the following assessment (Stokes 1868, 305):

Your account of the old Rosary has interested me; but I can only guess at its probable age, which I would suppose to be the sixteenth century. Had the figure of the Saviour remained, it would have determined its age at once. I scarcely think, however, that its age could be much earlier than the period I have named; for I have not found the use of pearls in any Irish ornaments of an older date than the fourteenth century, and that but rarely. They are usually of the fifteenth. I think your conjecture a good one—that the Rosary probably belonged to some of the Russell family. I am quite unable to say what is the material of the avis. The pearls may be Irish, and if so, of course the rosary too. Pearls were much used in Irish religious ornaments, in the fifteenth and sixteenth centuries.

George Petrie may not have been aware of the use of pearls in Irish religious ornaments before the fourteenth century but it appears that they were indeed being used. A list of church ornaments belonging to Stephen de Fulbourn, Archbishop of Tuam and Justiciar of Ireland, which were sent to

London after his death in the late thirteenth century, included a cross of pearls and an amice with pearls (Sweetman 1881, 45):

> 1293.
> Oct 5 93. Mem. That on Monday next after the feast of St. Michael, a.r. 21, Alexander of London, the clerk, received by the hands of Sir William de Estdene, Treasurer of Ireland, from the Chamberlains of Dublin, the underwritten ornaments which belonged to Brother S[tephen], formerly Archbishop of Tuam, then Justiciary of Ireland, namely, a chasuble of red samite, a great cross of pearls, two precious embroidered choir copes, a clasp for a cope with an image of the deity, and precious stones, a gilt crest for the head of the cope with divers shields and precious stones, and an amice with pearls, of varied work.

In medieval times, many of the freshwater pearls were used in ecclesiastical decorations such as on bindings of missals and other manuscripts (Gibbings 1945, 143), but apparently there are no surviving Irish examples. Unique tomes, such as the missal at the Library of Rouen, took 30 years of labour to complete (Farn 1986, 19). Pearls were still used in book-bindings in the sixteenth and seventeenth centuries. A Scottish embroidered binding of 1599, now in Christ Church Library, Oxford, features pearls, while an English one of *circa* 1630 in Worcester College has such a quantity of pearls that it will hardly lie flat (Barber 1971, 7).

Pearls were obviously in currency in the twelfth century, as can be seen from the letter of Gillebert to Anselm, and were used in the time of another bishop of Limerick, some three centuries later. The mitre of Conor O'Dea, Bishop of Limerick from 1400 to 1426, has 'the front and back enriched with jewels of semi-precious stones and pastes, the triangular reserves decorated with flowers and leaves formed of pearls' (see Figure 6.7). It is a fine 'example of medieval post-Conquest art in Ireland. It was made in 1418 and signed by the craftsman Thomas O'Carryd' (Walsh 1984, 7).

It is likely that most of the pearls used in Ireland in the late Middle Ages were native, but it is not improbable that merchants brought pearls from the East. We know, for example, that a Florentine jewel merchant travelled to Ireland in 1399 carrying jewels for sale (Labarge 1982, 13).

In the sixteenth century, in the period of the suppression of the monasteries, many ornaments of the Roman Catholic Church were hidden, and some were recovered many years later. An example is the find, some time between 1813 and 1819, of a remarkable treasure trove in the city of Waterford, estimated at the time to be worth £10,000. Some of the items found were ornamented with pearls and have been described as follows (Graves 1869, 242):

> ...a gold locket set with blue sapphires and pearls, which, when first

seen, had a painting on one side; but this faded at once on meeting the outer air. The last was a small, but very thick gold book, with rubies, emeralds, and pearls ornamenting the sides, having a cavity in the centre, supposed to hold a portion of the true cross.

Pearls were also used in Ireland for the embellishment of clerical vestments in the seventeenth century (Meagher 1928, 385).

*Medicinal*

In chapter five, the use of Irish pearls during prehistoric times as an elixir to prolong life was alluded to. A standard medical textbook of the Middle Ages, written in 1314 by Johannes Anglicus, the *Rosa Anglica* was translated into Irish in 1460 and was very popular in Ireland. It contains references to pearls being used in some of the medical preparations, for example to counter 'accidents' that come along with the fever in the illness Etica or Hectica (Wulff 1929, 108).

Poor pearls, such as those lacking lustre, were used by apothecaries in Ireland for medical preparations in the seventeenth century (Redding 1693, 660). Yet Charles Smith, himself an apothecary, who wrote of pearls in his histories of Counties Cork (Smith 1750), Kerry (Smith 1756) and Waterford (Smith 1746) makes no mention of this in the eighteenth century. Robert Boyle (1672), who was born at Lismore in Waterford, did not include pearls in his treatise on the virtues of gems, most probably because, rightly, he did not regard them as such in the true sense of the word.

Walter Raleigh delved into medicine, and his 'great cordial', which was used by Queen Anne, wife of James I, had among its ingredients a compound including pearl. In fact, it was still being written about and used by the physician to Charles II (Williams 1988, 215). Pearls were used as an antacid and astringent throughout the British Isles, and retained a central place in the world's pharmacy until the advent of scientific medicine in the late nineteenth century. Even today, the Japanese treat the common cold with pearl powder, while in Germany pearls are made into 'pep pills' (Joyce and Addison 1992, 46).

At one time, in Hatton Garden in London, a dealer would call on a regular basis to buy badly cracked and broken pearls for medical purposes in the Far East (Farn 1986, 131). Brown freshwater pearls are almost worthless (McCrea 1973b, 13) and Scottish ones with this colour are sent to India, where they are ground and sold as an aphrodisiac (Woodward 1994, 92). Similarly, the poorest ones, taken from sea mussels in the Conway Estuary in Wales in the nineteenth century were 'exported to India to be dissolved in the sherbet of the Nabobs!!' (D.C. 1830, 133).

*Uses of shells*

Shell fragments of the pearl-producing mussel *Margaritifera margaritifera* have been found in a sepulchral cave of the Neolithic Age in Wales (Jackson 1913, 321) but no such finds have apparently been made in Ireland (M. Cahill, National Museum of Ireland, pers. comm.; M. McCarthy, Environmental Archaeological Unit, University College Cork, pers. comm.). A related species, *Margaritifera auricularia*, which also produced pearls (see chapter seven), is known from the fossil record in England, where shells have been associated with stone axes and Neolithic implements (Preece 1988, 50).

It was probably while tasting the mussel for food that early man in Ireland discovered pearls. The flesh of the mussel is apparently 'extremely bad unsavory and unwholesome' (Copping 1740, 198), 'of an insipid disagreeble taste' (Harris 1744, 146) and 'seldom eaten' (Dubourdieu 1802, 314), but the shells have been used as spoons in Ireland from ancient times down to the middle of the eighteenth century. Thomas Dingley, the learned and industrious topographer who travelled through parts of Ireland between 1675 and 1680, observed that mussel shells were in general use as spoons, as they had been by the ancient Irish (Dingley 1675–80, 262):

> Spoons. In ancient times they knew not the use of them, so that they fed one another cross the table, at their first coming: instead of which they used *sliganes* as many do now a kind of muscle-shells so called.

In County Waterford, the shells were used as spoons by the poor people living near the River Blackwater in the eighteenth century (Smith 1746, 237):

> In summertime the country people near this river, when the water is low between Cappoquin and Lismore, gather up a species of Muscles of the larger kind, commonly called Horse-mussels, in, which, as I am well informed, a small kind of seed pearl has been found, and now and then a few of a larger size. It is not so much, it seems, either for the sake of the Muscle, or the thoughts of a pearl, that the people gather up the fish, but for the shells, which they use for spoons.

John Copping (1740, 198), Dean of Clogher, sent some pearl mussels to Hans Sloane in London, with a hastily and poorly written note in which he says that the poor people on the 'banks of the Bann' used the shells as spoons for eating their 'stirabout of oatmeal':

> According to promise the bearer carries the muscle kind in which the pearls are taken in the River Bann, although the upper part of it within five or six miles of Dromore, above forty from the lower Bann which falls into the Sea eight or ten miles from Colerain. The fish of this muscle is extremely bad unsavory and unwholesome, the shells however

of some use to the poor people on the banks of the Bann to eat their stirabout of oatmeal instead of spoons.

This is confirmed by Walter Harris (1744, 146), also writing on the River Bann in the middle of the eighteenth century, when he says that the shells are sometimes used by the poorer people instead of spoons. So it is evident that the shells of the mussel were used as spoons from a remote time until at least the middle of the eighteenth century.

The shells were used for holding soap by the people living near the River Roughty in the 1930s and 1940s (An elderly woman from near Kilgortaree, County Kerry, pers. comm.).

In Irish agricultural practice of the eighteenth and nineteenth centuries, the enrichment of the lime content of the soil was achieved in a number of ways, including by the application of seashells. In the latter century, the shells raised amounted to 59,496 tons, which were worth £5,000 a year to the country (Lucas 1969, 184, 200). The shells from the freshwater pearl mussel were also used to fertilize (lime) fields in County Tyrone in the nineteenth century. For example, Thompson (1856, 34) says that the mussel was taken in such quantity from the neighbourhood of Omagh in 1839 that 'the prisoners in the jail were employed in breaking the shells for manure'. It appears that seashells (cockles) were also used to make lime in the early part of the sixteenth century, as noted by the Four Masters (O'Donovan 1856d, 2190) and George Petrie (Stokes 1868, 161).

Mother-of-pearl (the inner layer of some shells) from large, thick shells was used for making the handles of knives and forks as well as other items of cutlery at the turn of the twentieth century. The best, whitest variety was from marine shells, such as the *Margaritifera maxima milii* from Australia, which was imported into and sold in London for an average of £180–220 per ton of shells at the beginning of the twentieth century (Lawrence-Hamilton 1902, 3). The shells of the freshwater mussel were used in mother-of-pearl products in Ireland up until relatively recently. For example, those from the River Nore were sent to Dublin up until about 40 years ago (Chesney *et al.* 1993, 290).

It appears that native pearls have been put to various uses throughout the ages in Ireland, and the shells from which they came have also been employed in a variety of ways. It is also apparent that various factors could trigger additional demand for them. When royalty wore pearls, for example, they became the vogue, thereby creating a demand for them as a commodity. Thus, as we have seen, when Queen Alexandra received some from County Galway, which were made into a brooch, this created a demand for Irish pearls. The various uses of pearls, as detailed above, give some indication of their demand through a very long period of Irish history, and this aspect of their history will be further developed and critically examined in chapter nine.

In order that pearls and their use in Ireland may be put in context, it is essential that their exploitation in other parts of the world be examined. Therefore, a survey of literature on freshwater pearls in other countries has been undertaken and an historical *résumé* of the findings is given in the following chapter.

*Notes*

[i]Nennius (*fl.*831) was a writer of the ninth century to whom the *Historia Britonum* is attributed despite, as James Ware noted, 'some copies do falsly bear the name of Gildas' (Ware 1705, 34). There are many versions of the *Historia Britonum*, including several different texts of *Lebor Bretnach*, the Irish version. Nennius says that he had collected information from the Irish annals and that he was told by the most learned of the Irish of Irish events—'Sic mihi peritissimi Scotorum nunciaverunt' (Cusack 1868, 69). Some of the Latin versions, including the most extensive edition in the British Library (Harleian MS 3859) contain 'De mirabilibus Hiberniae' or the 'wonders of Ireland' (e.g., Stevenson 1838, 61). At least one commentator (e.g., van Hamel 1932, xxviii), has suggested that Nennius was Irish, but this is generally thought highly unlikely and the considered opinion is that he was a Briton, most probably Welsh. It is believed that the work is a long compilation which was edited by Nennius in the ninth century and some MSS are dated 831 (Kenney 1929, 154). The 'wonders' are named by Nennius as pre-existing works that he transcribed, probably early in the ninth century (Morris 1980, 6), and that would place the reference to Irish kings wearing pearls in their ears to a more remote time. A later edition of the work (*c.* 910) came to Ireland and was worked on by Gilla Coemain (Kenney 1929, 155) and it is believed that the earliest manuscript of the 'Irish Nennius' was of the twelfth century (Todd 1848, 21).

[ii]J.C. O'Mahony (1991) Translation from Latin of passage in O'Conor's *Rerum Hibernicarum scriptores veteres. In litt.*, 20 July.

[iii]Either the date of the presentation of the pearls (i.e., 1907–08) or the reference to the person by whom they were presented is wrong, and it may be that the information was collected earlier and not edited prior to publication in 1908. The Dudleys' viceroyalty ended after the fall of Balfour's Government in December 1905 and the coming into office of the Liberals (Bence-Jones 1987, 108). Edward VII and Alexandra in fact came to Ireland in 1903, on their coronation visit, when they travelled to Connemara, and they may have received the pearls then. They did, however, return to Ireland in 1907, just after the 'Irish crown jewels' had been stolen (Perrin 1977, 93), but it was Lord Aberdeen who was Viceroy in 1907 during the visit. Therefore, the pearls were given either by the Dudleys on the 1903 visit or by the Aberdeens in 1907.

[iv]Gillebert (*c.*1060–1140). Variously called Gille, Gilbert, Gillebert, Gislebert (or Giselbert) and Giolla Easpuig (or Easpuic) in Irish, he was first Bishop of Limerick and Pope's Legate in Ireland (Murray 1840, 60–62; Watt 1972, 10). The twelfth century is regarded as the period of transition between the Celtic Church and that of the Middle Ages in Ireland and Gillebert was instrumental in some of the reforms carried out. Some time between 1110 and 1118 he convened a synod at Rath Breasail, near Cashel

in County Tipperary, which was attended by 25 bishops who then fixed the territorial boundaries of the dioceses of Ireland (Cotton 1851, 376). He corresponded with Anselm, Archbishop of Canterbury, whom he had known when the two were in Rouen, and sent him a gift of 25 pearls. His original writings were apparently destroyed, but there are some copies of the letter to Anselm extant: British Library, Cotton MS Claudius A. xi; Corpus Christi College, Cambridge, MS 135; Lambeth Palace Library, MS 59; Bibliothèque Nationale, Paris, MS 2478 (Ramsay (1991) *in litt.*: N. Ramsay (1991) Manuscript collections, British Library. *In litt.*, 23 April). James Ussher, later the Archbishop of Armagh, who is famous for dating more important events, borrowed a copy from Robert Cotton and dates the letter to Anselm at 1094 (Ussher 1632, 88–89). In the letter, however, Gillebert congratulates Anselm on his compromise with Henry I over investiture, thus dating the letter post-August 1107 (O'Hanlon 1875, 323; Kenney 1929, 761; Steinberg 1966, 38–39; Pike 1976, 89–91).

[V]P.J. Hamell, (1991) Translation from Latin of letter from Gillebert, Bishop of Limerick, to Anselm, Archbishop of Canterbury, written *c.* 1107. *In litt.*, 20 June.

# 7. Freshwater pearls and pearl fishing in Britain, Europe, Asia and North America

The purest gold that suffers no allay;
The pearl unbored, whose price no price can pay…
*Sir John Davies* (1569–1626), Attorney-General for Ireland, *A contention betwixt a wife, a widow and a maide* (1869, 274)

In order that Irish pearls and their exploitation can be viewed in a proper context, the following review of freshwater pearl fisheries around the world is given.

*Britain*

The pearl fisheries of Ceylon were operated, after the occupation of India, for a good number of years from 1796 onwards with great profit. From that year until 1809 the yield in one fishery alone was £517,842 (Markham 1867, 257). Although these foreign fisheries were run for government revenue, there is no evidence that this was the case for the native freshwater fisheries. Attempts by James VI (1566–1625), to control and license the pearl fishers in Scotland in the 1620s were resisted and subsequently failed (Green 1985/86, 31).

Pearl fishing in the rivers of Britain was an established industry long before the Roman Conquest (Streeter 1886, 233) and, as mentioned in the introduction, it has been said that pearls were a reason for that invasion. It is somewhat ironic that the area of most pearl production was never subjugated.[i]

The Roman writers Pliny (AD 23–79) and Tacitus (AD 55–120) both mention British pearls. The latter, in his *Life of Agricola*, says they came from the sea and were dusky or brownish: in the original Latin, 'Oceanus margarita, sed subfusca ac liventia' (Weise 1874, 280). Some of the Roman writers obviously regarded British pearls as of marine origin (Streeter 1886, 235) and, as will be seen, they do also come from the sea mussel. However, the Roman geographer and author of *De situ orbis*, Pomponius Mela (*fl.* AD 50), was aware that the rivers of Britain produced pearls: he said, 'flumina gemmas margaritasque generantia' (O'Conor 1814, xvi).

The Greek writer Origen (AD 186–254), who may have been repeating what the Romans wrote, called the British pearl cloudy and more obscure than Indian pearls, saying, 'Nebulosa autem est et margaritis Indicis obtusior' (O'Conor 1814, xvii).

Between the Boer War and First World War, according to one source (Pilkington 1991, 26), there were at least 500 full-time pearl fishermen on British rivers, with the vast majority of these plying their trade in Scotland. However, other estimates have put the number of British pearlers at 200 in 1906 (Kunz and Stevenson 1908, 80; Dakin 1913, 117). It is known that at the turn of the twentieth century there were over 100 full-time pearlers in Scotland (Armstrong 1973, 231). Nowadays it is estimated that, as well as one professional, a few score regular part-time pearl fishermen operate (Neale 1991). About 30 years ago the Earl of Cranbrook (1976, 90) established, from a firm of jewellers through which most British pearls are marketed, that less than half a dozen individuals made their living or a large part of it by pearl fishing.

The recent decline in the numbers of pearl mussels has been attributed primarily to pollution, as well as overfishing, in England and Wales, and to overfishing in Scotland (Young and Williams 1983, 35). Casual fishers, sometimes using sub-aqua equipment, have been particularly implicated, and it has been suggested that the best conservation measure would be to restrict pearl fishing to licensed fishermen using non-destructive fishing methods.

*England* There were active pearl fisheries in Devon and Cornwall in Roman times (Young 1984, 27). After the withdrawal of the Roman legions, the fashion for pearls declined, according to some writers, and it was not until about the twelfth century that they were again used in England. This has been attributed to the idea that the Anglo-Saxons were not artistic in the lavish manner of more southern races (Dakin 1913, 7).

That a ninth-century British writer (Nennius 831, 198) should include the occurrence of pearls in a lake as among the 'wonders of Ireland', would appear to substantiate the idea that they were not in use in Britain and could serve to illustrate the difference in society between the two islands at this period. Yet Bede (AD 672–735) writing a century earlier, in *Historia ecclesiastica gentis Anglorum*, says that excellent pearls of several colours were found in the England of his day (Bede 1955, 37).

It may well be that the Anglo-Saxons did not use pearls as much as other Europeans of their times, but it is known that their kings at some period had crowns decorated with pearls (von Hessling 1859, 185). In fact, Whitaker, in his *History of Manchester*, remarks that the imperial diadem of the sovereigns of the ancient Britons 'was sometimes encircled with an ornament of the mussel-pearls, as appears from the coins which have come down to us' (Jackson 1917, 83). It appears that although the effect of returning Crusaders carrying jewels and pearls caused an appreciation of the monetary value of such jewels, pearls were not extensively used for ornamentation in England before the twelfth century (Farn 1986, 19).

The famous sixteenth-century navigator Sir John Hawkins was granted a

Above: *Figure 1.1a*
The edible sea mussel, *Mytilus edulis*, which readily produces small 'seed pearls' in Irish waters.

Below: *Figure 1.1b*
The freshwater pearl mussel, *Margaritifera margaritifera*, which occasionally produces gem-quality pearls (in this case at toe of upper valve or shell) in Irish waters (Neil McCormick).

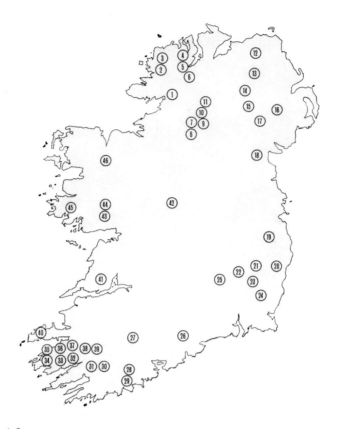

*Figure 1.2*

Index of places where pearls have been found in Ireland (with literature reference sources) as delineated on map Figure 1.2. The numbered locations start in County Donegal in the north-west and then proceed in a clockwise direction.

(1) L. Eske (Thompson 1856, 341); R. Eske (Anon. 1683b, 213; Moore n.d. c. 1980, 89)

(2) River near the Rosses (R.Y. 1833, 389)

(3) R. Clady (Milne 1907, 1)

(4) L. Fern (Milne 1907, 1)

(5) Ramelton [R. Leannan] (Barker 1862–65, 113)

(6) R. Foyle (W[elch] 1908, 90); McCrea 1973b, 13)

(7) R. Armey (A.N.N. 1960, 3)

(8) R. Swanlinbar (Oscar II 1973, 5)

(9) R. Coolebrooke (Redding (1688, 159; McCrea 1973b, 13)

(10) R. Drumragh (Anon. 1965b, 1)

(11) R. Strule (Redding 1693, 662; Willes 1760, 125; Camlin 1959, 10; Bryans 1964, 157)

(12) R. Bush (Milne 1907, 5)

(13) R. Bann (Harris 1744, 148; Barker 1862–65, 113)

(14) R. Ballinderry (Thompson 1856, 341)

(15) R. Blackwater (Weatherup 1974, 54)

(16) R. Lagan (Mulligan 1886, 21; W[elch] 1908, 90)

(17) R. Bann (Copping 1740, 198; Harris 1744, 148; Payne 1794, 174; Doyle 1854, 133)

(18) R. Kilcurry (Redding 1688, 662)

(19) King's River (Brosnan 1985/86, 47)

(20) R. Avoca (von Hessling 1859, 188)

(21) R. Doirín [Derreen] (MacDomhaill 1937, 88)

(22) R. Burren (Dingley 1675–80, 88; Dineley 1862, 46)

(23) R. Slaney (Synnott 1899–1902, 193)

(24) R. Slaney (Hoare 1862, 91; Streeter 1886, 244)

(25) R. Nore (Redding 1688, 160; Dublin Philosophical Society 1683–87, 183)

(26) R. Blackwater (Smith 1746, 237; A.M. 1892, 211)

(27) R. Blackwater (Quinn 1939, 37)

(28) R. Bandon (Grosart 1886, 66)

(29) R. Argideen (Smith 1750, 362)

(30) R. Lee (Smith 1750, 362; Holmes 1801, 175; Gibbings 1945, 143)

(31) L. Allua (von Hessling 1859, 188)

(32) R. Blackwater (Prendergast 1900, 148)

(33) R. Cumurah [Cummeragh] (Prendergast 1900, 148)

(34) R. Ini [Inny] (Prendergast 1900, 148)

(35) R. Behih [Behy] (Prendergast 1900, 148)

(36) R. Carrah [Caragh] (Prendergast 1900, 148)

(37) R. Laune (Smith 1756, 126; Hitchcock 1914, 210; de Dodd 1945, 160)

(38) L. Lein [Leane] (Nennius 831, 198; Dublin Philosophical Society 1683–87, 183; Hamilton 1867, 232; Hamilton 1885, 124)

(39) R. Flesk (Prendergast 1900, 148)

(40) L. Veagh [Gal] (Hart 1884, 220; Colgan 1914, 60)

(41) R. Cranny [Cloon] (Taylor 1928, 36)

(42) L. Ree (Pike 1976, 90)

(43) River at Oughterard [R. Owenriff] (O'Flaherty 1684, 53; Dutton 1824, 403; Buckland 1878, 334)

(44) L. Corrib (Maxwell 1832, 80; Buckland 1878, 336)

(45) R. Owentuidhe [Owentooey] (O'Flaherty 1684, 108)

(46) R. Moy (McCormick 1996, *in litt.*)

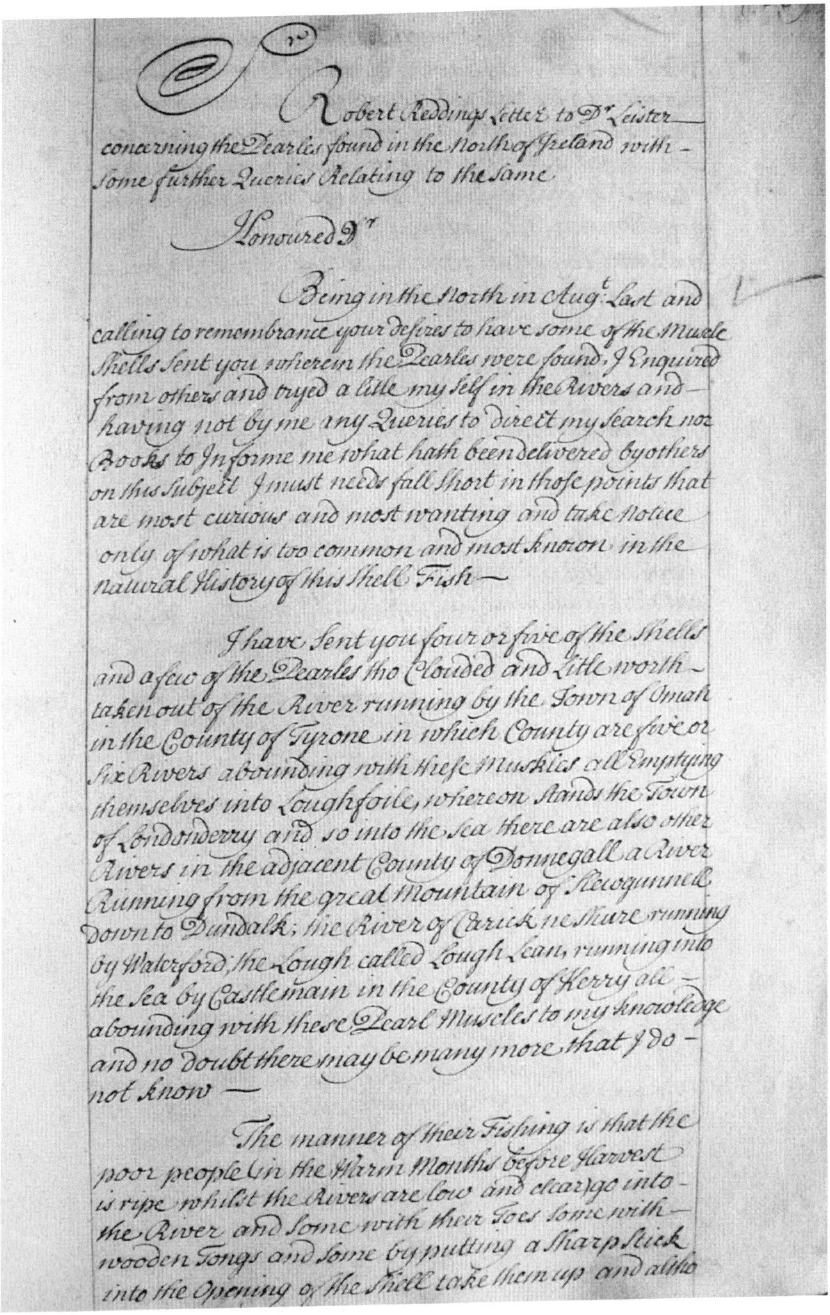

Robert Reddings letter to Dr Leister
concerning the Pearles found in the North of Ireland with
some further Queries Relating to the same.

Honoured Sr

Being in the North in Augt Last and
calling to remembrance your desires to have some of the Muscle
Shells sent you wherein the Pearles were found, I Enquired
from others and tryed a litle my self in the Rivers and
having not by me any Queries to direct my search nor
Books to Informe me what hath been delivered by others
on this Subject I must needs fall short in those points that
are most curious and most wanting and take notice
only of what is too common and most knowen in the
natural History of this shell Fish —

I have sent you four or five of the shells
and a few of the Pearles tho Clouded and Litle worth
taken out of the River running by the Town of Omah
in the County of Tyrone in which County are five or
six Rivers abounding with these muscles all Emptying
themselves into Loughfoile, whereon stands the Town
of Londonderry and so into the sea there are also other
Rivers in the adjacent County of Donnegall a River
Running from the great Mountain of Slewgunnell
Down to Dundalk; the River of Carick ne Shure running
by Waterford, the Lough called Lough Lean, running into
the sea by Castlemain in the County of Kerry all
abounding with these Pearl Muscles to my knowledge
and no doubt there may be many more that I do
not know —

The manner of their Fishing is that the
poor people (in the Harin Months before Harvest
is ripe whilst the Rivers are low and clear)go into
the River and some with their Toes some with
wooden Tongs and some by putting a sharp stick
into the Opening of the Shell take them up and altho

*Figure 2.1*
Part of copy of manuscript letter from Robert Redding to Martin Lister in
October 1688 concerning pearls found in the north of Ireland (Trinity
College, Dublin, MS 888/2, 63).

Above: *Figure 2.2*
Pearl fishers from Omagh in County Tyrone, photographed in the 1940s opening the pearl-producing mussels on the bank of the river which has just been fished (*Ulster Herald* 13 September 1947, 5).

Right: *Figure 4.1*
Tom Mullin from Omagh, pearl fishing in the 1940s with forked stick and glass-bottomed box (*Ulster Herald* 13 September 1947, 5).

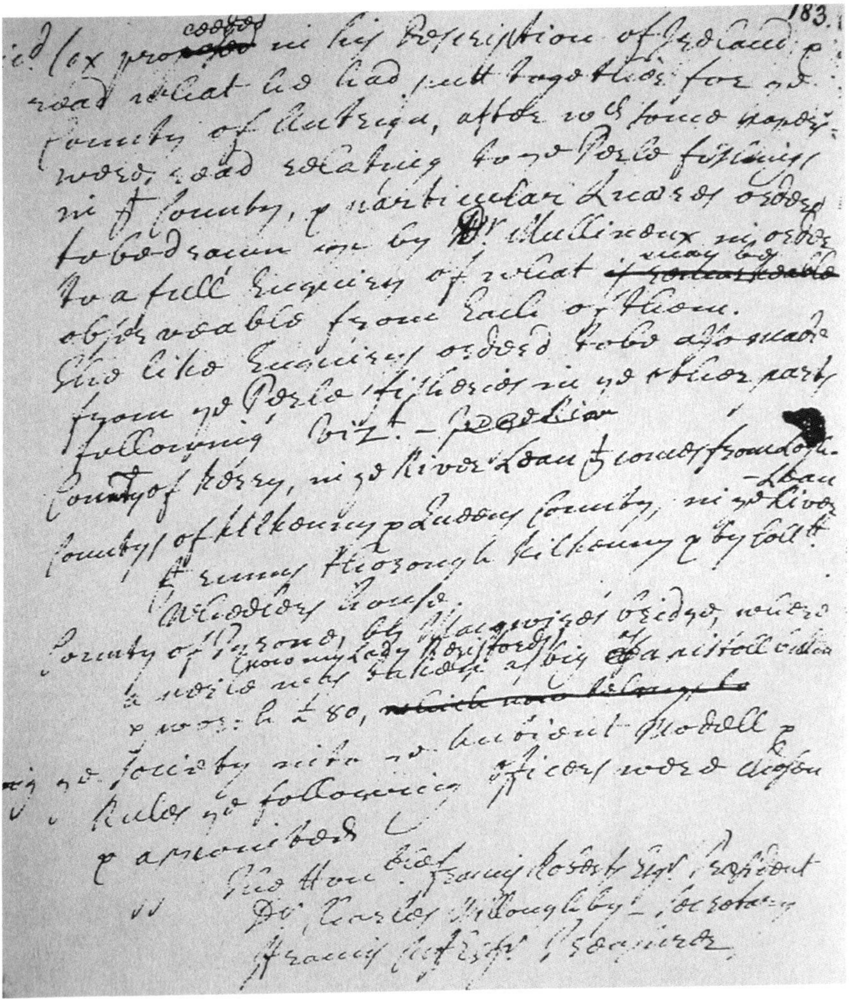

*Figure 4.2*
Part of minutes of the Dublin Philosophical Society meeting for 10 May 1693 relating to pearl fisheries (British Library, Add. MS 4811, 183).

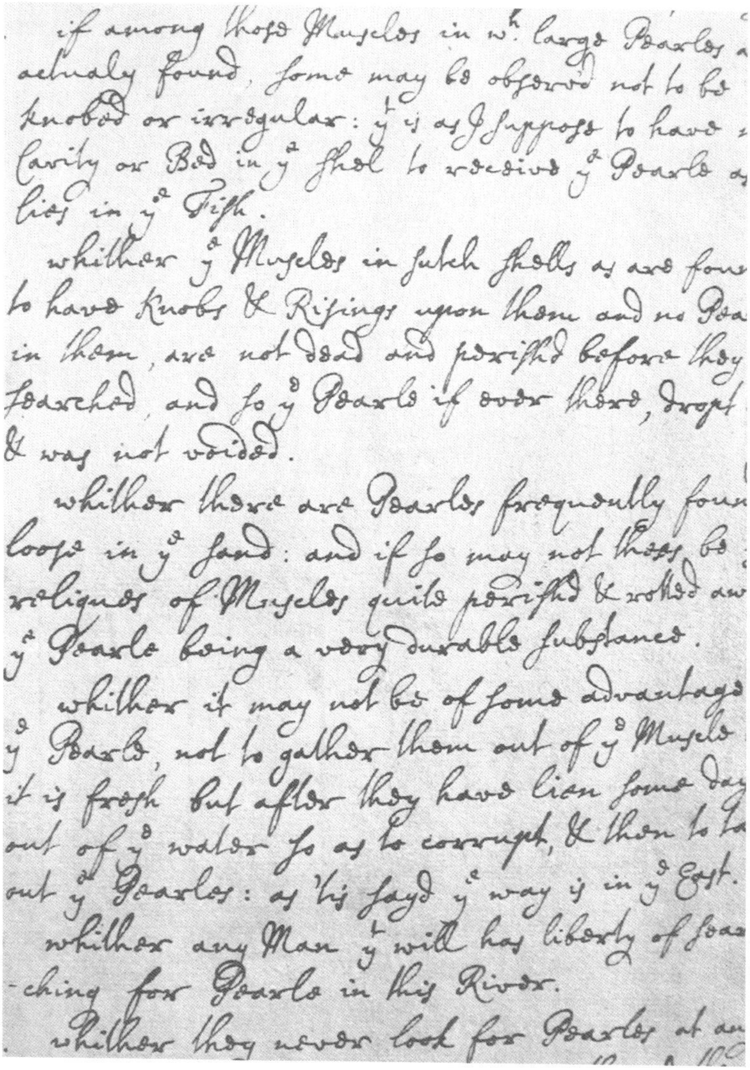

if among those Muscles in w:ch large Pearles a[re]
actualy found, some may be observed not to be
knobed or irregular: y:is is as I suppose to have [a]
Cavity or Bed in y:e shell to receive y:e Pearle a[s]
lies in y:e Fish.

whither y:e Muscles in such shells as are foun[d]
to have Knobs & Risings upon them and no Pea[rl]
in them, are not dead and perishd before they
searched, and so y:e Pearle if ever there, dropt
& was not voided.

whither there are Pearles frequently foun[d]
loose in y:e sand: and if so may not these be
reliques of Muscles quite perishd & rotted aw[ay]
y:e Pearle being a very durable substance.

whither it may not be of some advantage [to]
y:e Pearle, not to gather them out of y:e Muscle
it is fresh but after they have lien some day[s]
out of y:e water so as to corrupt, & then to ta[ke]
out y:e Pearles: as 'tis sayd y:e way is in y:e East.

whither any Man y:t will has liberty of searching for Pearle in this River.

whither they never look for Pearles at an[y]

*Figure 4.3*
Part of questionnaire directed to be drawn up by Dr Molyneux of the
Dublin Philosophical Society in 1693 to inquire into the existing
pearl fisheries in Ireland (Trinity College, Dublin, MS 888/2, 151).

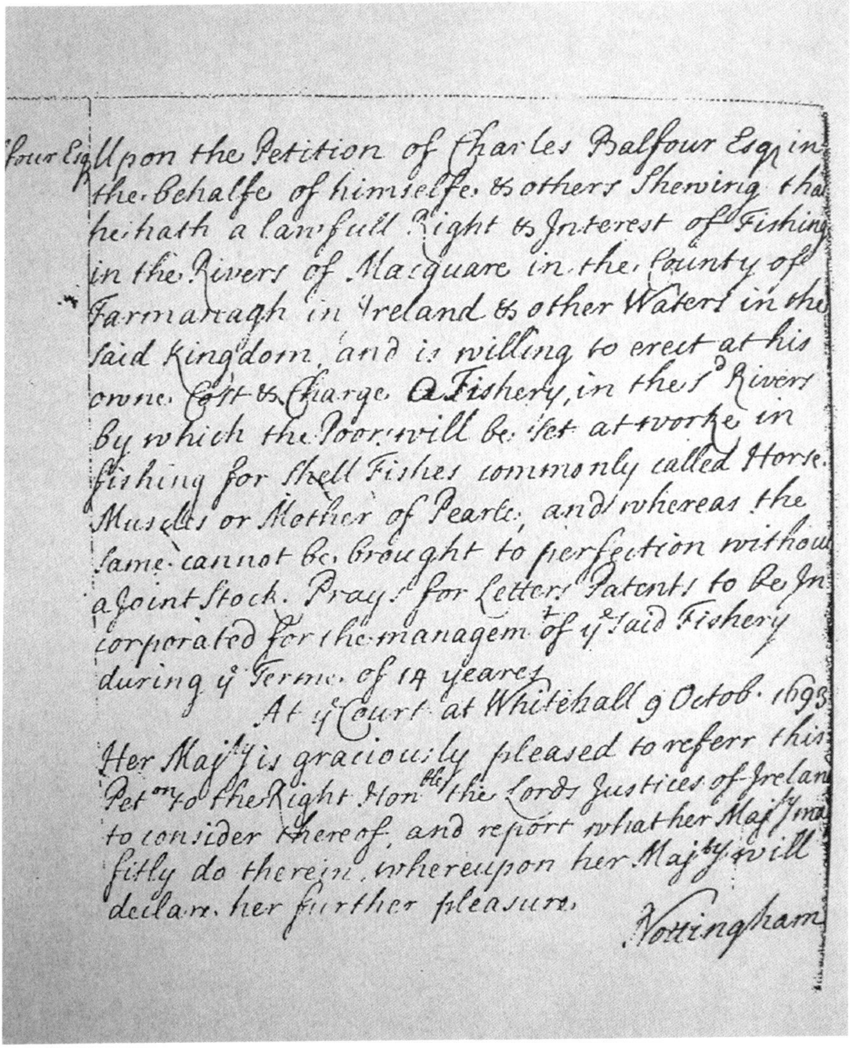

four Esq. Upon the Petition of Charles Balfour Esq. in
the behalfe of himselfe & others Shewing that
he hath a lawfull Right & Interest of Fishing
in the Rivers of Macquare in the County of
Farmanagh in Ireland & other Waters in the
said Kingdom, and is willing to erect at his
owne Cost & Charge a Fishery, in the sd Rivers
By which the Poor will be set at worke in
fishing for Shell Fishes commonly called Horse
Muscles or Mother of Pearle, and whereas the
same cannot be brought to perfection without
a Joint Stock. Pray.s for Letters Patents to be In
corporated for the managemt of ye said Fishery
during ye Terme of 14 yeares.

At ye Court at Whitehall 9 Octob. 1693

Her Majty is graciously pleased to referr this
Petn to the Right Honble the Lords Justices of Ireland
to consider thereof, and report what her Majty may
fitly do therein, whereupon her Majty will
declare her further pleasure.

Nottingham

*Figure 4.4*
Petition of Charles Balfour to the Crown in 1693 to establish a pearl fishery in the rivers of County Fermanagh (Public Record Office, London).

Right: *Figure 4.5*
Riverine head of the Bann sculpted by Edward Smyth for James Gandon's Custom House, built in the 1780s. The turban of linen represents the flax-growing and linen-weaving industries of the upper reaches, while the string of pearls sym-bolizes the pearl fisheries on the river (Department of the Environment, Dublin).

Below: *Figure 4.6*
Part of manuscript letter, dated 20 September 1762, from Edward Willes, the Lord Chief Baron, to the Earl of Warwick regarding the pearl fishery at Omagh in County Tyrone (National Library of Ireland, MS 806, 125–26).

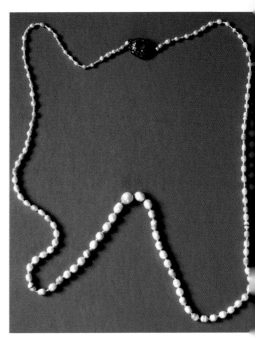

Above left: *Figure 5.1*
Romanticized depiction of pearl fishing in the west of Ireland (Lover 1844, 367, printed in London).

Above right: *Figure 5.2*
Necklace of pearls, from the River Slaney, passed down through a County Wexford family since the early part of the twentieth century (Private collection).

Below: *Figure 6.1*
Part of 'de mirabilibus Hiberniae' (the wonders of Ireland) from the ninth-century (AD 83?) *Historia Britonum* of Nennius referring to Lough Leane, in Kerry, where it reads (lines three, four and five), 'and in that lake are found many pearls which kings wear in their ears' (British Library, Harley MS 3859, 198).

Above: *Figure 6.2*
Equestrian portrait of King Charles I, by the Flemish painter van Dyck, showing a pearl hanging from his left ear (National Gallery, London).

Below left: *Figure 6.3*
Portrait of Sir Walter Raleigh in 1588, aged 34, wearing a double-pearl earring and a pearl bracelet. His belt is also embroidered with pearls (National Portrait Gallery, London).

Below right: *Figure 6.4*
Portrait of Katherine Fenton (d. 1630), second wife of the Earl of Cork, bedecked with pearls (Townsend 1904, 33, printed in London by Duckworth & Company).

Above: *Figure 6.5*
Self-portrait miniature of Richard Cosway (1742–1821) in Elizabethan costume; watercolour on ivory, set in a frame with pearls (National Gallery of Ireland).

Above right: *Figure 6.6*
Copy of early twelfth-century letter from Gillebert, Bishop of Limerick, to Anselm, Archbishop of Canterbury, the original of which accompanied a gift of 25 pearls (British Library, Cotton MS Claudius A. xi., 153).

Left: *Figure 6.7*
The mitre of Conor O'Dea, Bishop of Limerick from 1400 to 1426, showing the triangular reserves decorated with flowers and leaves formed of pearls. It was made in 1418 and signed by the craftsman Thomas O'Carryd (Reproduced by kind permission of Dr Donal Murray, Bishop of Limerick).

Above: *Figure 7.1*
Depiction of pearl fishing in Scotland in the seventeenth century (Geiger 1637, printed in Munich).

Left: *Figure 7.2*
The Abernethy Pearl, also known as 'Little Willie' (Cairncross).

Above: *Figure 7.3*
The Scottish pearl fisherman Neil McCormick fishing the River Spey in 1976
(Neil McCormick).

Below: *Figure 7.4*
Depiction of pearl fishing and uses of pearls in Sweden in the sixteenth century
(Olaus Magnus 1555, printed in Rome).

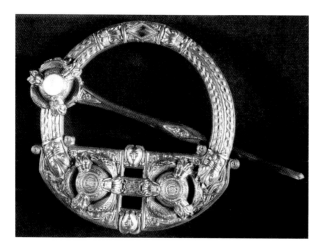

Above: *Figure 8.1*
*Domnach airgid* or Shrine of St Patrick's gospel; the only pearl remaining in its setting is shown in the inset illustration, a detail of one of the sides, in the lower left-hand corner (National Museum, Dublin).

Below: *Figure 8.2*
Gold brooch with pearl presented to Queen Victoria on her visit to Ireland in 1849 (National Museum, Dublin).

Above: *Figure 9.1*
Hundreds of empty shells found by the present author in the River Blackwater in County Cork during the summer of 1990, in the aftermath of the exertions of amateur pearl hunters.

Left: *Figure 10.1*
Armorial Bearings of Banbridge District Council showing the shield with two freshwater mussels, representing the ancient Banbridge pearl fisheries. Between them are the shuttle and spindle, representing the spinning and linen-weaving trade (Banbridge District Council).

patent for pearl fishing in the River Irt in Cumberland (Streeter 1886, 238). Having seen pearls on his travels in the Strait of Magellan, he intended to get rich by exploiting the pearls of his native country (Pennant 1812, 164). In the seventeenth century, a gentleman from the same county employed local poor people to collect pearls from the rivers, which were sold to jewellers in London for more than £800 (Kunz and Stevenson 1908, 162). The pearls from Cumberland were so noted that 'fair as Irton pearls' became a saying in the north country (Gibbings 1945, 143).

Other rivers in England were also fished for their pearls in former times, for example those in parts of Buckinghamshire, Shropshire and other counties in the seventeenth century (Streeter 1886, 239).

One English pearl fisherman, Peter Goodwin (1985), wrote a book on his 'conversion' to the trade and his experiences of fishing some English rivers, and later the Scottish rivers. He also fished for pearls in France, Germany, the United States and Canada. However, it was from the Scottish rivers, particularly a section of the Spey, that he earned a living, and he reckons that he and his colleagues took tens of thousands of pounds' worth of pearls there during the 1970s (Weir 1985, 294). He does not mention in his book, *The river and the road: journal of a freshwater pearl-fisher*, ever having fished the rivers of Ireland.

*Isle of Man*  The pearl mussel occurs on the Isle of Man, where the shells have in the past been used as scoops instead of spoons for broth and porridge. For example, George Waldron in his *Description of the Isle of Man* tells us the following (Harrison 1731, 49):

> I must not here omit that the first course at a Mank's feast is always broth, which is served up, not in a soup-dish, but in wooden piggins, every man his mess. This they do not eat with spoons, but with shells, which they call *sligs*, very like our mussel shells, but much larger.

Edward Forbes (1815–54) was the first resident and native-born Manx naturalist of any note. In the first of his many books, *Malacologia monensis*, a catalogue of the molluscs inhabiting the Isle of Man, which he wrote at the age of 22, he included information regarding the nomenclature of the Manx populations of the mussel. He goes on to say where it was found at that time and that it was fished for its pearls in former times (Forbes 1838, 45):

> In the Black river; common near Kirk Braddan Church. It was formerly much sought after by the inhabitants for the sake of the pearls, which it not unfrequently contains.

John Dixon, a noted nineteenth-century conchologist, had visited the Isle of Man on a few occasions to search this river for the shells of the pearl-producing mussel. Writing, in response to a query in *The naturalist*, from his base at the General Infirmary at Leeds in 1865, he tells of his quest (Dixon 1865, 81):

> As remarked by your querist, Mr. Parke, nearly all the Isle of Man hand-books inform us that *Unio margaritiferus* is found in the Dhoo, or Black River, near Kirk Braddan, and that it was formerly much sought after on account of the valuable pearls it sometimes contained. Acting upon this information I have, on more than one occasion, searched very diligently for this shell, commencing at Kirk Braddan and following up the course of the river past Union Mills and nearly to its source, but without finding a single specimen. The country people assured me that they used to be found by hundreds; that pearls had been obtained from them which sold for as much as a guinea each; that they still occurred in the river, though somewhat sparingly; and that very few now contained pearls. To remove all doubts as to their existence several half shells were shown to me. These are turned to a useful account by the thrifty Manx housewives who use them for scoops, and for scraping out the nutritious morsels of the porridge pot.

Obviously the mussel population of the river had, by that time, suffered an almost complete collapse owing to the exertions of the pearl seekers. Whereas the discarded empty shells could indeed be used as a kitchen utensil, live mussels were needed to produce pearls. Dixon did, however, meet with a man experienced in the art, who found some mussels for him:

> In the course of my enquiries, I met an old gentleman who not only gave me some curious facts as to the habits of this *Unio*, but also procured me some fine living specimens, one of which contained a small but not very brilliant pearl. This was Mr. Oates, of Kirk Braddan, through whose farm the Dhoo runs. He is a good specimen of an honest warm-hearted Manx farmer, and I trust caught no cold in catching me 'black mussels.'

He next describes the habits of the mussel and goes on to relate how pearl fishing was then carried out:

> *Unio margaritiferus* loves to lurk in the shallow and quick-running parts of the river, amongst the gravel and small stones, and as the shell generally burrows in a somewhat oblique position only a small portion is visible, and this being black and not unfrequently covered with a little moss, requires a well practised eye to detect it amongst the surrounding stones, for one of which it may be easily mistaken. It seems very

susceptible to the action of light, for under the full blaze of a bright midday sun it emerges more out of the gravel and protruding a portion of its body through the partly opened valves of the shell is the more readily distinguished. If the sun becomes overcast or the water above the shell be muddy it immediately closes, and, to a person not well conversant with it, is then very difficult to find. The country lads generally select a bright noonday to look for the mussels, and take them either by wading, or by thrusting the end of a long slender rod into the half open shell, which instantly closes upon it and it is then dragged to land.

Pearl fishing probably became current in the Black River in the sixteenth century, when it was prosecuted throughout the British Isles, particularly in Ireland, Scotland and Wales. The tradition of using the shells of the mussel as spoons and scoops was probably of longer standing. In parts of Ireland, for example, the poor people used these shells as spoons until at least the middle of the eighteenth century, and it is thought that this practice dated from ancient times (Lucey 2000, 78). There are many similarities between Irish and Manx traditions, signifying a common origin (Joyce 1903a, 79–80)[ii] and it is likely that the shells of the mussel were also used as spoons on the Isle of Man from a remote time. The current status of the mussel population in the Dhoo River is apparently unknown (Kerney 1999, 207).

*Scotland* Pearls were fished from the rivers of Scotland from a very remote time and were known to the Romans. That pearls from Caledonia were known on the Continent in the fourth century is evidenced by the following lines from Ausonius (*c.* AD 310–95) in his poem 'Mosella' (Curle 1931/32, 347):

> Tota Caledoniis talis pictura Britannis
> Cum virides algas et rubra corallia nudat
> Aestus, et albentes concharum, germina baccas,[iii]
> Delicias hominum locupletum, quaeque sub undis
> Assimulant nostros imitata monilia cultus.

Those in the possession of King Alexander I (*c.* 1077–1124) were celebrated in distant countries for their size and beauty (Anon. 1876b, 622). During his reign in the twelfth century, there was a market in Europe for pearls from Scotland (Kunz and Stevenson 1908, 160), although as trade with the East increased and the more brilliant ones came on the jewel market, they were regarded as of less value. This was effectively extended to exclusion by a statute of the Parisian goldsmiths in 1355, when it was enacted that no worker in gold or silver shall set any Scottish pearls with oriental ones, except in large ornaments or jewels for churches (Anon. 1876b, 622). By 1560, there was again a market for Scottish pearls in Europe and they were sent mostly to Antwerp

(Kunz and Stevenson 1908, 161).

A description of the regalia of Scotland has been given by Sir Walter Scott, and the workmanship indicated a date of origin of the fourteenth century (Kunz and Stevenson 1908, 419). Frank Buckland (1875, 273), who was interested in finding out about the pearls in the regalia, commissioned a lady in Edinburgh to look into the matter. She told him that the pearls were said to have been native, although she added that they were more like oriental ones in colour, as they lacked the slightly blue tinge which usually characterizes Scottish pearls.

Hector Boece (*c.* 1465–1536), who became principal of the recently opened university at King's College, Aberdeen in 1500 and whose name is Latinized as Boethius in his writings, made many references to Scottish pearls, which he described as not of small value, having a clear, shining whiteness, round and light. He says (Boethius 1627, 77), quaintly, that the mussels are taken up with the toes of the fisher, as the water depth might prohibit reaching with the hand, or, 'pedum digitis (nam manibus id sieri prohibet altitudo)'. Figure 7.1 shows a contemporary depiction of pearl fishing in the seventeenth century in Scotland.

John Lesley (1527–96), the Catholic Bishop of Ross who passed much of his life in exile after faithful service to Mary, Queen of Scots, wrote a Latin work on the origin, customs and achievements of the Scots, in which he praises the native pearls (Lesley 1578, 15):

> At vero margaritarum et copia et pretium magnum est, splendes-centemque ipsae candorem referunt, sed iis tamen quae ex oriente importantur paulo obscuriores.

In 1621, a superb pearl which was fished from a tributary of the River Ythan was presented by Robert Menzies, Provost of Aberdeen, to James VI (later James I of England). The King immediately set up a group of commissioners to manage and control all the major rivers in the north of Scotland where pearls were found. The new laws, however, were largely ignored or resisted by the locals, leading to the resignation of one of the commissioners, and the commission was eventually repealed in 1633 (Green 1985/86, 30–31). It has been said that the Scottish pearl trade was considered of such importance that it was worthy of the attention of parliament in the reign of Charles I (Anon. 1863, 11), but we do not learn to what degree.

During the eighteenth century in south-west Scotland, on the Rivers Dee and Doon, the locals fished for a group of about 30 merchants who visited Ayr for the summer season (Green 1985/86, 31). The slaughter of mussels continued into the early years of the next century and at times was so intense that there were complaints about the smell of the rotting flesh coming from the shell heaps on the river banks.

Between the years 1761 and 1764, pearls to the value of £10,000, from the Rivers Tay and Isla, were sent to London (Streeter 1886, 241). Thereafter, however, until about 1860, the pearl resources of Scotland were almost dormant and were rarely seen in the markets (Kunz and Stevenson 1908, 163). In 1861, a visiting German merchant had seen and then purchased some pearls kept by the cottagers as curiosities. Some accounts refer to him as 'M. Moritz Unger, a foreigner, settled in Edinburgh' (Anon. 1863, 11). Apparently at that time there was only one known pearl fisher in all of Scotland, whose pearls were sold to a private customer and never reached the jewellers (Anon. 1876b, 622). The merchant persuaded the people to collect more by paying high prices (Kunz and Stevenson 1908, 163) and this stimulated Scottish pearl fishing again, with hundreds going to the rivers in search of riches. Pearls to the value of £1,200 were collected in 1865, but the flurry of fishing did not last as the mussels were overfished (Dakin 1913, 9).

Apart from the problems of overfishing and the subsequent periods when few pearls could be found, there were serious commercial complications for the Scottish pearl fisher. The 'feast and famine' aspect of the Scottish pearl market lasted until the economic and political climate became more stable, and it is unlikely that pearling offered a full-time living for many until the nineteenth century. In the mid-nineteenth century the whole picture changed, as the syndicates, operated by 'tinkers', took over (Green 1985/86, 31):

> The syndicates fished the rivers in rotation, with their bases ranging from Stirlingshire to Aberdeenshire. Six to 30 members made up a family syndicate, and they continued to flourish until 1936, when the last group worked in Stirlingshire. Their organisation often included the services of a skilled lawyer, who could delay injunctions sought against the fishers by the local lairds. By the time a landowner managed to get his injunction, the fishers had left.

Only one heir of the syndicates remains in Scotland and was known as the last travelling pearl fisher—William Abernethy (see Box VII), who retired at the turn of the millennium. Abernethy's greatest pearl find is shown in Figure 7.2. Another Scottish pearler, Neil McCormick (see Box VII), who, with his sons, still fished the rivers of the British Isles up until recently, is shown in Figure 7.3.

In the late nineteenth century, a description of how two 'gipsies' fished the Tummell River, a tributary of the Tay, was given (Watkins 1896, 627–28):

> On the same river I saw a gipsy and his mate hard at work fishing for pearls. Their *modus operandi* was curious. Having chosen a much deeper reach of the river than I had experimented in, he had moored a large square box, like a big packing case, in the centre of the stream by means

of a rope tied at each end to a tree on the banks. He then reclined in the shade and smoked, while the younger man got in the box and pulled it from the side to the middle of the river. Then he lay down on it, and fixed on its edge in front of him a tin box tube, something like a milk tin, while he grasped a stout stick, six feet long, split at the lower end. Turning up his shirt-sleeves, he looked through the tin (thereby being able to survey the bottom), and groped about with the stick till he saw a likely mussel. The cleft of the stick was then pressed over it, and the shell thus secured. Without raising himself the lad withdrew the stick till his other hand could extricate the mussel and drop it at his left side, when the stick was again let down, and the same motions gone through. On an average the lad took up two a minute...When the boy had procured enough mussels to weigh down the boat, he pulled it along the rope to the side, landed, and broke open the mussels to see what luck had attended him.

Pearls found by these gipsies were sold to visitors at the shooting lodges or hotels in the neighbourhood. There were still a few travelling tinkers occasionally fishing in Scotland in the 1970s (Cranbrook 1976, 89). Up until recently, a few traveller families, in all about 15 people, still sold pearls to the Perth jewellers, Cairncross (J. Lochtie, pers. comm.).

Pearling was carried on by all sorts of people of all ages, and Frank Buckland (1875, 273) even tells of a blind old man who fished for pearls in a river in Sutherlandshire:

He used to wade into the river, and pick up the mussels off the bottom with his toes, his wife standing on the bank, telling him in which direction to go. When he had filled the bag which he carried round his neck with pearl mussels, he brought them to the bank for his wife to open. A pearl the size of a pea was worth £1.

The writer goes on to say how very sorry he was to hear of the poor man's tragic end. He had one day got out of his depth, fallen into a deep hole in the river and drowned.

Among the papers of George C. Hyndman (1796–1867), conchologist and founder member of the Belfast Natural History and Philosophical Society, there are many newspaper cuttings on Scottish pearls; one of these, from the *Edinburgh Courant* in September 1864, refers to a pearl found in the River Eske which weighed 27 grains and sold to a London jeweller for £100 (Hyndman 1843–57).

Towards the end of the nineteenth century, it appeared that the Scottish pearl-fishing industry was in decline, and Edwin Streeter (1886, 242) believed that there was little fishing then going on in the rivers. He also reckoned that

*Box VII*
## Pearl fisher profiles (Scottish)

*William Stormont Abernethy* of Tayside comes from a long line of pearl fishers, with his father and grandfather before him also having carried out the ancient craft. The tradition in the family, however, ends with him, as he is a bachelor and has no offspring. Now approaching his seventieth birthday, Bill Abernethy still fishes for seven months of the year and has, for some time, held the distinction of being known as the last remaining professional pearl fisher in Britain. He once earned a good living but now reckons he is doing well to gross £4,000 a year, and he blames pollution as well as amateur pearl hunters for the demise of the mussels on which he depends. In his time he has fished rivers throughout Britain and Ireland as well as on the Continent. He regularly took 70 to 80 pearls in a week's fishing, although most of these would have been only one to three grains in weight. In 1967 he found the greatest freshwater pearl of living memory, which is known as the Abernethy Pearl, and more affectionately as 'Little Willie'. At over 44 grains and 99 per cent round with a perfect lustre, it was valued at £20,000 in the 1960s, but is now regarded as nearly priceless. This gem is now displayed in the window, or held in the vault, of a Perth jeweller (see Figure 7.2). (Sources: Green 1985/86, 32; Neale 1991; Pilkington 1991, 26; Woodward 1994, 91–95.)

*Neil McCormick* (see Figure 7.3), who lives in Sutherland, became involved when he married into a traditional pearl-fishing family. In the 1950s, pearl fishing, combined with odd jobs such as raspberry picking, provided him with a fine income. As well as the rivers in Britain, he has fished throughout Europe and North America. He is a regular visitor to Ireland and fishes the known pearling rivers north and south with his two sons; in 1914 his father-in-law fished a pearl from the River Moy in Mayo which purchased him a horse and cart. In the 1970s he recognized the decline in population numbers of the mussel as a result of overfishing and pollution in the rivers he fished in Scotland, and was instrumental in having research projects on population dynamics and conservation strategies initiated at Aberdeen University. In an effort to conserve stocks, he uses pliers to open a mussel slightly, searches for pearls, and marks the shell with an X, 'so that any other pearl fisher who was educated to this practice would bypass this mussel', realizing that it had already been examined. Prior to this mussel-friendly method of examination, he and other pearlers opened the shells completely, which destroyed the hinge and muscle keeping the two valves of the shell together, thus effectively killing the mussel. He is not optimistic about the future of his craft as the mussels, and hence pearls, become more elusive.
(Sources: Woodward 1994, 90–91; McCormick 1996, *in litt.*; BBC 1 *Countryfile*, 8 April 1996.)

because of its reputed interference with ordinary fishing, pearl fishing was being discouraged at that time.

Since then, pearl fishing has continued, with some professional fishers as well as amateurs operating. Two donations of Scottish river pearls were made to the museum of the Society of Antiquaries of Scotland in 1967 (Anon. 1967/68, 204).

During the 1990s there was a decline in the freshwater pearls coming on the market. The jewellers Hamilton & Inches of Edinburgh paid some £2,500 to pearl fishermen for pearls in 1990 and £1,000 in 1994, but were offered none in 1995 (A. King, pers. comm.). This might indicate that the pearlers were disposing of their pearls elsewhere, but is more likely to represent the decline of the trade. The Perth jewellers, Cairncross, which traditionally handled more than 50 per cent of the trade in Scottish pearls, had been offered very few good ones (six or more millimetres in diameter) recently and noted a steady decline in the 1990s (J. Lochtie, pers. comm.). It would appear, therefore, that the recent decline in the Scottish pearl trade is real and the present period may, as in former times, represent the start of a falling-off in pearl fishing which will remain at a low level until the mussel stocks have again regenerated. What is different now is that pearl fishing has become regulated in Scotland, as elsewhere in the British Isles. In 1998, the freshwater pearl mussel was given full protection in the UK under the Wildlife and Countryside Act, making it illegal to take or kill any freshwater pearl mussels.[iv] The protection also includes pearl fishing using special tongs.

*Wales* Shell fragments of the pearl mussel have been found in a sepulchral cave of Neolithic Age in Denbighshire (Jackson 1913, 321), and it is probable that these people also knew of the pearls produced by this mollusc collected from the local rivers.

According to Welsh Celtic myth, pearls were apparently credited with life-giving powers and were used to embellish a sacred vessel known as the 'mother-pot', with the hope that they would impart extra potency to the holy waters which it contained (Joyce and Addison 1992, 33). This 'mother-pot', perhaps the same as the 'cauldron of Ceridwen' (Bonwick 1986, 7), later became the Holy Grail of Arthurian legend, the object of the chivalric quest for immortality. Here there is a parallel with the tradition of the magi in Ireland using a pearl to prolong life (see chapter six).

During or before the sixteenth century, there was obviously a freshwater pearl fishery on the River Conway in the north of Wales, as the following lines from the *Faerie queene*, written by the poet Edmund Spenser[v] when he was living at Kilcolman Castle in County Cork (Morris 1869, xxxvii), show:

> And Conway, which out of his streame doth send
> Plenty of pearles to decke his dames withall…

A variation on this theme is given by Michael Drayton (1563–1631), an admirer of Spenser (Collier 1888, lix), in his *Polyolbion*:

> She meets with Conway first, which lyeth next at hand
> Whose precious orient pearle that breedth in her sand…

A pearl from the Conway was presented to the Queen of Charles II, Catherine of Braganza (1638–1705), by her chamberlain, Sir Richard Wynne of Gwydir, which is apparently retained in the Royal Crown (Kunz and Stevenson 1908, 161; Dakin 1913, 10). Pearls were still found in the Conway, between Llanrwst and Betws-y-Coed, in the nineteenth century and fetched a much higher price than those taken from the sea mussel lower down in the Estuary (Garner 1873, 427).

In the seventeenth century, pearls were also fished from the River Clun in Montgomeryshire (Streeter 1886, 239). According to Streeter (1886, 236), the Welsh pearls were mostly of a dull colour. In fact, he had received one from the mouth of the Conway that was quite black.

In the Conway Estuary, a pearl fishery also existed, in the nineteenth century, where pearls were taken from the common sea mussel *Mytilus edulis*. Many of the inhabitants of that part of North Wales apparently obtained their livelihood entirely from collecting the pearls (D.C. 1830, 132). Indeed, one lady, under a charter, was said to 'net' nearly £1,000 a year from this business (Murray 1830, 451), although it is not clear if her fishery was for the freshwater mussel further upstream in the River Conway.

How the sea mussels were collected in the Conway Estuary, and the technique used for extraction of the pearls, was given at the time (D.C. 1830, 132–33):

> When the tide is out, they go in several boats to the bar at the mouth of the river, with their sacks, and gather as many shells as they can before the return of the tide. The muscles are then put in a large kettle over a fire to be opened; and the fish taken out singly from the shells with the fingers, and put into a tub, into which one of the fishers goes bare-footed, and stamps upon them, until they are reduced into a sort of pulp. They next pour in water to separate the fishy substance, which they call *solach*, from the more heavy parts consisting of sand, small pebbles, and the pearls, which settle in the bottom. After numerous washings, until the fishy part is entirely removed, the sediment, if I may so term it, is put out to dry, and each pearl separated on a large wooden platter, one at a time, with a feather; and when a sufficient quantity is obtained, they are taken to the overseer, who pays the fisher so much per ounce for them.

At the beginning of the twentieth century, London dealers had, during some seasons, agents present for purchasing these pearls which, depending on quality, sold for eight to thirty shillings per ounce (Kunz and Stevenson 1908, 168). Recent studies on the sub-tidal mussels of the Conway have shown that the occurrence and abundance of pearls increased with mussel size (Fernandes and Seed 1983, 114). Today the presence of seed pearls in this mussel is regarded as a potential deterrent to the widescale commercial use of the species as food.

*Europe*
Almost all of the European countries can be said to have rivers which have contained pearls (Taburiaux 1985, 64), and the following represents a summary of information gleaned from various literature sources. The pearls on the Continent have been taken almost exclusively from the same mussel that occurs in Ireland, *Margaritifera margaritifera*, but they were also occasionally found in a related species, *Margaritifera auricularia*, which once lived in large rivers over most of Western Europe, but now is apparently on the verge of extinction, being recently only recorded from the lower River Ebro in Spain (Altaba 1990, 271).

*Austria* The Austrian Empire at one time encompassed Bohemia, Moravia and Hungary as well as parts of Italy, Dalmatia, Bavaria, Switzerland and Poland. The River Ilz was famous for its beautiful pearls (Payne 1793b, 314) which were reputedly the choicest in Lower Bavaria (Kunz and Stevenson 1908, 172). In the early part of the twentieth century, the shells were collected for the mother-of-pearl industry (Wells *et al.* 1984, 151) as well as for their pearls, but pearl fishing is apparently no longer prosecuted there (Wells and Chatfield 1992, 112). A study in the northern part of Lower Austria has found that even dense mussel populations are endangered (Georgiou 1992, 1).

*Belgium* The pearl mussel occurs in streams and rivers of the Ardennes (Wells and Chatfield 1992, 113) and was apparently still being fished for its pearls in Wallonia recently (Gaspar *et al.* 1990, 20).

*Czech Republic and Slovakia* The pearl fisheries of the River Wotawa were worked since the middle of the sixteenth century (Kunz and Stevenson 1908, 178). Count Adolf Schwarzenberg owned a fabulous collection of pearls taken in the rivers of his land (Taburiaux 1985, 63), which were exhibited, together with the apparatus used in his fishery, at the Bohemian Exposition held at Prague in 1791 (Kunz and Stevenson 1908, 178).

Sometimes the fisheries of Bohemia, then part of Germany, were successful enough to gain notice internationally, as the following from the *Gentleman's magazine and historical chronicle* (Anon. 1811, 373) shows:

> The fishery for pearls in the rivers of Bohemia, has been unexpectedly successful this year, especially in the neighbourhood of Rosenberg and Frauenberg. The river Moldau yields pearls not surpassed by those obtained in the East, and they are sold as high as 60 florins each.

Between Pilsen and Budweis, on the River Wotawa, a pearl fishery was conducted in the late nineteenth century (Streeter 1886, 247); these towns, however, are traditionally associated more with beer than with pearls. The River Queiss had been famous for its pearls since the sixteenth century (von Hessling 1859, 179) and was still yielding some fine specimens in the early part of the twentieth century (Kunz and Stevenson 1908, 176). As a result of eutrophication (or enrichment) of water courses, due mainly to intensification of agriculture, the populations of pearl mussels have shrunk and are now restricted to the headstreams in forest parts of the higher-altitude areas in the Bohemian crystalline region (Hruska 1992, 182).

*Denmark* Populations of the pearl-producing mussel have declined, owing mainly to pollution, and unsuccessful introductions have been made to some rivers (Wells and Chatfield 1992, 113). Pearls were fished in Jutland in the early seventeenth century by a Greenlander, for the Governor of the castle at Kolding, but the fishery ceased when the fisherman became ill and died (Kunz and Stevenson 1908, 179–80). In 1734, Charles VI of Denmark asked the King of Saxony to send an experienced fisherman from the Vogtland fisheries to assess the rivers of his dominion (which then included Norway). The subsequent report was so promising that he was apparently awarded a pension for life (Taburiaux 1985, 63). Pearl fishing had evidently ceased in Denmark by the early part of the twentieth century (Kunz and Stevenson 1908, 179).

*Finland* The pearl mussel has been collected extensively for pearls since about 1750, and in the following 200 years the species underwent a catastrophic decline (Wells *et al.* 1984, 150). Pearl fishing has been banned in Finland since 1955, but the discovery of a heap of mussels on the banks of a river in Karvianjoki in the south-west during the 1980s indicates that it still occurs illegally (Valovirta 1990, 59–61). The pearls found there at the beginning of the twentieth century were chiefly sold in Russia (Dakin 1913, 90).

*France* Pearls have been exploited from the Vologne, a river in Lorraine, since the sixteenth century (Taburiaux 1985, 62). The fisheries were managed to some extent in the eighteenth century, with the Dukes of Upper Lorraine maintaining a certain amount of control over the fisheries by permitting fishing only during the summer months. An essay written on the fisheries in

1779, however, notes that while pearls were plentiful in the previous 60 years, they had then become scarce (Taburiaux 1985, 62). In the mid-nineteenth century, unsuccessful attempts were made to stimulate pearl production by mussels in a stream in Aveyron (Streeter 1886, 250). In the River Charente, which flows into the Bay of Biscay south of La Rochelle, there was a pearl fishery which was still in operation at the beginning of the twentieth century (Kunz and Stevenson 1908, 171). Apparently the mussel exploited there was the species *Margaritifera auricularia* which is now believed to be extinct in France. Pearls were found in many other rivers in western France and, although they were small, they were reputed to have a good colour (Taburiaux 1985, 62). Pearls were being fished in France into the 1920s and one of 40 centigrammes, which is equivalent to eight grains, was taken in the River Ance in Lozère in 1928 (Anon. 1928, 4). The pearl mussel *Margaritifera margaritifera* is now protected, and still occurs in some of the smaller rivers of France but has declined in many others (Wells and Chatfield 1992, 113).

*Germany* The main fisheries were in Saxony in the north and Bavaria in the south; those in Bavaria were in Upper Franconia (along the River Main and part of the Rhine), Upper Palatine (on the border with Czechoslovakia) and Lower Bavaria (on the small tributaries of the Danube) between Ratisbon and Passau (Taburiaux 1985, 62). Those in Saxony were chiefly located in the basin of the White Elster and its tributaries (Streeter 1886, 247).

Early in the sixteenth century, pearls were collected from the rivers of Bavaria, and those from Lake Ilz were reputed to be the finest in Lower Bavaria (Taburiaux 1985, 63); the Bishop of Passau had the right to the pearls from the region and a law of 1579 decreed that anyone convicted of poaching on his reserves should be hanged (Kunz and Stevenson 1908, 172).

It has been estimated that as many as 445,000 pearls were taken from the Bavarian fisheries in the years between 1600 and 1857 (Kunz and Stevenson 1908, 173).

In Saxony, particularly in Vogtland, the fisheries were active from the sixteenth century and were under state control from the early part of the seventeenth century (Streeter 1886, 248); in 1621, Elector Johann Georg I declared them to be a royal privilege and a superintendent was appointed to oversee the fishing (Taburiaux 1985, 63). For almost two centuries from 1719, when Vogtland passed to the Electorate of Saxony, a record existed for nearly every pearl obtained, and the fishery was still in operation at the beginning of the twentieth century (Kunz and Stevenson 1908, 173). The fisheries were systematically worked, with a close season operating, and with sections also being 'rested' for ten to fifteen years at a time to allow the mussel stocks to recuperate.

In the late eighteenth century, Payne (1793b, 248), describing Saxony, said that 'in the White Elster are found pearl muscles that have beautiful pearls, some of them as large as a cherry stone'.

In the nineteenth century, in an effort to conserve stocks, a non-destructive method was used to examine the mussels for pearls: the mussels were opened gently with a small iron implement and, if no pearl was found, were returned to the water uninjured. In the early part of the twentieth century, however, pollution due to the development of manufacturing industries reduced the abundance of mussels, and the fisheries subsequently declined (Kunz and Stevenson 1908, 175).

The pearl-fishing industry still flourished in Bavaria and Saxony at the turn of the twentieth century (Synnott 1899–1902, 193). The fisheries were carefully looked after, with the rivers being inspected in spring and the fishing taking place in summer (Dakin 1913, 90). The development of manufacturing industries in Saxony and the resultant pollution of the rivers in the early part of the twentieth century led to the decline in the pearl industry there (Kunz and Stevenson 1908, 174–75).

There has been an overall decline of populations of the pearl mussel (Wächtler 1986, 225), which is now largely restricted to Bavaria, as well as the Saxonian Vogtland and Elster regions of the former East Germany (Wells *et al.* 1984, 148). In North Bavaria, pearl-mussel stocks have declined by some 90 per cent since the beginning of the twentieth century, owing largely to water pollution (Bauer 1988, 240).

*Hungary* This country formerly formed an important part of the Austrian dominions. The native pearls have from time immemorial been popular with Magyar women, and were worn with the national costume (Kunz and Stevenson 1908, 179). The crown and coronation mantle of the Hungarian regalia have many pearls (Kovács and Lovag 1988, 60) which are probably of freshwater origin.

*Latvia, Lithuania and Estonia* In the seventeenth century, pearls were collected by the peasants of Livonia (now Latvia) who forwarded them to Moscow for sale. Then, under Swedish rule, it was decreed that the pearls from Livonia should not be exported, but should instead be sold to officers of the Crown at a fixed price. The locals objected to being compelled to sell the pearls to the King's (Charles IX's) commissioners. The fishery soon dwindled, but again revived with the lifting of restrictions after the annexation of Livonia to Russia (Kunz and Stevenson 1908, 182). By the middle of the eighteenth century, the fisheries were again very productive, and the Crown awarded 30 to 60 roubles for every half ounce of pearls, depending on quality, to the nobility on whose rivers they were collected. However, owing to the cost of supervision of the fisheries, which eventually exceeded their revenue, they declined, and by 1774 very few pearls were produced (von Hessling 1859, 199).

In the seventeenth century, pearls were also found in Lithuania (Geiger

1637, 2), and some of the streams of Estonia furnished pearls before the development of manufacturing industries destroyed most of the mussel stocks there in the early part of the twentieth century (Kunz and Stevenson 1908, 183).

*Luxembourg*  No specific information on pearl fishing was found in literature searches. The mussel, which has declined recently, was formerly plentiful, and pollution is cited as a major factor (Collins and Wells 1987, 134).

*The Netherlands*  The pearl mussel does not occur in the Netherlands, but the related species *Margaritifera auricularia* formerly occurred and was undoubtedly exploited for its pearls, as was the case elsewhere in Europe. In the seventeenth century, pearls were collected by royalty (Coomans and Brus 1989, 49), and many of these would have come from fresh water.

*Norway*  Between 1691 and 1718, the pearl fisheries were under special supervision as a royal prerogative of the Queen of Denmark (Kunz and Stevenson 1908, 180), and in 1734 the rivers were assessed to determine their suitability as pearl fisheries (see above for Denmark). According to Erich Pontoppidan (1754, 309), Bishop of Bergen, the Norwegian pearl fisheries were placed under the jurisdiction of the Diocese of Christiansand in 1751. The returns from the fisheries gradually decreased, and by the early part of the nineteenth century they had ceased to be fished systematically, although good pearls have been found through the years, right into the twentieth century (Kunz and Stevenson 1908, 180). The pearl mussel is still widespread in Norway, but has declined owing to a number of factors including pearl fishing (Wells *et al.* 1992, 116).

*Poland*  Since the sixteenth century, some of the tributaries of the River Oder produced pearls. In the early part of the eighteenth century, the destruction of mussel beds by people searching for pearls was such that the Government issued a decree recommending their conservation (von Hessling 1859, 179). The pearl mussel was common in Lower Silesia in former times but has declined, mainly through pollution, and may even be extinct there (Wells and Chatfield 1992, 116).

*Russia*  The widespread occurrence of pearls in the streams throughout most of the country probably led to them being adopted as a national ornament, and they were widely worn by women and girls in the nineteenth century (Kunz and Stevenson 1908, 184). In the 1850s, in the province of Olonetz, the brooks were fished by 'young maidens' who could have them pierced for a couple of kopeks each. Von Hessling refers to 'junge Mädchen fischen und ein Bauer durchbohrt sie, das Stück zu 2 Kopecken' (von Hessling 1859, 196). Also in the nineteenth century, a necklace made of pearls from the River Pouentschanka was presented to Tsarina Katharina Alexcewna (von Hessling 1859, 196).

Further north, in Archangel, the rivers flowing to the White Sea and Arctic Sea provided pearls for many centuries, but were of small return by the beginning of the twentieth century (Kunz and Stevenson 1908, 184). Little information regarding the exploitation of pearls is available for the period between the formation of the Soviet Union in 1917 and its dissolution (Woodward 1994, 101). Owing to exploitation and pollution, the pearl mussel is now only found in undisturbed rivers and streams of the European part of the former USSR. Large numbers were known from at least 75 rivers in the Kola Peninsula at the beginning of the twentieth century, but were apparently heavily overfished since then (Wells and Chatfield 1992, 116).

*Spain and Portugal*  Spain and Portugal mark the southern limit of the pearl mussel's distribution in Europe. While local fishing has probably taken place, there appears to be no specific information on freshwater pearls. In a survey of the rivers which formerly supported the mussel, three rivers in Galicia had populations, but none were found in Portugal (Bauer 1986, 8). Spain is the last refuge for the larger of the two pearl-producing mussels, *Margaritifera auricularia*, which recently has only been found in the basin of the River Ebro. The nacre or mother-of-pearl of the shell of this species was formerly used to manufacture knife hilts, especially by the people of the riverside village of Sastago (Alvarez 1998, 114).

*Sweden*  The pearl fisheries of Sweden were in operation from an early period and, in the middle of the sixteenth century, Olaus Magnus (1555, 476, 800–01), Archbishop of Uppsala, described how the pearls were procured and the uses to which they were put (see Figure 7.4). He tells that the fishermen brought the pearls to the coastal areas to sell to girls and women, both rich and poor, who, he says, used them extensively in personal decoration.

About the middle of the eighteenth century, the celebrated naturalist Linnaeus (1811, 104) gave an account of the pearl fisheries of Swedish Lapland after a visit there. In the late eighteenth century, the pearls found in the rivers of Lapland were remarkably valuable (Payne 1793a, 144). In a study of the Pärläven (pearl-river), a river in Arctic Sweden, it was found that mussel populations were much thinner than they had previously been, as a result of pearl fishing which had apparently been intensive in the past (Hendelberg 1960, 156). The pearl mussel, although declined in numbers and locations, still occurs from Scania to Lapland and is now protected and listed as a threatened species (Wells and Chatfield 1992, 116–17).

*Asia*

The rivers of Siberia, Manchuria and China have supported pearl fisheries in the past (Kunz and Stevenson 1908, 65).

*China* Freshwater pearls were known to the Chinese by the beginning of the first millennium BC (Clark 1986, 80) and in the nineteenth century a large industry was based on cultured pearls. It is said that more than 5,000 families, who were also involved in farming silkworms, were engaged in pearl production in the villages of Chung-kwan and Siau-chang (Streeter 1886, 258). The mussel used in China, *Dipsas plicatus*, was impregnated with various nuclei, such as spherical beads and even images of Buddha, around which the mollusc laid down nacre to form the pearls (Kunz and Stevenson 1908, 288).

*India* All around the coast of India pearls have been found, and those from the Gulf of Manaar supported large fisheries in ancient and more modern times. It does not appear that freshwater pearl fisheries were of any consequence. Pearls have, however, been found in a freshwater mussel, *Lamellidens marginalis*, particularly in ponds in West Bengal. In a recent study it was found that some four per cent of mussels examined contained small pearls, and it was suggested that this could form the basis for a viable industry by either pearl fishing or pearl culture (Raut and Biswas 1989, 105).

*Japan* In Japan in the nineteenth century, small pearls were obtained from freshwater mussels (Streeter 1886, 81), but this country is better known for its marine pearls, particularly the cultured varieties. Soon after their initial success with cultured saltwater pearls, Japanese pearl farmers experimented with freshwater mussels in Lake Biwa. This was so commercially successful that, up until relatively recently, all freshwater pearls coming on the market were called 'Biwas' (Ward 1995, 40–41). In the 1980s, however, pearl production diminished, owing to industrial pollution entering the lake. The gap in the market has now been filled by freshwater pearls from China (Ward 1995, 41).

*Siberia and Manchuria* Pearls were found in the rivers of northern Siberia in the early part of the eighteenth century (Kunz and Stevenson 1908,147). The pearl-mussel industry was still of importance in Manchuria at the beginning of the twentieth century, having been carried out there for hundreds of years (Kunz and Stevenson 1908, 146). Payne (1793a, 106), writing on eastern Tartary in his *Universal geography*, noted that 'In some of the rivers which fall into the Saghalianula are considerable pearl fisheries, which are carried out with much art. The Tartars throw themselves into the waters without fear.' An account of the occurrence of pearls in the Asiatic part of the former USSR was given by von Hessling (1859, 201–02). The same pearl mussel as is found in Ireland, *Margaritifera margaritifera*, reaches its eastern limit of distribution around Kamchatka and in Japan (Ellis 1978, 12) where it occurs on the island of Hokkaido (Koba 1933, 175). Because pearls have, from the earliest times, been fished from southern Manchurian rivers, in Kamchatka and on the south coast of the Sea of Okhotsk, it has been suggested that the earliest settlers in Japan were prehistoric pearl fishers (Mackenzie 1994a, 334).

*North America*

The British colonizers along North America's Atlantic coast and the French explorers in the north and west all found Native Americans wearing pearls. There are more than 200 species of freshwater mussels in North American rivers (Burch 1973, v) compared with only three in Ireland and six in Britain (Lucey 1995, 1). Some of these, including the pearl mussel which occurs in Ireland (*Margaritifera margaritifera*), have been important producers of pearls and mother-of-pearl, particularly in the nineteenth century.

*Canada* The pearl mussel occurs along the Atlantic drainage of Canada from Labrador southwards, and is especially abundant in Newfoundland and Nova Scotia (Clarke 1981, 248). In the nineteenth century, pearls were collected in the streams of Quebec, to the north of the city of the same name, and in the districts bordering the St Lawrence River (Streeter 1886, 252), as well as further north in the province around the Ungava Bay region (Kunz and Stevenson 1908, 281). Some of these pearls, weighing from three to 70 grains, were exhibited at the Colonial Exhibition of 1886.

The jeweller who exhibited the pearls went on an expedition for three weeks in August 1885 in search of pearls, but only located two good specimens and complained that the 'streams which are richest in Pearl-mussels are but little known, except to Indians and backwoodsmen who take care to keep the localities as secret as possible' (Streeter 1886, 252).

Edwin Streeter (1886, 253) believed that Canadian pearls had a great future, as many were of a large size, and in beauty they were nearer to the oriental than any other river pearls then known. Kunz and Stevenson (1908, 281–82), however, thought them generally of little value, although they report a single pearl being sold for $1,000 in 1905.

*United States* Native Americans have exploited freshwater pearls since at least the early centuries AD and used them for personal adornment (Ward 1985, 221). The British and French colonists discovered freshwater pearls in the basins of the Ohio, Mississippi and Tennessee Rivers (Ward 1995, 10).

In the nineteenth century and the early part of the twentieth century, the American freshwater fisheries were considerable, and the total value of pearls and shell together was estimated at £200,000 in 1906 (Dakin 1913, 91). In the late nineteenth century, the eastern part of Arkansas was one of the most productive pearling regions and was apparently exploited by Native Americans two centuries before that (Kunz and Stevenson 1908, 259, 263). In 1895, a surveying team working on the White River found pearls in the mussels to the value of about $5,000. Within a year, all the streams in Arkansas had been searched by people attracted to the area by news of finds. A pearl-fishing industry developed, centred at Black Rock, in which more than 1,000 people were employed, and within three years the fisheries in Arkansas had yielded pearls worth more than $500,000 (Kunz and Stevenson 1908, 263–64).

Pearls have also been found in Ohio, Texas, Colorado, Mississippi and Wisconsin, with those from the latter state reputedly the finest (Taburiaux 1985, 60). Pearls were systematically fished in the Miami River in Ohio in the nineteenth century, when the season lasted from June to October, with one of 46.5 grains found in the 1880s (Streeter 1886, 251). The rivers and lakes of the Mississippi Valley formed an important industrial enterprise, yielding annually more than half a million dollars' worth of pearls in the late nineteenth and early twentieth centuries (Kunz and Stevenson 1908, 252). Mississippi River mussel shells are again in demand to make pearls, but it is for nuclei for the Japanese cultured-pearl industry (Koch 1989, 25).

Attempts at developing a freshwater cultured-pearl industry in North America at first proved unsuccessful; a recent study ruled out *Corbicula fluminea* as a suitable candidate species for the artificial production of pearls (Kropf-Gomez 1993, 1). There is now a flourishing American freshwater cultured-pearl industry, but it takes from three to five years to cultivate the finished article, compared with just a year in most saltwater operations.

Many good pearls have been found in the north-east of the US, with one taken from a stream in New Jersey fetching £400, while some have also been fished from the rivers of Florida in the south-east (Streeter 1886, 251–52). It was the discovery of a pearl weighing 93 grains, at Notch Brook near Patterson in 1857, that stimulated the fishery in New Jersey; that pearl was sold to the Empress Eugénie for 12,500 francs (Dakin 1913, 91).

Some British pearl fishermen have fished the rivers of the US, and in 1990 a group of Scottish pearlers went to New York State, where in a fortnight's fishing, enough pearls were collected to cover the cost of the trip (Woodward 1994, 121–24).

The vast freshwater mussel beds which produced the pearls also became a major source for a different product. Until plastic replaced it, mother-of-pearl, chiefly from the Persian Gulf, was used to make buttons. After 1891, the main source of mother-of-pearl was from freshwater mussels in the United States, and it is still used to make buttons for high-quality clothes (Ward 1995, 53). The development of plastics led to the decline in the US mother-of-pearl industry in the period between 1937 and 1940 (Wells *et al.* 1984, 110). The uses to which the shells of such mussels were put in Ireland were discussed in chapter six.

*Overview of freshwater pearl fisheries in Britain, Europe, Asia and North America*
In overviewing the foregoing short history of the freshwater pearl fisheries

worldwide, some aspects become clear. It is apparent, for example, that the industry was at its height in Britain and Europe in the seventeenth and eighteenth centuries, while in North America, the late nineteenth century was the period in which it prospered. The fisheries were still in operation in the early part of the twentieth century, but subsequently went into decline. Not enough information is available to make any meaningful assessment of freshwater pearl fishing in Asia.

*Estimated value of freshwater pearl production in 1906*

The total value of freshwater pearl fisheries and the number of pearlers employed was included in an estimate of the fisheries around the world in 1906 (see Table 7.1). As to estimating the number of persons employed in the pearl fisheries of the world, and the aggregate local value of their catch, Kunz and Stevenson (1908, 79) found no great difficulty for some regions such as Ceylon, Venezuela, Australia, the Persian Gulf, the Red Sea, the Gulf of California and the islands of the Pacific. But, they say, 'in the rivers of America, as well as of Europe and of Asia, where neither experience nor costly equipment is required for the industry, and pearls to the value of very many thousands of dollars are obtained by men, women, and even children, on pleasure bent, as well as in the widely fluctuating professional fisheries, the problem is far more difficult'.

At the beginning of the twentieth century, the majority of pearl fishers for the British Isles would have been located in Scotland, after which Ireland (particularly Ulster) would figure, followed by Wales. It is known that at that time there were over 100 full-time pearlers in Scotland (Armstrong 1973, 231). From Table 7.1 it can be deduced that the river-pearl fishers in the US and British Isles would have made £15 per head on average, while their counterparts in Europe earned £20 each based on these figures. The corresponding wage for the Asian river pearler for that year would work out

*Table 7.1*

Estimated total value of pearls taken in rivers and the number of pearl fishers in 1906.

| Region | Local value | Number of pearl fishers |
|---|---|---|
| Asia (China, Japan and Siberia) | £80,000 | 20,000 |
| United States | £130,000 | 8,500 |
| Europe | £20,000 | 1,000 |
| British Isles | £3,000 | 200 |

(Sources: Kunz and Stevenson 1908, 80; Dakin 1913, 117.)

at £4.

If the number of fishers in Ireland was conservatively estimated at 50, then we can give the total sum of £750[vi] as the local value of the Irish fishery for that year. However, some 50 years previously we know that one jeweller alone bought some £500 worth of native pearls in a few years, so that the calculation of value of the fishery must be grossly underestimated.

Having given a summary of what is known of freshwater pearl fisheries elsewhere, it can be deduced that while in Ireland they were more widespread than in most other countries of Europe, they were not as well managed as a resource than in some countries such as Germany, where attention to detail, particularly as regards record keeping and conservation of the mussel, was practised.

In the following chapter a direct comparison between the exploitation of alluvial gold and that of river pearls in Ireland, which have much in common, will be made.

*Notes*

[i]The Roman Conquest was incomplete, as it never touched northern Scotland and never seriously affected southern Scotland (Fletcher 1913, 25).

[ii]The Irish evidently mastered the Isle of Man, and Irish literature abounds with references to the constant intercourse kept up by the parent people with those of their little insular colony. Though the Norsemen wrested the sovereignty of the island from them in the ninth century, they did not succeed in displacing either the Gaelic people or their language. The best possible proof of the Irish colonization and complete and continued occupation of the island is the fact that the Manx language is merely a dialect of Irish—spelled phonetically, but otherwise very little altered.

[iii]Pearls were called 'shell berries' in early poetry. In this stanza, Ausonius describes how the whole scene is like Scotland, in Britain, where the tide recedes to reveal the white berries that grow in mussel shells.

[iv]Under Schedule Five of the Wildlife and Countryside Act 1981, which was strengthened in March 1998 to give freshwater pearl mussels full protection, it is illegal to fish for pearls, and to sell or advertise the pearls even if they were collected before that date. Jewellers can apply to the Scottish Executive for a licence to sell pearls legally acquired before 1998.

[v]Spenser first came to Ireland in 1580 as secretary to Lord Grey of Wilton, who succeeded Sir William Pelham as Lord Deputy.

[vi]Nevertheless, we find at that time pearls being sold in Scotland and Ulster for £50–£70 each.

# 8. Gold in Ireland: a comparison with pearls

Of the streams all the mould
Stones precious and gold…
*Friar Michael of Kildare* (b. 1280), *The land of Cockaygne* (n.d.)

It is difficult to find an activity or industry with which the exploitation of pearls in Ireland may be compared. For a variety of reasons, however, but chiefly because both can be described as 'river treasure', the exploitation of alluvial gold offers a useful comparison.

Just as pearls were said to have lured the Romans to Britain, so gold has been cited as the chief attraction that Ireland offered to invaders (Macalister 1949, 9). The native stores of gold also made Ireland a country with which it was desirable to trade (Fletcher 1922, 135). Having little native tin, Ireland had to trade (see Box VIII) with tin-bearing regions during the Bronze Age (*c.* 1800–300 BC), and during those 1,500 years gold from the County Wicklow rivers and streams, in the form of dress-ornaments, was exported (Evans 1977, 31). It is intimated in the *Annals of the Four Masters* (O'Donovan 1856a, 43), that gold was first discovered during the reign of Tighearnmas, King of Ireland, who died in the Age of the World 3656 (*c.* 1600 BC).

Like pearls and the other precious substances, the appeal of gold was to the senses, with early man initially being attracted to its colour and lustre (Clark 1986, 50). Like the alluvial sources of gold, the river and lake pearls were probably exploited in Ireland from very early times.

In the Bronze Age, the alluvial deposits of certain rivers were rich in gold and this was collected from the river gravels. It appears that the Bronze-Age goldsmiths all but exhausted that supply, so that it has been said that Ireland will never again be a gold-producing region (Macalister 1949, 15)—at least, not until the technology to extract the gold from the mother lode has been developed. To date no efforts at exploitation have ever proved a commercial success, though the deposits in County Wicklow were worked by the Government for a few years towards the close of the eighteenth century (Freeman 1950, 287). In 1995, conditional planning permission was granted to a company for an open-cast gold and silver mine at Cavanacaw, Omagh, County Tyrone which, it was estimated, would produce gold and silver to the value of some £4,000,000 each year (Moriarty 1995, 16). That discovery of

---

*Box VIII*
## Trade in precious materials

That the ancient Irish traded with the Phoenicians, exchanging native pearls for the technique of producing dyes, has been suggested. What is more certain is that in the early Bronze Age, gold ornaments, mainly lunulae, were manufactured, chiefly from the gravels of the County Wicklow rivers, and exported to Britain and the Continent.

Finds of amber (a form of fossil resin which came from the shores of the Baltic) and faience (an artificial gemstone of glass which came from Egypt and the Near East) show that these luxury items were being imported, probably in exchange for the gold and bronze objects Ireland was exporting about 1500 BC. There is some evidence that Continental- and British-made Iron-Age beads reached Ireland before the Roman period. Glass beads were not manufactured in Ireland until the fifth or sixth century, when they were again apparently popular as items of decoration. Draconite or dragon-stone, a red gemstone, may have found its way to Ireland from the Continent in early times and occasionally been used among the higher classes. According to the *Libel of English policie*, written about 1430, silver and gold were then still among the exports of Ireland.

Pearls are less durable than many other precious materials and may well have been used but have not survived preserved in the Irish archaeological record. Those buried with the daughters of a Roman general, who died in AD 407, were lacklustre and apparently fell into dust, while the other ornaments were intact when found in 1526.

It is uncertain at what period pearls first came into use as ornaments and charms. Necklaces of shells (littorinids) have been found in Ireland dating to the Neolithic period, indicating either their talismanic or precious status. In the sixteenth century, several of the Cornish ports show exports of clams from Ireland which, given their high price of five shillings each, were unlikely to have been oysters. Longfield was uncertain of what exactly was then meant by the term, beyond the fact that it probably referred to some variety of bivalve. Given their high individual price and the fact that they were sent in small numbers (three, four or five at a time), it could be conjectured that these were pearl mussels for stocking English rivers.

(Sources: O'Conor 1814, xvii; Moore 1837, 2; Anon. 1838, 189; Kunz and Stevenson 1908, 12; Joyce 1903b, 433; Joyce 1906, 229; Longfield 1929, 51; Guido 1978, 39; Mitchell 1989, 39–40.)

---

gold in the Sperrin Mountains has led to an upsurge in gold exploration, but mining developments planned in County Mayo were blocked on environmental grounds (Sheridan 1996, 39).

It is interesting to note that gold in the streams coming from the Sperrins had been exploited some 340 years previously. Gerard Boate, writing in 1652, had been informed that a man who had found about one eighth of an ounce of gold in the River Moyola, which rises on the borders of Counties Tyrone and Londonderry, concluded that it indicated a source in the mountain whence it flowed (Boate *et al.* 1755, 69):

> …out of a certain rivulet in the county of nether-Tyrone, called Miola (the which rising in the mountains Slew-galen, and passing by the village Maharry, falleth into the nortwest corner of Lough Neagh, close by the place where the river Bann cometh out of it) he had gathered about one dram of pure gold; concluding thereby, that in the aforesaid mountains rich gold mines do lye hidden. For it is an ordinary thing for rivers, which take their original in gold-bearing mountains, to carry gold mixt with their sand…

How the alluvial deposits of gold arose and why little further from these will be found has been explained by Praeger (1950, 31):

> But the gold was obtained not in its original position in the rocks, whence it occurs in very small quantity, but in alluvial deposits of gravel, the result of prolonged washing down of former rocks destroyed by the action of weather and streams; in this detritus the heavy metal became concentrated. So far as they were accessible, these gravels have now been worked out; and until a few further million years have sifted more gold out of the rocks, there is little to be obtained; human endeavour is powerless to again produce that concentration of gold that might make its winning worth the labour involved.

The alluvial gold was exploited by the Bronze-Age people in Ireland and worked by their craftsmen (Herity and Eogan 1977, 116):

> As in modern times, it is likely that the gold used during the Bronze Age was acquired by sieving or 'panning' the gold-bearing river gravels. Alluvial gold is rarely found in nugget form. Usually it consists of small flakes or grains. When a sufficient amount was collected this was melted into an ingot and from that it could have been hammered or cast into the required shape.

Like pearl fishing, gold prospecting in the late eighteenth century was carried out by the poorest people of the district, using very simple equipment, and as with pearls, the gold that was garnered was sold to local jewellers. The practice was still going on at the turn of the twentieth century (Cole 1902, 22):

Probably the really profitable transactions were those of the peasantry, who from time to time stored up a little gold, which they had washed out by the most primitive means, and brought it for sale to the jewellers in Dublin. It is currently reported that this practice still continues.

In fact, as recently as 1973 a Dublin journalist, Des Moore (n.d. *c*. 1980, 109), had seen panning being carried out along the Gold Mines River in County Wicklow. The earliest prospecting in the Gold Mines River area appears to have been undertaken around 1770 by a local schoolmaster. It was also stated that a Dublin jeweller around this time obtained four or five ounces of gold annually for 11 or 12 years from a peasant of the vicinity (Kinahan 1883, 269). In 1785, a boy, while fishing in the river, found a piece of about one quarter of an ounce. This did not excite any interest locally as the find was considered to be lost property. The real gold rush started in September 1795, when normal work ceased in the area as everybody set about the search. Their methods have been described by Reeves (1971, 76):

> Since gold mining was a new experience to the people their methods of extraction were rather crude and inefficient. Household tools (shovels, bowls and sieves) were used in the search. In their efforts to work as much ground as possible their washings were hurried with the result that much gold escaped their search, so much in fact that the waste heaps afforded a profit on reworking. This state of affairs persisted until fifteenth October, 1795, when a party of the Kildare Militia was dispatched from Arklow to take possession of the deposit by order of the Government. The local gold-diggers retired peaceably.

It was reported (Kinahan 1883, 268) that the gold found near Ballinascorney Gap, County Dublin, was carried in quills into the city for sale by the peasants of the district. It was reckoned that the Dublin jewellers, on average, purchased yearly in the period 1796–98 gold to the value of about £2,000 (Brash 1871, 526). Similarly, it is known that one Dublin jeweller alone purchased native pearls worth £500 in a few years of the 1850s (von Hessling 1859, 189).

In 1796 a French royalist, an *émigré* from his native land because of the Revolution, came to Ireland and visited the area of County Wicklow where gold had been found (de Latocnaye 1917, 47–50). He tells of some lucky finds of gold, even by children, in the streams; but he adds that nothing is ever heard about the many who had lost their time and even their lives in unfruitful searches. He had been informed that since 1795, several hundreds or even thousands of country people searched the streams in the area until the Government forbade any more prospecting, enforcing it with a military guard. The largest find in that time was apparently a nugget of 22 ounces which was worth over 80 guineas; it had been estimated that gold to the value of several thousand pounds had been collected.

Thus, apart from being carried on in rivers, pearl fishing and panning for gold in Ireland have many similarities which may be summarized as follows. Both were carried on from an early period; both were prosecuted by the poorer classes; both required no particular skills or elaborate equipment; both produced luxury items fetching relatively high prices for the finder; demand for both of the products was governed by limited sources of supply; both products were sold directly to jewellers in some instances; both products were used together in items of ornamentation and personal decoration. Also, because great numbers of shells had to be opened without success, pearl fishing has been said to resemble gold digging (Anon. 1863, 11). It is interesting to note that about £4 an ounce was paid for gold during the gold rush in County Wicklow in the 1790s, while shortly after that time the average price for a good native pearl was about £6. Nowadays also, the two are worth approximately the same price—about £240.

Jackson (1991, 75) has reckoned that gold occurs at some 130 localities in Ireland. These include the Delphi Valley in County Galway and the flanks of Croagh Patrick in County Mayo. The localities also include Curraghinalt in County Tyrone, where conservative estimates of reserves of some 300,000 ounces of gold have been established by drilling.

At these localities, however, the gold occurs in bedrock, and was probably unavailable to the Bronze-Age metalworker. Gold won during the Bronze Age would have come from placer deposits, as nuggets and flakes in the sands and gravels of the streams and rivers of the country. Many of these are known;[i] two of the most prolific areas are the Gold Mines River and the other rivers draining Croghan Kinshela in southern County Wicklow, and the river system of the Sperrin mountains in County Tyrone. Several nuggets of gold of extraordinary size were found in the stream in Ballinasilloge of which one weighed nine ounces, another weighed 18, and a third weighed 22 ounces (de Líon *c.* 1968, 21).

Like in Ireland, large quantities of gold and pearls were apparently produced in Scotland in early times (Curle 1931/32, 347). Recently, large deposits of gold have been found in England, in some areas so rich that it had seeped into streams in sufficient quantities to be panned, with the biggest of these in Devon. Minmet, a Dublin-based gold-mining company, bought a government licence to investigate the area's potential, and prospectors were due to start work in 1996. Initial studies have suggested that several hundred thousand ounces could be expected. With an ounce of mined gold worth about £240, the attraction for companies could be great. In some of the areas the rocks are so rich in gold that, according to the British Geological Survey, people could make a living out of panning the rivers (Leake 1996, 6).

*Gold and pearls: how they have been ranked*

The Romans ranked pearls as their most precious commodity, even above gold. They sent so much gold to India in exchange for pearls that a serious trade imbalance developed and the Roman economy weakened significantly. It has even been suggested that Rome's weakness for pearls ultimately contributed to the decline of the Empire (Joyce and Addison 1992, 88). The Chinese also valued pearls above gold and held them inferior only to jade (Clark 1986, 81).

In Ireland, gold has always ranked highest among the precious materials, as can be evidenced by a visit to the National Museum in Dublin or the Ulster Museum in Belfast. Since gold occurred as a native metal, it did not require smelting, and was merely melted in crucibles prior to being poured into moulds. Alternatively, as gold is extremely soft and malleable, it could be worked into artefacts by hammering or beating (Jackson 1991, 75). Richard Brash (1871, 523), after listing the major treasure finds, concluded that gold was the predominant metal in use for personal ornaments in Ireland, with the quantity of silver relics being very small. This is not surprising, since gold has been used in manufacture—mostly of personal and dress ornaments—in Ireland from about 2000 BC, while silver was not similarly used until the sixth and seventh centuries AD (Teahan 1990, 1).

With regard to pearls, it is not clear when these were first exploited. The earliest written reference is the ninth century, but is apparently copying something already written down (see chapter six) and that may even have come from oral tradition. The large collection of gold ornaments in the National Museum show that the gold of the river gravels was industriously collected (Macalister 1949, 15). The pearl cannot compare with gold in its uses in Irish social history, although it has been used for a long period and continues to be an item of ladies' fashion (see chapter six).

*Pearls and gold in the same rivers*

Freshwater pearls sometimes have a golden tinge to their colour. Charles O'Conor (1814, xvii) quotes Origen, the Greek writer of the third century, saying that the British pearl in the colour which overlays its surface has the appearance of gold—'Britannica, inquit, Margarita, colore quo ejus superficies imbuta est, auri speciem refert.' The colour of Scottish pearls is said to depend upon the minerals of the host river, and sometimes has a golden sheen (Green 1985/86, 29). It has been reasoned that the imparting of the golden colour to some pearls is due to deposits of gold in the streams they come from, as the following (Anon. 1928, 4) suggests:

> This freshwater pearl, which is purple-hued, is tinged with gold, a peculiarity which is explained by the fact that the streams of the region wash down quite considerable deposits of alluvial gold.

Jean Taburiaux (1985, 77–78), a French pearl specialist, quotes a note read to the Academy of Science in January 1924, which also explains the same phenomenon:

> In certain rivers which flow down the Central plateau, small mussels are found in which fine pearls are sometimes found of some value. In one of these mussels, the author found a pearl of medium size with a piece of shining yellow metal. Upon chemical examination, it was discovered that a golden plate was forming part of the pearl and a small piece of this could be seen on the surface. The presence of gold in the pearl can be explained by the fact that the rivers and waterfalls of the area often carry pieces of gold.

In this case it would appear that a piece of gold was indeed incorporated into the pearl. However, whether the explanation of a golden hue in other instances is scientifically sound is questionable, as many of the colour effects are not due to the presence of actual pigment but rather to the phenomena of reflection and refraction (Dakin 1913, 63).

In the Wotawa (a gold- and pearl-bearing brook) in Austria, pearl fishing and washing for gold were carried out side by side in the nineteenth century (Kunz and Stevenson 1908, 178). There is no direct evidence that gold and pearls were exploited from the same rivers in Ireland but, given that some of the rivers, particularly in Counties Wicklow and Tyrone, contained both alluvial gold and the pearl mussel, it is likely, though the two activities were probably not carried on at the same time.

*Gold and pearls used together*

Native gold and pearls were used together in jewellery in Ireland. An example was an old gold ring which had a pearl set in it, dug up in the garden at Furness, County Kildare in May 1898, which was afterwards exhibited at a meeting of the County Kildare Archaeological Society (Mayo 1899–1902, 57). The inside of the gold band had the inscription, 'Wicklow Gold & Slaney Pearl'.

The two have been used together on the outer cover of the *Domnach airgid* (see Figure 8.1)[ii] or Shrine of St Patrick's gospel, the original inner part of which contained a copy of the four Gospels said to have been used in Ireland by the patron saint (Cusack 1868, 134).

A gold brooch with a pearl was given to Queen Victoria by the Fellows of Trinity College, Dublin, on the occasion of her visit to Ireland in 1849 (see Figure 8.2). It is a copy of a brooch dated about AD 800 which was found in County Cavan (Teahan 1990, 15). The pearl used in the brooch came from Lough Eske in County Donegal, while the gold is likely to have come from County Wicklow. It is said that one of the pearls on Queen Victoria's coronation crown came from County Galway (Whilde 1994, 215). A 22-ounce gold nugget, from the Ballinasilloge Stream, was made into a snuffbox for the melancholic George III (de Líon *c.* 1968, 21). It is interesting to note that King George III, who reigned from 1760 to 1820, and his wife Queen Charlotte, should both possess the produce of Irish rivers—he a snuffbox of County Wicklow gold, and she a necklace of County Down pearls (see chapter six).

*Government intervention*
In the late eighteenth century, Ireland entered a period of comparative prosperity following the brief peace (Beckett 1973, 241). In the period between 1700 and 1780, trade with Britain increased fourfold in real terms and the Dublin parliament sought to encourage native industry (Ó Grada 1995, 43). In 1795, the Government became interested in Wicklow gold. In the following year, the business of its extraction was taken up by the Government at a place called Croghan Kinshela. It has been calculated that at least £10,000 was paid to the country people for gold (Brash 1871, 525) collected before the Government took possession of the works.

Some estimates of the total quantity of gold extracted by Government workings have also been reported, but they vary so much that the highest estimate is almost ten times the lowest. For example, one account has it that in about two years 945 ounces were collected, which sold for £3,675 (Kane 1845, 220) while another has estimated that the mine workings produced from 7,440 to 9,390 ounces of gold with a value of £28,855 to £36,185 (Kinahan 1883, 275). Apparently the cost of the workings and of various trials made in search of the original deposit of the gold exceeded the return. The workings, having been interrupted by the troubles of 1798, were apparently not again resumed (Macalister 1949, 125).

Unlike with gold, no attempts were apparently made by the Government to control, or become involved in, the pearl fisheries. Pearls do, however, figure in some Government correspondence, but mostly in a cursory way. Sir William Pelham, the Lord Justice, kept a journal of his expedition from Limerick to Dingle in 1580 (the original of which was preserved among the State Papers of the year 1580, No. 52) which was later dispatched to Lord Burghley.[iii] Under the date 26 June, Pelham's scribe entered the following (Hitchcock 1914, 210):

> The twenty-sixth, after storing of Castel Magne with victuals, we marched thence towards Cork, through part of Desmond, the Erle of Clancartie's countrie, and camped that night by the fayre river of Lawyn between the 'Palace', one of Clancartie's chiefe houses, and Downlogh, a house of O'Sullivan More's, rased by the Erle of Ormond in the last war of James Fitz-Maurice. The river hath in it many big muscles, wherein are found many large pearls.

In a letter dated 11 July 1580, from 'Edward Fenton to Walsyngham' (Secretary Walsingham) relating the daily occurrences of his journey through Munster, it is noted, 'much pearl found in Lough Leane' in County Kerry (Hamilton 1867, 232). It could be speculated that this Captain Fenton[iv] may have exploited the pearls of his 'home' waters.

Walter Raleigh had also fought in the wars in Munster and was allocated lands forfeited by the Earl of Desmond. It is possible that he exploited or received local pearls, as Richard Boyle, who bought his lands and who became Lord Justice of Ireland in 1629 (Townsend 1904, 171), did some few years later.

In a letter, dated 18 February 1589, from 'Sir Warham Sentleger[v] to Walsyngham' regarding the elopement of 'the Earl of Clancarthy's daughter', the lake at Castle Lough near Killarney is mentioned, 'where there is great store of orient pearl found' (Hamilton 1885, 124).

Colonel Maurice Hussey, of Flesk Bridge in County Kerry, wrote to Secretary Dawson at Dublin Castle in December 1702, informing him that he had collected some Kerry stones for him and would send them at the first opportunity. He goes on to say (Prendergast 1900, 147):

> I send you a little Kerry pearle to put in the top of your seale, if you think fit; if not, though it is very inconsiderable and a mere trifle, it may purchase you a salute or a smile from some of the fair sex, who are generally taken with such trifles; if it does, I have my end in sending it.

Obviously, Dawson had people around the country who supplied him with pearls and other precious stones. From the printed calendar summarizing British departmental correspondence for 1683–1714 (Burke 1882, 141–42), the originals of which were destroyed in the fire at the Four Courts in 1922, it is apparent that during July and August 1709, a Mr Thomas Putland in London corresponded with Secretary Dawson in Dublin on three occasions with regard to a pearl reputed to weigh 62 carats and be worth £400. The first letter, dated 26 July 1709, is summarized as follows:

> *From Thos Putland to Joshua Dawson.* Acquaints M$^r$ Dawson that he 'went to Prince Eugenes head w$^{ch}$ is now y$^e$ signe of the Black Bogg Anglice Newgate to enquire for Sir Richard Blackham where he lay for some times suspected of coyning but came out upon the Act of indemnity' understands Sir Richard is poor and believes if 'the Pearle is worth £400', it would long since have been gone; but will try & find out where he is.

The content of the second letter, dated 4 August 1709, is so much summarized as to tell us nothing:

*From Thos Putland to Joshua Dawson.* Sir Richard Blackham and 'the Pearle'.

The third letter, apparently dated 9 August 1709, is somewhat more revealing:

*From Thos Putland to Joshua Dawson.* Sir Richard Blackman's [*sic*] pearl, which, if Sir R's statement of its weight 62 carrats be true, is the largest pearl in the Queen's dominions—Strange story told by Sir Richard about it, and its non production.

From the summaries of the letters[vi] we do not learn of the origin nor the destination of the pearl in question. It can be surmised, however, that because it figured in State Papers the likelihood is that the pearl had originated in Ireland and was apparently smuggled out of the country. Why the Government was interested in tracing the pearl, however, remains a mystery; pearls could, as will be conjectured in chapter nine, have been subject to crown duties. Thus it can be seen that pearls have been mentioned in official correspondence but not, as far as the surviving record shows, in a way to suspect that the Government was ever interested in their exploitation.

While gold and pearls show many similarities in their exploitation and uses in Ireland, the main difference was that the Government never invested in the latter as it had, for a short time, in the former. In the next chapter the extent to which private enterprise invested in pearl fishing will be examined among the reasons to establish why it never became an industry of national importance in Ireland.

*Notes*

[i]Gold has been found in a number of rivers and streams in various counties in Ireland: the river near Crossmolina (the Deel), County Mayo; the Moyola in Counties Tyrone and Londonderry; the streams flowing into the Glendun in County Antrim; the Dodder near Rathfarnham, County Dublin; tributary streams of the Barrow in hills near St Mullins, County Carlow (Kinahan 1883, 267–69). It was, however, the rivers and streams of an area of County Wicklow that were systematically searched for their gold. These include the tributaries called the Ballycreen Brook, the Mucklagh and Killahurler Brooks, the Ballintemple Stream, the Gold Mines River, the Ballinvalley (Aughatinavought) Stream, the Coolbawn Stream as well as the Aughrim, Ovoca and Ow Rivers (Kinahan 1883, 277–79). As well as the above the following counties are named as having gold-producing districts: Clare, Kildare and Wexford (Joyce 1906, 245).

[ii]The *Domnach airgid* is apparently the most precious relic of its kind as it contained a

considerable portion of the copy of the Gospels which was used by St Patrick during his mission in Ireland (Wakeman 1891, 312). The original box, made of hollow yew, was given by Patrick to St MacCarthainn of Clogher, County Tyrone, and is now in the National Museum in Dublin. It has tinned bronze plates ornamented with interleaved bands against a hatched background dating from the eight to ninth centuries. An outer cover is of silver plated with gold which was added in the mid-fourteenth century by the native Irish artist John O'Barrdan (Stokes 1878, 98). This external cover has a representation of the Holy Ghost, as a dove, enamelled in gold, and the corners were enriched with pearls which were most probably native (Petrie 1838, 16). Only one of the original four pearls remains in its setting today (see Figure 8.1).

[iii]Formerly Sir William Cecil, Queen Elizabeth's minister who, on the death of Sir Francis Walsingham, succeeded him as Principal Secretary.

[iv]Captain Edward Fenton, who was the circumnavigating uncle of Katherine Fenton, wife of the Earl of Cork, had an altercation on a voyage with Captain, later Sir, John Hawkins—the same who was granted a patent for fishing for pearls in the River Irt in Cumberland (see chapter seven)—after which he lost court favour and had to retire into private life (Townsend 1904, 59).

[v]In *Historiae Catholicae iverniae compendium*, written by Philip O'Sullivan Beare and printed at Lisbon in 1621, Sir Warham St Leger is referred to as 'Governor of Leix' and later as 'an English knight, and President of Munster' (Byrne 1903, 97, 130); the Four Masters call him 'deputy of the Governor of the two provinces of Munster' (O'Donovan 1856d, 2161).

[vi]Searches carried out at the Public Record Office in London and the Public Record Office of Northern Ireland in Belfast, as well as the initial search at the National Archives in Dublin, failed to locate any copies of the original letters.

# 9. Decline, demand and supply

Pearls sometimes taken in these muscles and now but rarely (the people being better employed in the linen manufacture)…
*John Copping*, Dean of Clogher, *Letter to Sir Hans Sloane* (1740, 198)

In the previous chapter it was established that the Irish Government at no time invested in the native pearl fisheries as it had, albeit not very successfully, for a while in the exploitation of gold. In this the penultimate chapter of the history of Irish pearls, the reasons for the decline of native pearls on the market will be examined critically. Included among the factors to be detailed are: lack of supply owing to industrial development offering more attractive or regular employment; the effects of pollution and overfishing on the pearl–producing mussel; lack of demand through competition from alternatives; and the lack of private enterprise or investment.

*Industrialization*
Up until the latter part of the eighteenth century, the economy of Ireland, as in the rest of Europe, was largely based on agriculture and household industry. But from then on, the factory began to replace the household as the centre for productivity at an increasing rate (Galbraith 1958, 19). In Ireland prior to the 1680s, Ulster had been sparsely populated and was the most backward of the four provinces. But following an influx of settlers from Scotland and the north of England it developed rapidly (Cullen 1987, 24). With the exception of Ulster and a few other centres, Ireland remained by and large unaffected by the industrial expansion of the time. Even in Ulster there was a great contrast between the western and eastern parts regarding the extent of industrial development, with the proximity to Britain and its markets being a major factor for the expansion of linen and cotton industries in the latter.

The decline of the pearl-fishing industry in East Ulster appears to coincide with the development of the linen industry in the late seventeenth century. Following the removal of the duties on Irish linens by the British Government in 1696, the industry became well established before the turn of the century, with good prospects of markets in England. The success of this industry in the eighteenth century was to have a tremendous impact on economy and society in Ulster (Crawford 1975, 9). The upper Bann, which supported an important pearl-fishing industry from at least the middle of the seventeenth century to the middle of the eighteenth (see chapter four), became the focus of the linen industry in Ulster, and by the nineteenth century was one of the outstanding linen-manufacturing and linen-bleaching districts of the province (Gribbon 1969, 159).

In the eighteenth century a number of bleach greens had been established on the River Bann, and these would have affected the water quality and caused a decline in the populations of the pollution-sensitive pearl-producing mussels. The demand for water in the nineteenth century, particularly between 1830 and 1836, when the linen trade was at the zenith of its prosperity, led to the construction of reservoirs (Gribbon 1969, 160). This involved regulating the flow of water as well as impeding the passage of salmonid fish on which the mussel's larval stage depends, and therefore would also have been inimical to its general ecology and well-being.

Consequently, the pearl-fishing industry on the River Bann was affected both directly and indirectly by the linen trade. Apart from offering more gainful employment, it led to the erection of weirs and regulation of flow, as well as pollution. In chapter four it was shown that contemporary sources attributed the decline of the pearl fishery in the middle of the eighteenth century to pollution from the bleach works along the River Bann. That it was still being polluted in the following century and pearls were then rarely found is confirmed by Smyth (1875, 12), who reported:

> The Upper Bann was formerly celebrated for its trout-fishing, which has been much injured of late years by the discharge of flax steep-water into the river, instead of lifting the flax out of the water when the water is low. It is said if some improvements were made in the weirs,[i] salmon would come up the river...Pearls have been found in rare instances.

Dubourdieu (1802, 315), speaking of the pearl fisheries of the Lagan and Bann at the end of the eighteenth century, says that 'The business now is nearly given up, nor are the pearls found of sufficient value to tempt people, for the chance of finding them, from their more regular and more profitable occupations.' This area of eastern Ulster would have had the option of alternative employment in the linen trade from an early stage, culminating later in the great linen mills being concentrated in the Lagan Valley (Kennedy 1987, 101) which would have brought pollution as well as mass employment. Yet the destruction of the pearl-fishing industry of the Lagan has been attributed by one source to the formation of the Lagan Canal (W[elch] 1908, 90).

The situation in the west of the province was different with regard to industrial expansion, and pearl fishing survived to a much later time in such areas as Counties Donegal, Tyrone and Fermanagh. A pearl fisher, James Brogan of Omagh, told the notable conchologist and photographer Robert Welch that he could 'remember the day [probably in the mid-1800s] when as many as thirty or forty men and women from the town would be seeking their fortunes, looking for pearls, on the river Strule' (Ross 1988, 44). Even as late as 1908, pearl fishing in the streams of County Tyrone was classed as a regular employment by some newspapers of the time (e.g., Anon. 1908, 5). The river known in the seventeenth century as Maguiresbridge (Coolebrooke), in County Fermanagh, appears to have been fished for its pearls down to the very recent past. We also hear of pearls being taken in the rivers of County Donegal in the twentieth century.

After the seventeenth century, nothing further is apparently recorded of certain pearl fisheries in the south of the country—for example, the River Bandon in County Cork and the River Laune in County Kerry. Although an attempt to establish a woollen manufacture at Bandon, where raw wool and technical know-how were available, failed due to a lack of capital in 1617 (Beckett 1973, 27), linen manufacture was carried out there for a time following the establishment of the town, then known as Bandonbridge, by Richard Boyle, Earl of Cork (Townsend 1904, 45). Later in the town, there were 17 tanneries along the river (Ó Gráda 1995, 325). The Laune, on the other hand, was not affected by pollution, nor would its hinterland have offered much in the way of alternative employment.

Thus, while it was undoubtedly carried on there, nothing much is heard of pearl-fishing activity in Munster in the eighteenth century. The culture of pearl fishing may have been part of Daniel Corkery's 'hidden Ireland' (Corkery 1924).[ii] It is possible that the activity became more secretive and may have had an underground existence, particularly in the repressive early part of the century, with the result that little of its prosecution came to notice at the time.

*Overfishing and pollution*
The Earl of Cranbrook (1976, 89) has asserted that freshwater pearl fishing, while destructive, is no more so than taking fish or shellfish to sell for food. Such an assertion, however, takes no account of the low population-recruitment potential of the species, and is analogous to saying that shooting elephants for their ivory is no more destructive than killing rabbits for food. The life-history strategy of the mussel (*Margaritifera margaritifera*) with its high fecundity and long lifespan, coupled with the reliance on an encysting glochidial stage,[iii] is indicative of a low population-recruitment potential (Ross 1988, 109), so that exploitation of such a species is not the same as for one such as the sea mussel (*Mytilus edulis*). Apart from giving the mussel the distinction of being among the longest-living animals, the very slow growth leaves its population at a high risk of damage from overfishing.

The decline of the industry after the seventeenth century in Ireland has been attributed to overfishing alone by one writer who said, 'Little discrimination was used in the search for pearls. Small and large, young and old, the mussels were gathered and killed, with the result that the industry gradually decayed' (Meagher 1928, 385). There are contemporary accounts of the decline in the occurrence of mussels and their pearls in the following century. For example, Edward Willes (1762, 125) writing in the 1760s, stated that the people around Omagh maintained that the 'pearls were formerly more plentifull than they are at present'.

Populations of the pearl-producing mussel had apparently declined throughout Ireland by the early part of the twentieth century according to Stelfox (1911, 122), a leading conchologist of the time, who wrote that they were 'Seemingly scarcer than in former times in many rivers, perhaps owing to the depredations of the pearl-searchers and their wanton destruction'. This is more or less confirmed by Dakin's (1913, 90) comment that 'The Irish fishery seems to have died out—the shellfish being much less common now than formerly.'

Recent studies have shown that records exist of up to 6,000 mussels being fished in a single day in northern rivers (Mackie 1992, 25). Local pearl fishermen admitted taking 4,000–5,000 mussels, of an estimated total of about 200,000, from the River Owenea in County Donegal in 1982 (Ross 1988, 109). Similarly, Dr Eugene Ross, who studied the pearl mussel, found thousands of empty shells on the banks of rivers in the west of Ireland in the 1980s (MacConnell 1987, 4); once, he came across thousands of freshly opened mussel shells where the air in the vicinity was full of the smell of rotting flesh. Hundreds of empty shells have been found by the present author in the River Blackwater in County Cork (see Figure 9.1) during the summer of 1990, in the aftermath of the exertions of amateur pearl hunters.

It is likely that some rivers, particularly in the north, were heavily fished, but the pearl mussel is still relatively widely spread in the country though its populations are very much reduced in size. One pearl fisher who, in 1973, in his eightieth year, was still collecting pearls, reckoned that he had probably handled 500 pearls, of which at least 100 were 'good', taken by him from rivers in Ulster (McCrea 1973b, 13). If, as the pearl collectors say (Camlin 1959, 10), only about one in a thousand shells contains a pearl, then it is not difficult to appreciate the destruction that could occur to mussel stocks even by single fishers. As a general rule it can be said that about one mussel in a hundred contains a pearl, and only one per cent of these are of any value as jewels.

The destruction of the thousands of mussels required for a successful pearl-fishing operation results in a population collapse likely to take 50 years or more to recover. It has been said that there is no possibility of a sustainable fishery (Moriarty 1994, 20) although one in Saxony, which was managed properly, survived into the twentieth century until the stocks of mussels were depleted by industrial pollution (see chapter seven). Similarly, the fishery at Banbridge survived as an exploitable resource for more than a century, which would imply that it was also effectively managed; this is implicit from a press advertisement of 1732 which informed that 'A new breeding bed had recently been erected for the propagation of the mussels' (Robb 1939, 6).

A County Tyrone man from Sion Mills, in whose family pearl fishing has been a hobby for five generations, blames pollution for the demise of the pearl mussel in the tributaries of the Foyle (McGrath 1996, *in litt.*). Indeed, one such tributary, part of the famous pearling River Strule around Omagh, was seriously polluted by a large spillage of a toxic wood-preservative compound in recent years. Other pearl fishermen, perhaps predictably, have also blamed pollution rather than pressure from overfishing for the loss of mussel stocks (McCrea 1973b, 13). It is likely that since the twentieth century, and particularly since the 1960s, pollution has played an increasing role in the demise of the mussel.

It would appear that down through the centuries to the present time, the pearl-producing mussel has been heavily fished throughout Ireland. Today, most of the world's wild, natural pearl-producing molluscs have vanished because of overfishing and pollution, so natural pearls are rarer than ever before (Matlins 1996, 25).

*Competition and alternatives*
The quality of the native pearl must be evaluated to try to establish if it could ever have compared and competed with its rivals from the traditional sea fisheries, particularly those from Ceylon and the Persian Gulf.

Pearls from the River Strule in County Tyrone were exhibited in a cabinet made of Irish bog oak at the Great Exhibition of 1851 in London. The *Dublin Daily Express* of May 1851 (apparently in a special supplement published on 2 May) included a description of the pearls among the most important Irish contributions. The piece was copied in the *Tyrone Constitution*, a newspaper whose proprietor was a keen collector of Irish antiquities and who in fact sent the exhibit, as follows in the issue of 16 May (Anon. 1851a, 1):

> Mr. Nelis of Omagh. Omagh Pearls. Amongst the raw materials and other Irish produce displayed in the Exhibition, is a case of river pearls, many of them of extreme purity and of a large size, found in the Strule, at the town of Omagh, county Tyrone, and contributed by Mr. Nelis, proprietor of the *Tyrone Constitution* newspaper. These pearls are found in shells, resembling those of large muscles, and when taken at the proper stage, are of remarkable purity, possessing a soft and gentle brilliancy peculiarly their own. At other stages of their formation, however, they are quite dark and valueless. The case contains specimens, apparently found in all the periods of formation, as well as the shells in which they are produced. These pearls have long been held in high estimation in the fashionable world, and, being now very rare, are of considerable value.

The glowing patriotic account of the pearls in the Irish newspapers, however, was not shared by the juries, who apparently judged them inferior to other pearls on display from Ceylon (Report by the juries 1852, 164).

These Irish pearls were again shown at the National Exhibition in Cork in 1852 (Maguire 1853, 349). A primary objective of the organizers of the Cork exhibition was to highlight potential growth areas in the Irish economy (Davies 1975, 56). It would appear, however, that the pearls were shown mainly for their intrinsic interest, as they were exhibited under a section headed 'Curiosities and Natural History' (Maguire 1853, 349). However, the necklace shown in the frontispiece of this book, with its placard of fine Tyrone pearls, would attest that one jewellery company at least believed that their exploitation was capable of being developed into an industry in the late nineteenth century.

Irish jewellery, which included pearls, was also exhibited at Crystal Palace— for example, 'W. Griffiths, Grafton Street, Dublin…Irish harp brooches, with Irish beryl, pearls and diamonds' (Anon. 1851b, 4). At the turn of the twentieth century, Dublin jewellers still exhibited Irish pearls for sale, but specimens seen by Nicholas Synnott (1899–1902, 193) were apparently very small and, according to him, hardly deserving of any great commendation.

Nevertheless, we find even in the twentieth century reports extolling native pearls. Before writing an article on Ulster pearls, C. Douglas Deane (1965, 7) went to Edinburgh Castle in 1964 to see the Crown of Scotland which, he says, contains seven pearls from Scottish rivers. He concluded that a selection of pearls shown to him in Omagh compared favourably with those in the Scottish regalia. Even down to the 1980s, valuable pearls have been found in the rivers of County Tyrone and one such was sold in London for £200 (see chapter four).

The late Dr Arthur Went (1947, 45) of the then Department of Fisheries, writing after the Second World War, said that the mussel was widely spread in Ireland 'and the only reason why they are not now fished for the contained pearls appears to be that the oriental pearl has superseded the native'. The mussel was, of course, then still being fished for its pearls but not, apparently, on the same scale as in previous times, and this had indeed a lot to do with the availability of oriental cultured pearls as well as more gainful employment.

In some countries in Europe, records were maintained and the fisheries managed so that rivers were fished, under licence or by appointment, on a rotating basis in an effort to preserve the stocks of the pearl-producing mollusc. In the Vogtland fisheries, for example, complete accounts were kept for almost two centuries from about 1719 (Kunz and Stevenson 1908, 173). The Scottish fisheries were the most extensive and best organized of those in these islands, and although some mussel beds were managed, many others were worked to exhaustion. Following a falling-off in demand for Scottish pearls at the beginning of the nineteenth century (see chapter seven), they were again in fashion in the 1860s. The reasons for the revival were given by none other than Charles Dickens (1869, 125), in his weekly publication, where he attributed the new demand as follows:

> ...partly to the recent failure of the Manaar fisheries in Ceylon, partly to the cheapness of the western gem, and in some measure, perhaps, to the fact that large quantities of Scottish pearls have been purchased by Queen Victoria and Queen Eugenie; Some fifteen years ago these pearls were scarce and lightly esteemed; but owing to the exertions of a German merchant, and the care taken by him to select and exhibit the best specimens, the trade, which had languished for about a century, has very largely revived, and is now recognised as a legitimate branch of the business of the dealer in precious stones.

Similarly, in Ireland, increase in demand has been boosted from time to time by various events, as when Queen Alexandra received pearls from County Galway on her visit in the early part of the twentieth century, and when cultured pearls from Japan were unavailable during the Second World War.

Although river and sea pearl fisheries differ somewhat in their *modus operandi*, they have many things in common—not least that both produced the same commodity, albeit from a slightly different source. Thus, an examination of the cause of the decline of the fishery of the Persian Gulf, which was a huge industry and the main source of wealth there, might prove instructive in pointing to similar factors in the demise of the Irish fisheries. The decline there bears many similarities to what apparently happened in Ireland, and has been chronicled in the following terms (Field 1984, 185–203):

> In practice only a few shells had any pearls at all, and almost all of these were seed pearls. The entire fleet of the Gulf would produce the pearls for only two top-quality necklaces of exactly matching, perfectly rounded specimens in a season; even to find two matching tear-shaped pearls for a pair of earrings a crew would have to open tens of thousands of shells. The industry was based on there being a very large number of people—about 40,000 at the height of the industry in the first thirty years of this century—prepared to spend months at sea for a pittance...At the beginning of the 1930s[iv] the precarious economy of the Gulf was struck by disaster. The Japanese invented cultured pearls. The arrival of these pearls on the international market was accompanied by a change in fashion. By the 1930s the rich ladies of Europe were no longer wearing long ropes of pearls strung many times around their necks, as they had in the first two decades of the century. More serious was the effect of the Depression, which cut demand for all types of

luxury goods in the industrialised countries. From the early 1930s prices sank rapidly. By the late 1940s they were only 10 or 20 per cent of the level of 1928–9…The number of boats in pearling was reduced slowly. There was a good catch and a slight recovery of prices in 1937. A few years later, at the beginning of the Second World War, the merchants hoped that there would be a revival, with the same surge in demand that there had been during the First World War, when people in Europe had bought pearls for hoarding. Further hopes were raised in 1945, when there was another good catch and a small rise in prices caused by the low level of stocks and the destruction of Japan. On both occasions the merchants and divers' hopes were disappointed. By the later 1940s pearling employed only a tenth of the numbers it had employed in the early decades of this century. Within a few years the industry was dead. There is no question that it was the introduction of the Japanese cultured pearls and the Depression that caused the suffering of the Arabian population during the 1930s. Yet these were not the main factors in the decline of the numbers engaged in pearling. The industry faded away because the oil companies that arrived in the Gulf in the 1930s and 1940s offered easier and more rewarding employment. Even if there had been a recovery in pearl prices after 1945, pearling would never have competed with the attraction of the oil industry.

If the clock was turned back 200 years and the situation changed to Ireland, then an almost identical epitaph could be written for the pearl fishery on the Bann by substituting linen for oil. No mention was made of the effects of overfishing in the Gulf as it has been in other sea fisheries—for example, in Ceylon and in the opposite side of the Gulf of Manaar off the shores of Tinnevelly; when the stocks in the latter were fished out in the 1860s it was suggested that those from the Persian Gulf be used in restocking (Markham 1867, 260). It could also be added in regard to the Gulf (and again there is a similarity with the linen industry of the mid-eighteenth century in Ireland) that once the companies started production, the industrialization and subsequent oil spillages leading to pollution would not be conducive to pearl fishing.

Ireland, then, did show certain similarities and certain differences with the Gulf fisheries. It is curious to note, *prima facie*, that there was not the same fall in price for Irish pearls in the period between the two Wars as that documented for the Gulf. We see that a good pearl fetched £25 in the 1920s (McCrea 1973b, 13) and up to £50 in the late 1930s (Loudan 1943, 2). However, in real terms it would appear that there was indeed an effective devaluation by the 1940s, as we find that the price of a good pearl only fetched the same (Mullin 1947, 5) as 20 years previously. Yet we do hear of what were referred to as 'good pearls' being sold for very low prices—for example, 7s 6d

(38p), in County Carlow by a writer in the 1930s (MacDomhaill 1937, 88) but he may have been referring to an earlier period. The information regarding the prices of native pearls at these times is rather meagre and an assessment of the true price would need to be based on far more data. The decline in the supply of pearls from the Gulf would have left a gap in the market which may well have been filled by that from freshwater fisheries.

*Supply*

The supply of a commodity can, as we have seen, be much affected by excessive exploitation, such as with overfishing in the case of the pearl-producing molluscs, leading to a rise in price.[v] Conversely, it would be expected that profusion of goods on a market should result in a uniform lowering of prices for that particular commodity. This, however, does not necessarily happen with luxury goods. Quality remains an essential factor, especially in a narrow field bound by aesthetic values, like the jewellery trade (Taburiaux 1985, 223). Thus quantity, through open competition directed towards improving quality and constant promotion of products, can in turn create demand.

According to one source, the discovery of diamonds in Brazil in the eighteenth century resulted in a decrease in interest in pearls, which was only revived in the late nineteenth century with the commercial production of cultured pearls (O'Hara 1986, 192). It was not until the twentieth century (*c.* 1920), however, that the technique was perfected in Japan and so these would not have come on the market until then. In the case of luxury items such as pearls and diamonds, the laws of supply and demand may not always appear to apply, as the example of what happened to the latter in the 1920s shows (Anon. 1926, 6):

> By the 1920s there was a virtual glut of diamonds in the markets of the world. There were attempts by the four main companies, which controlled most of the mines in South Africa, to co-operate with the smaller enterprises, that dealt with alluvial diamonds, with a view to the restriction of output until the glut on the markets was eased. Among the reasons for the over-rapid production in the middle of that decade (of the last year) was a greatly increased demand in America and France. The inflated wealth of the United States has put extravagant luxuries in the reach of the multitude. In France, on the other hand, the demand for gems seems to have been stimulated by financial circumstances which have made people distrustful of money as a form of wealth secure against fluctuation in value. Strange are the circumstances which govern value in exchange! The growth of the popularity of diamonds is regarded by merchants as the chief danger to the diamond trade. Once diamonds lose rarity, a revulsion of favour will send their price

tumbling, and the stones that the Frenchman hoards will prove as fickle as the franc.

Generally, as its price falls, a commodity becomes cheaper relative to its substitutes, and it is therefore easier for the commodity to compete against these substitutes. In the case of scarce goods that possess value, such as natural pearls, only a portion of the demand for them can be satisfied. The price of such commodities cuts off all demand which is not prepared to pay, and in this way demand is equated to supply.

During the whole of the eighteenth century, pearls were apparently somewhat scarce as a result of both the Ceylon and Red Sea fisheries being unproductive. The most plentiful supplies during that time came from the Persian Gulf and from freshwater supplies. At this period, however, diamonds became fashionable owing to the discovery of new reserves (see above) and to improved methods of cutting and preparing them. But in spite of this rival, the pearl continued in favour, and by the end of the nineteenth century it was more sought after and more valuable than ever (Dakin 1913, 10).

During that century, there were discoveries of pearl banks off newly settled countries, such as Australia, where they became one of the sources of wealth to the colonists. Thus, the growing value of the pearl in the early part of the twentieth century was not due to a decrease in the source of supply, but to an ever-increasing demand for a gem which, as Dakin (1913, 10) puts it, 'never seems out of place for personal adornment or in any scheme of decoration'. Shortly afterwards, however, the production of the Japanese cultured variety did change the pearl market.

*Private enterprise*

It was outlined in chapter eight that while native pearl resources were mentioned in official correspondence, the Government never became involved in their exploitation as it did for a period, at the end of the eighteenth century, with regard to alluvial gold. In the eighteenth century, the inland fisheries were the subject of constant regulation by parliament, and proved very valuable properties to those who owned them, but they never developed on such a scale as to be worth notice as a national industry (O'Brien 1977, 172). In the previous century the same was probably true of the pearl fisheries, but by the middle of the eighteenth century it appears that the business of pearl fishing had largely declined; very few finds of pearls come to notice in the last decade of the eighteenth century. As with the inland fisheries generally, and salmon in particular, pearl fishing may have been lucrative to the owners of the rivers of a century before. Early in that century the salmon of the River Foyle and the eel fishery of the River Bann were well known (Beckett 1973, 28).

We know that river pearls were highly prized in the late seventeenth century, but perhaps in later years the quality of the product was deemed too poor to compete with those coming from Ceylon and elsewhere. In the late sixteenth century and during periods of the seventeenth, wars and rebellions, as well as severe restrictions on Irish trade, may have dampened any enterprising zeal. We see that in 1639, for example, the Governor and company of the copper mines in England were granted a monopoly of working the copper ore in Ireland, but the outbreak of rebellion prevented any use being made of the grant (O'Brien 1919, 56). We have seen in chapter four that during the rebellion of 1641, property at the fishery near Banbridge, which included mussels and pearls, was destroyed or stolen. Despite the restrictions imposed by English trading policy, the 25 years of Charles II's reign, from 1660 until 1685, were a period of unusual peace and economic expansion in Ireland (Simms 1989, 206). As Dickson (2000, 26) has observed:

> The world was not yet turned upside down, however. Rents continued to be paid normally until 1688 when cattle mortality, bad harvests and an acute scarcity of coin first diminshed proprietors' incomes. Nor was commerce initially depressed, for Irish exchequer receipts reached record levels in 1686, with a marked decline only setting in during 1688.

Although the Jacobite War (1688–90) is said to have halted economic life (McNeive n.d., 106), conditions probably improved afterwards towards the end of the century. We find that Robert Redding (1688, 140) travelled to County Tyrone and spent some days there in August 1688 observing work at the pearl fishery. This was before the war began, as William of Orange landed in November of the same year and James II left England the following month (Foster 1988, 141).

In the 1690s, Ireland recovered with remarkable rapidity from the devastation of war, as it had in the past (Beckett 1973, 155), and we find that a petition to the Crown was made in October 1693 to establish a pearl fishery in the rivers of County Fermanagh (see chapter four).

Other factors may also have contributed to a lack of industrial adventure with regard to the exploitation of pearls. In early Irish law, treasure trove was usually deemed to be either in whole or in part the property of the finder (Ó Cróinín 1995, 71). Just as the wool licence duty was a lucrative branch of revenue in the time of Charles II, so profits on treasure trove were subject to what were called casualties—one of a number of small miscellaneous duties payable to the Crown (O'Brien 1919, 199). Pearls may have been deemed treasure trove, and the duty payable might have further served to make the activity of their exploitation less lucrative and the business more secretive. In a manuscript *sine loco et anno* (Anon. n.d., 181–219), whose date of compilation may be fixed with certainty at 1623 and whose authorship has been attributed to Sir Henry Bourchier (Boucher),[vi] afterwards Fifth Earl of Bath (O'Brien

1923, ii), it is proposed that pearls taken in Irish rivers should be subject to Crown duties (Anon. n.d., 183):

> The pearls there of value should be looked after…The royalties there be of some value, for there is whale and sturgeon often taken and great store of pearl taken there in many places, whereof one was sold for £80 and another for £30 lately…and all this usurped by private men which be mere royalties. In law all the ambergrease and pearl of any value that there hath been gathered all this time past being admitted to be royalties (whereof I doubt not for my part) may be recovered against the usurpers upon an action of account brought against them by the king…And these commissioners may very convenniently enquire of such casualties and other advantages that His Majesty was entitled unto and yet usurped by private men, or secretly compounded for, or rated at a base value by the ordinary officers; as be outlaws' and felons' goods, waifs, strays, wrecks of the sea, forfeitures of bonds, fines, amercements, royalties, pearls of any note, ambergrease and the like.

After all, the increase of the royal revenues doubtless formed the principal object of James's colonizing schemes (Moore 1846, 171). We have seen in chapter seven that after being presented with a superb pearl from Scotland in 1621, he had set up a group of commissioners to manage and control the pearl fisheries there, but the commission failed owing to local resistence and was repealed after his death. We do not know when, or indeed if, such taxes were first levied in Ireland but the duty on pearls and other precious stones was abolished by the parliament of 1727–32 (Kunz and Stevenson 1908, 367).

For whatever reason, just as the Government did not get involved, neither did private individuals invest in the native pearl fisheries on a large scale. In summary, it could be said that by the time Ireland reached a climate of political and economic stability, the pearl-fishing industry had declined.

Even by the middle of the eighteenth century, Ireland apparently was not equipped with the wherewithal to exploit such natural resources as pearls, if contemporary commentators are to be believed. In a letter to the Earl of Warwick from the Munster circuit in 1760, Edward Willes (1762, 94), the Chief Baron, having given an account of pearls found in the rivers there as well as in the 'river of Omagh in the north of Ireland', goes on to say:

> Your Lordship may perceive by this account that nature has furnished us with precious things perhaps equal to our mother of England, but we are not yet arriv'd to that degree of skill, nor indeed have we abilities in point of money to make the most of natural advantages providence hath bless'd us with. If we were richer it wou'd be better for our good mother England, for really and truly all our riches center there. The current cash

of this kingdom, by the best calculation, does not amount to more (if so much) as a million, and was it not for our linnen manufactory, which brings us in about that sum annually, we shou'd not have cash to go to market with. The exportation of beef, pork, butter, tallow and fish is indeed a great assistance to us but as it is, cash is a very scarce commodity with us. I am told from the prerogative office, where wills and inventories are registered, that the articles of cash in the house makes but a very mean figure in the inventories of most of the gentlemen even of very large estates.

It can be deduced from this that there was an inability, for want of expertise and money, to exploit the pearls and other natural resources in the middle of the eighteenth century. As Chief Baron, travelling throughout the country to the various court sittings, Willes was in a very good position to 'judge' the state of the country. By the end of the century, pearl fishing as an industry in Ireland had all but ceased.

The freshwater pearl fisheries throughout the greater part of Europe were also past their peak and were in decline by the end of the eighteenth century. This would signify a common causative agent acting against the industry. In fact, a few issues can be identified as contributing to the demise: improved social conditions leading to better employment; industrial expansion leading to pollution of rivers; the fact that the pearl-producing mussel was easily overfished; and the fact that the pearls were only rarely comparable in lustre to their saltwater rivals.

We find that at the beginning of the twentieth century, the total value of pearls taken in European rivers was estimated at £20,000, with the equivalent calculation for Britain and Ireland given as £3,000 (see Table 7.1 in chapter seven). Between the years 1761 and 1764, pearls to the value of £10,000 were sent to London from the Rivers Tay and Isla alone in Scotland (Streeter 1886, 241). The Scottish trade is still the most vibrant of these islands although, as shown in chapter seven, a recent real decline is apparent there in the past few years. The remaining pearlers, who make a large part of their income through pearls, could be numbered on the fingers of one hand.

These pearl fishers come to Ireland on a regular basis and, together with a few locals, mainly dispose of the pearls through two jewellers in Scotland. As outlined in chapter seven, these two outlets have experienced a sharp fall in the number of good freshwater pearls being offered for sale in the past decade. This illustrates that even in Scotland and Ireland, where the largest stocks of mussels occur, a handful of fishers and their families cannot be supported. Most of these pearlers rely on the mussel for their livelihoods and thus operate their own methods for conserving stocks by employing non-destructive fishing techniques. This would serve to illustrate that even with non-destructive methods being employed, the existing stocks of mussels are not sufficient to provide a sustainable fishery for the few remaining professional pearlers. Most of the amateurs and casuals plying the trade, however, do not conserve the mussel and all those examined for their pearls are usually destroyed.

Pearl fishing is a very ancient craft throughout most of Europe and as such should not be banned out of hand. Rather, the traditional pearl fishers should be encouraged to carry on their trade in a non-destructive way. In an effort to conserve the mussel, guidelines on pearl fishing have been proposed by the Council of Europe's Standing Committee of the Convention on the Conservation of European Wildlife and Natural Habitats (1992, 1).[vii]

In the next, and final, chapter, the story of Irish pearls will be brought to a close by summarizing what has gone before and drawing a conclusion on their place in the social and economic life of the country.

*Notes*

[i]A report on the Bann drainage work in 1906 included a proposal for removing weirs to facilitate the passage of salmon upstream (Binnie 1906, 15). Because the pearl mussel depends on salmonid fish (trout and salmon), as it is parasitic on such fish in its larval stage, anything that affects their number will inevitably also affect mussel populations.

[ii]Although regarded as simplistic by some, the general concept is now long established as an aspect of the interpretation of the eighteenth-century economic and social history of Ireland (Cullen 1988, 1).

[iii]The stage at which the larval parasite becomes encysted on a salmonid fish.

[iv]It was, in fact, the preceding decade, the 1920s, in which the Japanese cultured pearls were perfected.

[v]This, of course, only holds true if demand is unchanged or increasing.

[vi]He may have seen, or heard about, river pearls while travelling through Munster as a commissioner inquiring into the condition of the army, when he was received at Bandon in 1622 by the Earl of Cork (Townsend 1904, 75), who we know had many collected from the river of the same name.

[vii]The Committee has recommended the establishment of the following: a list of authorized methods of pearl fishing; a minimum size of pearl mussel; a close season; a prohibition of fishing outside the hours of daylight; a code of practice for pearl fishing. Today pearl fishing, in both Northern Ireland and the Republic of Ireland, requires a licence as the mussel is protected by law.

# 10. Discussion and conclusion

When a prize of that value is discovered, it sets the people all at work to put into the pearl Lottery…by Degrees the adventurers, not meeting with the same Success, the Humour of pearl Fishing subsides, and is neglected, 'till some lucky person by accident meets with a good pearl, and this set's them all at work again…

*Edward Willes, Letters on Ireland* (1762, 125)

Having garnered as much information as is desirable on the topic of pearls in Ireland, some discussion and conclusion of their historical status must be given. It has been said that economic history, at its simplest level, entails gathering together the facts of economic and social life in the past. This much, at least, has been achieved in the present work regarding pearls. The more difficult part is to place interpretations on these facts (Othick 1987, 224). In the discussion to follow, an attempt will be made to bring the various strands put forward in the chapters together, and by so doing reach a conclusion about the socio-economic and socio-cultural significance of native pearls.

The foregoing chapters support the view that pearls played a part, albeit a small one, in economic and social history in Ireland. That pearls were a basis for a minor industry for a time before the middle of the eighteenth century has been a central theme in the dissertation. After that period, however, pearl fishing declined and it was never an industry of national significance.

The epigraph given at the beginning of this chapter, written more than 240 years ago, is an apt summary of the nature of pearl fishing in Ireland after it had passed from being a minor industry to a largely opportunist occupation. Fishing in many areas in Ireland was cyclical in nature, as we saw regarding Scotland in chapter seven. Some 200 years after Willes was writing, we find that the same river he was referring to, the Strule in County Tyrone, suffered again from overfishing. When there was an increase in demand for freshwater pearls because of the halt in supply of the Japanese variety during the Second World War, there was an upsurge in the level of fishing. Such pressure of fishing is self-limiting, as eventually the mussels, and therefore the pearls, become rare. As the fishing effort subsides the stocks of mussels recover. This occurred in the Strule in the 1950s, according to an inspector of fisheries for the area (Camlin 1959, 245); we find that in the 1960s more pearls come to notice, indicating an upsurge in fishing as the cycle begins again.

Up until the seventeenth century, information regarding pearls in Ireland is very limited. No archaeological evidence of pearls, nor of the pearl-producing mussel, has apparently been found (M. Cahill, National Museum of Ireland, pers. comm.; M. McCarthy, University College Cork, pers. comm.). Pearls are, unless looked after properly, much less durable than other precious stones and may not have survived in the archaeological record. It is likely that in prehistory they were, like alluvial gold, exploited, and as much is intimated by one source who believed they were probably used for trade with the visiting Phoenicians. Similarly, we have seen, but again without an authority, another source maintain that the magi (or druids) as well as the Tuatha Dé Danann used pearls as elixirs.

The early references of the Christian era show that pearls were used in personal adornment as well as in ornamentation and decoration of artefacts. While no evidence exists that women in early Ireland used pearls, there is evidence regarding kings, from the testimony of Nennius based on the oral tradition. However, it is likely that they were items of personal adornment for both sexes. They are mentioned in passing as being exploited from a river in the *Senchus mór* (part of the ancient law code of Ireland) which was written down and modified, it is said under the auspices of St Patrick, from pagan origins in the fifth century. They were apparently exploited during the so-called Dark Ages—from the fifth century until AD 1000—when for a time Ireland is said to have enjoyed a 'golden age' and when many artistic items, both ecclesiastical and secular, were manufactured. Many of these artefacts, some of which had pearls in the decoration, made during that period, were probably lost in the Viking raids.

We have provided evidence, in a letter written by the Bishop of Limerick in the first decade of the twelfth century, that pearls were then in currency. Similarly, they were used in the thirteenth century as shown in the list of church ornaments belonging to the Archbishop of Tuam. In the following century they continued to be used, as they were in the early fifteenth century when another bishop of Limerick had a mitre, referred to in chapter six, decorated with them (see Figure 6.7). We have it on the authority of George Petrie that pearls were much used in Irish religious ornaments in the fifteenth and sixteenth centuries. The Anglo-Norman ladies of Geraldine Ireland used them lavishly in personal adornment, as did ladies of succeeding generations down to the present time. Outside the country there was a demand for them too, and we find that English ladies of the Georgian period specified Irish pearls when ordering items of jewellery.

In the late sixteenth century, the Elizabethan adventurers such as Walter Raleigh and Richard Boyle, arrived in Ireland bent on making their fortunes by expropriating Irish lands. They were forerunners of the entrepreneurs and colonists who were to expand the British frontier across the Atlantic (James

1995, 19). Raleigh brought Cornish miners to exploit the minerals (Williams 1988, 92) and there can be little doubt that he was aware of the pearls in the River Blackwater on which his castle at Lismore stood. We know from the *Lismore papers* that Boyle, who purchased Raleigh's lands in Ireland, was aware of native pearls and bought many taken from the river in Bandon. Pearls are mentioned in the official dispatches to London during the wars in Munster and it has been speculated in chapter one that the soldiers cantoned near Killarney exploited them from Lough Leane and the River Laune. Raleigh had fought in these wars and from a portrait which was painted in 1588, where he is seen not only wearing a pearl in his left ear but with his tunic bedecked with them (see Figure 6.3), his fondness for them is obvious.

It is only from the seventeenth century onwards that any material evidence to do with pearls and their exploitation emerges. We saw, in chapter three, that pearls from the River Foyle were among the inducements offered to the people of London to settle in what was then County Derry. There is no evidence that these settlers subsequently worked the tributaries of the Foyle for pearls, and it would appear that in western Ulster the natives exploited the pearls in the seventeenth century, as they had prior to the Plantation. On the eastern side of Ulster, which had been settled largely by lowland Scots since 1610, the Bann and other rivers were systematically searched for their pearls and it was a successful industry there until the middle of the eighteenth century, when it was superseded by the linen industry. Coming from Scotland, these people, unlike those from London who settled in the west of the province, would have had knowledge of pearl fishing as they brought with them their own tradition, their own institutions, and their own way of life (Clarke 1989, 191). The fishery at Banbridge was obviously in place for some time before the middle part of the seventeenth century as we know that property there, belonging to a John Ware (or Weir), was destroyed or stolen during the Rebellion of 1641. That name and the names involved in the lease of the fishery in the eighteenth century, namely Majores, were certainly of settler stock, and the latter sold their interest in the fishery to a Scot, Hugh McClaine of Greenock, in 1736 (Robb 1939, 6).

Similarly, in Bandon in Cork, founded by Richard Boyle and settled with people from south-west England, the pearl fishery was probably managed in the seventeenth century. We have no definite information, however, save what the Earl himself has left us regarding the pearls from there, where his cousin, a jeweller, procured them for him. Nothing apparently is heard of the fishery after that time, although it is said locally that Queen Victoria had a necklace of Bandon pearls. As in some areas in eastern Ulster, the town did thrive for a time owing to the linen trade, and thus had alternative employment. Later, a huge cotton mill supported a corduroy industry that employed about 2,000 weavers for almost 30 years and it also at one time had as many as 17 tanneries (Ó Gráda 1995, 325).

The lack of minerals has frequently been mentioned as one of the causes of the slight industrial developments of Ireland, yet the north-east managed to attract both coal and the steel necessary for its shipbuilding (Freeman 1950, 211–12). We have seen that it was also in that part of the country that the new settlers in the seventeenth century set up what was probably the most systematic pearl fishery in the country from a natural resource, before turning their attention to the linen trade. It would seem that, for whatever reason, the same enterprising ethos was absent in most other parts of the country.

After the Restoration in 1660, some of the dispossessed were given back their holdings, but there were more claimants on Irish land than the total area of the island could possibly accommodate (Chart 1920, 35). It has been suggested that in the economic recession of the following decade, searching for pearls was a proud alternative to begging for survival, and that it may even have enabled the dispossessed to rebuild their lives and buy back their holdings (Meagher 1928, 385). In chapter three, the average price for a good pearl for that time was computed at £3.50, the equivalent to a year's wages, while an acre of land was priced at £2. If, as we have seen, the pearls were sold direct to the gentry, they could fetch for the seller ten times that amount, and it is plausible that land was purchased through their sale.

After that time, pearl prices appear to fluctuate but were generally about equal to a week's, rather than a year's, income, except in particular times for a specific reason. Examples of this were in the Edwardian period when they were extremely popular, and during the Second World War when there were no alternative varieties available. Contemporary sources from different parts of the country appear to quote more consistent prices for pearls in the former period than for other times, when they seem to vary depending on to whom and where they were sold. One difficulty with the price of a commodity such as pearls is that each one is different and individually valued—unlike, for example, an ounce of gold, whose price will be universal at a particular time.

The main reason for considering the various uses of pearls was to establish the extent of the demand for them. In earlier times, as well as for personal adornment, they were used to decorate artefacts and ecclesiastical garments and accessories. They were often sold locally to merchants and direct to jewellers in Omagh, Belfast, Dublin, Cork and other centres on internal markets. But many were also disposed of outside the country. The latter markets included London, Edinburgh and even places as far afield as Paris. Although it would appear that most freshwater pearls in these islands are nowadays marketed through the Scottish trade, particularly in Edinburgh and Perth, London was, and continues to be, the best market for pearls of a fine quality. Thus an emphasis on fashions there, given in chapter six, is justified.

From the earliest times, one of the main uses of pearls has been personal adornment, even among men, and they were worn as earrings both in very early times and in the sixteenth and seventeenth centuries. A definite bias against men wearing them has come to light in this study, particularly among some nineteenth-century scholars, and has been incorporated into the folklore of one particular region of Ulster. We have seen, in chapter six, that they were used in ornamentation and decoration from an early time, but many of those in the older artefacts appear to have perished or fallen out, as the example of the *Domnach airgid*, with only one of the original four pearls remaining in its setting, illustrates (see Figure 8.1).

As well as the pearls, the shells of the mussel were used, particularly as scoops or spoons, by the poor from an early time until at least the middle of the eighteenth century. They were also used as a dressing on base-poor soils, and it is interesting to note in this context that the natural occurrence of the mussel, unusual for a mollusc that builds robust shells of calcium carbonate,[i] should be in areas where the water and the soils are low in calcium.

The main reasons for the effective demise of the pearl fisheries in the eighteenth century were given in chapter nine, and may be summarized as the improved social conditions leading to better employment, as well as competition from largely superior pearls from the other dominions increasingly making their way onto the markets. Added to this, the effects of pollution owing to the industrial expansion of the time, and the fact that the mussels were a vulnerable resource that was easily overfished, were contributing factors.

The idea of a 'hidden Ireland', first espoused by Daniel Corkery (1924) in relation to Munster in the eighteenth century, was touched upon in relation to pearls and their exploitation. While a critic of the general concept in the sense in which it was originally promulgated, L.M. Cullen (1988, 36), has conceded that in fact 'several hidden Irelands—if we compartmentalise studies—must exist, in the sense that there are aspects or dimensions to what happened in human activity and experience that escape the prying eye of the historian'. This, it would appear, epitomized the activity of pearl fishing in the early part of the eighteenth century, when many pearls are likely to have been smuggled out of the country and sold in London. The period of the Penal Laws alienated a large proportion of the population and many activities may well have become more secretive. It is possible that some, such as pearl fishing, had an underground existence. It is interesting that the only two instances where pearls apparently come to notice in the early years of the eighteenth century are references in the correspondence to Secretary Dawson in Dublin. It is of further interest to note that one of these relates to a small pearl found in Munster (see chapter eight).

Just as Corkery sought to explain his concept of a 'hidden Ireland' through the study of Irish poetry and culture of eighteenth-century Munster, the present dissertation has surveyed, *inter alia*, mythology, folklore and literature to establish the extent to which a pearl culture existed in Ireland. The conclusion to be drawn from that part of the study is that while pearl exploitation is mentioned in Irish literature, stretching from when the ancient laws were first written down to Anglo-Irish writings of the twentieth century, it could never be said that pearls have entered into the culture in any prominent way. They have largely been used symbolically and allegorically in Irish poetry, prose and music, but have also been used by those involved in the Gaelic Revival of the nineteenth century, where they were woven into historical novels. The native pearl has been used in some stories to symbolize religious salvation or simply as fashion accessories and bridal ornaments, to represent purity, but also to signify the patriotic homeland, producing as it does such a pure and precious gem.

The legacy of pearls is found in very few local names and only a possible couple of rivers or lakes could, from their names, be identified as having some association with pearls.

The native pearl may have been overlooked as a commodity by historians as a result of inaccurate or misleading translations; a definite bias against pearls by two Irish scholars of the nineteenth century, John O'Donovan and Eugene O'Curry, has been identified. How scholars of their calibre, with their knowledge of the Gaelic language, could respectively interpret the Old Irish word for pearl as 'onyx' and 'gem' is beyond credulity. That they may have been sceptical that pearls occurred in Ireland is no excuse, as a good translator, or indeed historian, should never meddle with material handed down from previous generations. If this duo, as well as others, who unwittingly wrongly translated references to pearls in the seventeenth, eighteenth and nineteenth centuries, had been less judgemental in their undertakings—or, in the case of the latter, more accurate in their renderings—then perhaps native pearls might have received more attention.

At the same time as O'Donovan and O'Curry were writing, as we have seen in chapter five, the authors of historical novels were weaving the native pearl into their stories. Thus, knowledge of the occurrence of pearls in Ireland was current in the nineteenth century and ignorance cannot really be proffered as an excuse. It is difficult to rationalize the attitude of O'Donovan and O'Curry except to conclude that, for whatever reason, both showed an antipathy to pearls.

The main difficulty with an economic evaluation of pearl fishing in Ireland is the lack of any central sources. Thus we have been left nothing regarding the numbers employed or engaged in the pearl fisheries. Even when we come to establishing prices for pearls, the contemporary sources do not appear to agree and uniform values cannot therefore be given for particular periods. What has been established is that they were highly prized, and priced, up until about the middle of the eighteenth century, after which the more plentiful supplies coming on the market from Ceylon[ii] and elsewhere superseded them.

Pearl fishing and gold prospecting in Irish rivers were compared and contrasted in chapter eight, and found to have many aspects in common. While both riverine pearls and gold may be considered as natural resources, only the former could be regarded as renewable. If, however, the mussels from which pearls came were not treated carefully by efficient management of the resource, their supplies, like alluvial gold, were quickly exhausted.

Unlike in the United States, which now has a productive freshwater cultured-pearl industry (Matlins 1996, 43), attempts by the pearlers in County Tyrone at producing or enhancing pearls in this manner in Ireland in the 1930s and 1940s proved unsuccessful. An artificial-pearl[iii] industry did thrive in Belfast for almost 50 years, up until recently. Although individuals will probably always search for pearls, the sea pearl fisheries, like those in fresh water, are effectively extinct as industries. They were doomed to failure in Europe after the advent of the Industrial Revolution, but survived much longer in the sea fisheries of the Third World. They could only survive so long as those involved worked for small remuneration and so long as large stocks of the raw material, the pearl-producing molluscs, also survived. As elsewhere in the ascent of man, such as the transition from hunter-gatherer to farmer, the natural progression was therefore to seek to control the production of pearls. This has been done, most notably in salt water in Japan, but also in fresh water in China and latterly in the United States, through the cultured-pearl industry.

Native pearls, as well as being part of the heritage of the poorer classes, were associated with the womenfolk of the Ascendancy. The tradition among the Anglo-Irish, begun in the seventeenth century, of taking the pearls from the local rivers for necklaces for the lady of the 'big house', continued down to the third decade of the twentieth century, the twilight of their period. Similarly, folklore and legend regarding pearls have survived, particularly in the south-west and north-west of the country. It is of note that these differ, in that the legends regarding pearls in the latter area, such as the idea that they fade when worn by men, or the story about finding a large one, buying out several townlands but eventually falling victim to misfortune, appear to be of much more recent origin than those in the south-west.

In terms of sociological and cultural studies on a wider scale, it is very interesting to note the similarities between some of the legends relating to pearls in Ireland and elsewhere, suggesting, perhaps, a common origin. For example, we have seen in chapter five that the legends regarding the origin of pearls in two lakes, Lough Leane and Lough Gal in County Kerry, where they are respectively formed by showers and guarded by a serpent, have parallels with the legendary tales in China[iv] and India as well as Polynesia. This aspect has been interpreted as part of the survival of what E. Estyn Evans (1957, xiv) has called archaic elements of the Indo-European culture.

Ireland in the middle of the twentieth century still retained many ancient customs (Freeman 1950, 165) but these became more threatened, particularly by sophistication, as the century and indeed millennium drew to a close. Even Ulster, which was the most industrialized of the four provinces, has held on to many old traditions, and it appears that many of these which were strongest there, including pearl fishing, have also survived longest there.

The decline of pearl fishing in Ireland appears to have corresponded with the advent of the linen trade in some areas with a causal connection identified in eastern Ulster. As an industry in Ireland it was apparently finished by the last quarter of the eighteenth century, or about the time that Adam Smith was publishing *The wealth of nations* (1776). Although some parts were impoverished, others were prosperous and the economic, social and cultural level of Irish civilization in the late eighteenth century compares favourably with that in many other regions of Western Europe (James 1995, 153). By that time, however, the majority of pearl fisheries both in Ireland and the rest of Europe were past their heyday, and the opportunity offered by the new prosperity came too late.

Such an industry, it could also be advanced, had had its day and had no place in the new mechanical age of the late eighteenth and early nineteenth centuries. The impression is gained from contemporary sources that pearls were then treated as curiosities rather than commodities that could be the basis for an industry.

The heyday of the freshwater pearl fisheries came much later in North America. The first English colonies in what is now the United States were settled[v] about the same time as Ulster but freshwater pearls were not exploited there commercially until some 280 years later. As an industry there, the pearl fisheries were considerable in the late nineteenth and early twentieth centuries, being worth about $500,000 annually.

Why the pearl fisheries never became an industry of national import in Ireland was assessed in chapter nine, where the reasons for their ultimate decline were outlined. The failure fully to exploit native pearls was apparently due to lack of investment in the fisheries, as well as the absence of the managerial knowledge and skills necessary to harvest a sustainable yield of such a resource. By the time, towards the end of the eighteenth century, that conditions were conducive to industrial development and the necessary entrepreneurial skills were present, the opportunity for the pearl fisheries had passed and industries which offered more secure investment were beginning to thrive.

It could also be argued that given the nature of the exploitation of the resource, like gold, it was always doomed to failure. Yet, unlike that commodity the raw material for pearls—the mussel—is a renewable one. Because of the nature of the mussel, which has a very slow growth rate and does not reproduce until it is around 12 years of age (Young and Williams 1983, 48) it can sustain a fishery only if managed in a non-destructive manner. Although the fishery at Banbridge was managed and survived for more than a century, generally in Ireland each mussel examined was destroyed in the search for the hidden pearl.

The actual quality of the native pearl was questioned, also in chapter nine, particularly in relation to those from Ceylon. It would appear that the Irish pearl was generally inferior to its saltwater rival, although fine specimens have been, and continue to be, found from time to time. Thus, *ipso facto*, it could be construed that the supply of a dependable source of quality product may also have been among the factors which impeded the development of the pearl fisheries as an industry in Ireland.

Of all the elements of pearls covered, the most adequate sources have been to do with fishing methods. Good contemporaneous accounts, in four centuries, have come down to us and a selection of these were used to give a chronological account of how the pearlers harvested the pearls. The most striking feature to emerge from that examination is the survival of the simple forked (or cleft) stick as the fishing implement during all that time. Thus, there has been no effective evolution of techniques in the prosecution of pearl fishing over some 300 years, pointing to its antiquity based on traditional methodology. It is curious to note that in most of the countries of Europe where pearl fishing was prosecuted, the forked stick has been a universal piece of equipment. Similarly, with regard to extraction of pearls, as we have seen in chapter two, the methods were also largely crude and the shells were routinely opened and searched using a knife and the fingers. A few exceptions to this have been outlined, such as when the mussels were fished on a large scale from the Rivers Bann and Slaney, where slightly more sophisticated extraction methods were employed. We can also conclude on the evidence presented that the seventeenth century saw the greatest level of intensity of fishing for pearls in Ireland.

Somewhat surprisingly, perhaps, the activity of pearl fishing was not strictly a male preserve and there are instances of female pearlers from the seventeenth century onwards. Because no elaborate equipment was required, almost anyone, as with gold panning, could partake in pearl fishing of rivers. It would accordingly make economic sense for the pearler to work freelance, unless (as was the case in some European countries) the fisheries were under state, royal or even Church control, which in practice appears to be what happened in Ireland and Scotland. It is in this particular aspect that the main difference with the sea fisheries, where a seagoing vessel—and hence capital—was necessary, is found. In both the marine and freshwater pearl fisheries, vast numbers of molluscs were destroyed in the search for pearls. In the rivers of Ireland, just as in Scotland and elsewhere in Europe where a conservation strategy was not employed, this led to temporary crashes in populations. Fishing would be curtailed until stocks had recovered—hence the cyclical nature of pearl fishing in these islands, characterized by periods of 'feast and famine' in terms of pearl production.

Pearls were apparently fished systematically in more than one location in Ulster (the Rivers Strule and Bann), Leinster (the River Slaney) and Munster (the River Bandon) in the seventeenth century. There are, however, records of pearls from 21 of the counties in Ireland, and from all four provinces. Thus, while greatest effort was concentrated in particular areas, there was a wide geographical spread of pearl-fishing districts in Ireland.

Although no attempt was made, owing to lack of suitable data, to quantify the numbers engaged in pearl fishing at any given time, we know that at one period in the middle of the nineteenth century as many as 40 people, both men and women, plied the trade on the Strule in County Tyrone. Nor has it been possible, again for want of adequate data, to estimate the value of the fisheries at any time, although a figure of £3,000 was given in chapter seven for the local value of the fisheries of the British Isles in 1906, when they were in terminal decline. The corresponding figure for the number of fishers, even at that late period, at 300 is similarly most probably a conservative estimate. That period, the first decade of the twentieth century, was to be the final phase of the fisheries as an industry, save for a brief reprieve during the Second World War, before the introduction of the cultured Japanese variety, and more widespread freshwater pollution dealt a final blow in most countries. In countries of relatively unpolluted rivers, such as Scotland and Ireland, the activity was still prosecuted, though largely on a part-time basis.

One of the chief reasons for the decline of the pearl fisheries was, as outlined in chapter nine, the availability of more regular and gainful employment in the late eighteenth century. This was particularly true in the case of the Bann and Lagan fisheries, where the linen and cotton industries, both directly and indirectly, led to their demise. Pearl fishing, for a number of reasons, was always a clandestine activity[vi] to some extent, but it became even more secretive in the time of the Penal Laws, particularly, so it would appear, in Munster, after which it never apparently regained its former momentum. Two centuries later, in the 1920s, the perfecting of cultured pearls, chiefly from Japan, sounded the final death knell and since that time pearl fishing in Ireland, despite the respite during the Second World War when the Japanese variety was unavailable, has become a low-level activity.

A history of pearls in Ireland has been given and, although the fisheries never became a national industry, they nonetheless survived into the twentieth century in some areas. However, they are absent from all treatises on Irish social and economic history. The economic history of Ulster, from such treatises, is dominated by the linen trade, but before its advent pearl fishing was a viable enterprise—so much so that its legacy is in a coat of arms of the town of Banbridge dating from about 1870, which has the pearl mussel as one of its emblems and indicates its importance in the history of the town (see Figure 10.1).

Further to the west of the province, on the other hand, it appears that while the mussel was industriously fished for its pearls, the trade never developed beyond a part-time occupation. Yet in that area, and particularly around

Omagh, it has endured as such or as a pastime for some right down to the present, and it is also there that the folklore or legend regarding pearls has survived longest.

In the previous chapter the economic aspect of pearls not obeying the laws of demand was touched upon. At first sight it might appear that pearls are exceptions to the law of demand, as they exhibit what economists have termed the Veblen effect—they are commodities wanted solely for their high prices. This really is in the realm of theoretical economics and is difficult to prove one way or the other. There are, however, good and poor pearls and the quality of each individual specimen will dictate its worth within a range of price for the commodity based on criteria such as quality, colour and size. Most cases of what appear to be exceptions to the law of demand are in fact changes in demand (Watson 1982, 231–32) and we have seen that an increase in the supply of pearls, as well as the availability of substitutes, did not dent the desire to purchase the commodity. The perfecting of the culturing techniques in Japan led to some control of the size and shape of pearls, and they could only be distinguished from the natural by an expert. This development did dent the market for freshwater varieties and, through a lessening demand for natural pearls, led to the demise of many traditional fisheries.

The systematic pursuit of natural pearls, although diminished, is still undertaken, as no imitation or cultured varieties can match some of those occurring naturally, and for these there will always be a niche in the market. The supply of, and demand for, pearls in Ireland was inextricably linked, in that owing to its very long life cycle, the native pearl-producing mussel was easily overfished. It is only in the last decade that the activity of pearl fishing in Ireland has been regulated, through the issuing of licences, and the mussel is now protected by law in both the Republic of Ireland and Northern Ireland.[vii] It is likely that the imposition of a licensing system will once again make pearl fishing an even more clandestine activity, as apparently happened in the eighteenth century during the period of the Penal Laws.

In chapter seven, the information on the worldwide freshwater pearl fisheries was surveyed. As already iterated, some of those in Central Europe survived as industries down to the first decade of the twentieth century, when industrial pollution all but eradicated the pearl-producing mussel from the rivers. There, the governments of Bavaria, Saxony[viii] and Bohemia had supervised the industry and only granted a licence to fish any stretch of water about once in every 12 years. It was said of such a restriction that 'had it been imposed on our fisheries [i.e., those of the British Isles], might have saved a vanishing industry' (Shipley 1908, 5). Thus, overfishing was squarely blamed for the demise of the fisheries in these islands but, as we have seen, it was only one of the factors involved. Where a conservation policy was apparently implemented in Ireland, such as in the Bann fishery in the seventeenth and eighteenth centuries, the industry flourished for a time—in the case of the

Banbridge fishery, for something in the order of 100 years.

The Dublin Philosophical Society, founded in 1683 by William Molyneux, was interested in actively promoting the pearl fisheries by gauging their worth. This we learn from the minutes of its meeting for 10 May 1693 and from the subsequent questionnaire drawn up to inquire into their operations. Also in 1693, a petition was made to the Crown to establish a pearl fishery in the rivers of County Fermanagh. We hear nothing further, however, of such proposed ventures. Perhaps a degree of mercantilism entered into the situation: parliament and not the monarch was by then making the economic policy.

It was in the last decade of the seventeenth century that the full effects of the restraints on Irish commerce were felt. The early part of the following century, however, was even worse, with the imposition of Penal Laws. By the 1780s, though, it appears that the impetus for the exploitation of pearls had passed. From then until the close of the century, some industries, such as copper and gold mining in County Wicklow, were stimulated by parliamentary grants. But these, as well as the fishing industry, which also had been encouraged by bounties and premiums granted by the Irish and English parliaments, prospered for a short while and then declined owing to the political unrest towards the end of the century.

The inland fisheries, like the pearl fisheries, never developed into an industry of national significance as the sea fisheries did from an early time. From the earliest times the rivers were fished or trapped, by the monks amongst others, for salmon and eels. The salmon has, unlike the eel and pearl mussel, been propagated artificially[ix] for commercial purposes and is the most important of the inland fisheries species. The inland fisheries have, since at least the sixteenth century, been controlled by the proprietors of the rivers, first by the native earls and later by the new Ascendancy.[x] It may well be that in the seventeenth century this impeded the development of the salmon and pearl resources, while in other European countries, royal or state control of the latter was common and appears to have worked well.

The overall conclusion to be drawn from this study is that while it has an interesting history in Ireland, the native pearl has, both culturally and economically, only ever been of local importance. It is nonetheless part of the cultural and industrial heritage of Ireland and, as such, deserves to be documented.

*Notes*

[i]The shells are built up slowly with calcium carbonate during the mussel's long lifespan.

[ii]Britain took control of Ceylon, and thus of its pearl fisheries, in 1796.

[iii]See chapter one. Whereas natural and cultured pearls are produced in rivers, lakes and bays by living molluscs, artificial or imitation ones, also known as 'faux' and 'simulated' are not created by any living creature except man.

[iv]In Chinese literature there was a connection with the moon, where it was referred to

as the night-shining pearl. This connection between the pearl and the heavens is found in the Gaelic language, where *néamh* is the sky or heaven and *némann* (or *néamhainn*) the pearl, with both names derived from the root *nem*.

[v] The first English colonies were settled by the Plymouth Company and the London Company. The freshwater pearls were used by Native Americans prior to the arrival of European settlers.

[vi] It was probably seen as, or mistaken for, poaching by the largely hostile riparian proprietors.

[vii] It is necessary to obtain a licence for the taking of pearl mussels: from the National Parks and Wildlife Service in the Republic of Ireland and the Environment and Heritage Service in Northern Ireland.

[viii] As would be expected, those in Saxony, supervised with Teutonic efficiency, were the best managed of those in Europe and a record exists of practically every pearl obtained at one fishery for nearly two centuries (Kunz and Stevenson 1908, 173).

[ix] This is due to a complicated life cycle in both cases. However, recent advances in the development of techniques to culture the pearl mussel have been made for this endangered species (e.g., Moorkens 1996, 50; Preston *et al.* 2002, 1).

[x] See chapter four: the Earl of Desmond's forfeitures in 1584 included a productive salmon and pearl fishery.

# Bibliography

## Books

ADAMS, W.F. (1932) (Reprint 1980) *Ireland and Irish emigration to the New World from 1815 to the Famine*. New Haven (Reprint Baltimore).

ANMYL, J.B. (ed.) (1922) *Geiriadurur saesneg a chymralg*. Carmarthen.

ANON. (1683a) *England's vanity or the voice of God against the monstrous sin of pride in dress and apparel*. London. (Quoted in Ribeiro 1986.)

— (1855) *The Irish pearl: a tale of the time of Queen Anne*. Place of publication not given but almost certainly Dublin.

— (1865) *Ancient laws of Ireland*, vol. i. Dublin.

— (1876a) *Leabhar breac, the speckled book*. Dublin.

— (1876b) *A history of the earth and animated nature by Oliver Goldsmith*, vol. vi. London.

APPLEBY, J.E. (1992) *A calendar of material relating to Ireland from the High Court of Admiralty Examinations 1536–1614*. Dublin.

ARMSTRONG, N. (1973) *Jewellery: an historical survey of British styles and jewels*. London.

ARMSTRONG, R.A. (1825) *A Gaelic dictionary*. London.

BACON, F. (1626) *Sylva sylavarum*. Londini.

BARBER, G. (1971) *Textile and embroidered bindings*. Oxford.

BARTSCH, P. (1968) *Mollusks*. New York.

BAUER, M. (1904) *Precious stones*. London.

BECKETT, J.C. (1973) *The making of modern Ireland 1603–1923*. London.

BEDE (1955) *A history of the English church and people*. Harmondsworth.

BENCE-JONES, M. (1987) *Twilight of the Ascendancy*. London.

BEST, R.I. and BERGIN, O. (eds.) (1929) (Reprint 1970) *Lebor na huidre: book of the dun cow*. Dublin (Reprint Galway).

BEST, R.I. and O'BRIEN, M.A. (eds.) (1965) *The book of Leinster formerly lebar na núachongbala*, vol. iv. Dublin.

de BHALDRAITHE, T. (1959) *English–Irish dictionary*. Baile Átha Cliath.

BINNIE, A.R. (1906) *Bann and Lough Neagh drainage*. Dublin.

BOATE, G., MOLINEUX, T. *et al.* (1755) *A natural history of Ireland*. Dublin.

BOETHIUS, H. (1627) 'De animantibus terrestribus volatilibus, aquatilibus Scotiae', in *Republica sive status regni Scotiae et Hiberniae* (Ex officina Elzeuiriana. Place of publication not given but probably Leyden).

BONWICK, J. (1986) *Irish druids and old Irish religions*. New York.

BOURKE, U.J. (1877) *Sermons in Irish-Gaelic by the Most Rev. James O'Gallagher*. Dublin.

BOYLE, R. (1665) *Occasional reflections*, vol. iv. London.

— (1672) *An essay about the origine and virtues of gems*. London.

BROWN, T. (ed.) (1836) Appendix to *A history of the earth and animated nature by Oliver Goldsmith*, vol. iv. Glasgow.

BRYANS, R. (1964) *Ulster: a journey through the six counties*. London.

BUCKLAND, F. (1875) *Log-book of a fisherman and zoologist*. London.

BUCKLAND, F.T. (1878) *Curiosities of natural history*. London.

BURCH, J.B. (1973) *Biota of freshwater ecosystems. Identification manual no. 11: freshwater unionacean clams (Mollusca: Pelecypoda) of North America*. Washington.

BYRNE, F.J. (1987) *Irish kings and high-kings*. London.

BYRNE, M.J. (1903) *Ireland under Elizabeth: chapters towards a history of Ireland in the reign of Elizabeth*. Dublin.

CAMDEN, W. (1789) *Britannia, translated from the edition published in 1607, enlarged by the latest discoveries by R. Gough*. London.

CHART, D.A. (1920) *An economic history of Ireland*. Dublin.

CIPRIANI, C. and BORELLI, A. (1986) *Precious stones*. London and Sydney.

CLARK, G. (1986) *Symbols of excellence*. Cambridge.

CLARKE, A.H. (1981) *The freshwater molluscs of Canada*. Ottawa.

COLLIER, J.P. (1888) *The poetical works of Edmund Spenser*. London.

COLLINS, N.M. and WELLS, S.M. (1987) *Invertebrates in need of special protection in Europe*. Strasbourg.

COOMANS, H.E. and BRUS, R. (1989) *Parels en parelmore*. Scheveningen.

CORKERY, D. (1924) (Reprint 1977) *The hidden Ireland; a study of Gaelic Munster in the eighteenth century*. Dublin.

COTTON, H. (1851) *Fasti ecclesiae Hibernicae*, vol. i. Dublin.

CROOKSHANK, A. and GLIN, Knight of (1969) *Catalogue of Irish portraits 1660–1860*. London.

CULLEN, L.M. (1987) *An economic history of Ireland since 1660*. London.

— (1988) *The hidden Ireland: reassessment of a concept*. Mullingar.

CUSACK, M.F. (1868) *The illustrated history of Ireland*. Kenmare.

DAKIN, W.J. (1913) *Pearls*. Cambridge.

DAVIES, J. (1869) *The works*, vol. i. London.

DAY, A. and McWILLIAMS, P. (eds.) (1990) *Ordnance survey memoirs of Ireland*, vol. iv. Dublin.

DEENEY, D. (1900) *Peasant lore from Gaelic Ireland*. London.

DICKSON, D. (2000) *New foundations: Ireland 1660–1800*. Dublin.

DOYLE, J.B. (1854) *Tours in Ulster*. Dublin.

DUBOURDIEU, J. (1802) *Statistical survey of the County of Down*. Dublin.

DUTTON, H. (1824) *A statistical and agricultural survey of the County of*

*Galway*. Dublin.

ELLIS, A.E. (1978) *British freshwater bivalve Mollusca*. London.

EVANS, E.E. (1957) (Reprint 1988) *Irish folk ways*. London.

— (1977) *Irish heritage*. Dundalk.

EVANS, H.M. and THOMAS, W.O. (1989) *Y geiriadur mawr*. Dyfed.

FARN, A.E. (1986) *Pearls: natural, cultured and imitation*. London.

FARRELL, M.J. (1928) (Reprint 1996) *Young entry*. Oxford.

FIELD, M. (1984) *The merchants: the big business families of Arabia*. London.

FISHER, P.J. (1966) *The science of gems*. New York.

FLETCHER, C.R.L. (1913) *An introductory history of England*. London.

FLETCHER, G. (ed.) (1922) *Ireland*. Cambridge.

FORBES, E. (1838) *Malacologia monensis.* Edinburgh.

FOSTER, R.F. (1988) *Modern Ireland 1600–1972*. London.

FREEMAN, T.W. (1950) *Ireland: its physical, historical, social and economic geography*. London.

GALBRAITH, J.K. (1958) (Reprint 1977) *The affluent society*. London.

GANTZ, J. (1981) *Early Irish myths and sagas*. London.

GEIGER, M. (1637) *Margaritologia, sive dissertatio de Margaritis*. Monachii.

GIBBINGS, R. (1945) *Lovely is the Lee*. London.

GOLDSMITH, O. (1744a) *An history of the earth and animated nature*, vol. v. London.

— (1774b) *An history of the earth and animated nature*, vol. vii. London.

GOLLANCZ, I. (1936) *Pearl: an English poem of the fourteenth century*. London.

GOODWIN, P.J. (1985) *The river and the road: journal of a freshwater pearl-fisher*. London.

GRIBBON, H.D. (1969) *The history of water power in Ulster*. Newton Abbot.

GRIFFIN, G. (1862) *The invasion*. Dublin.

GROSART, A.B. (ed.) (1886) *Lismore papers*, vol. iv. Privately published.

GUIDO, M. (1978) *The glass beads of the prehistoric and Roman periods in Britain and Ireland*. London.

van HAMEL, A.G. (1932) *Lebor Bretnach: The Irish version of the Historia Britonum ascribed to Nennius*. Dublin.

HARRIS, W. (1744) *The antient and present state of the County of Down*. Dublin.

— (1745) *The whole works of Sir James Ware concerning Ireland*, vol. ii. Dublin.

HARRISON, W. (ed.) (1731) *A description of the Isle of Man by George Waldron, Gent*. Douglas.

HARRY, H.W. (1990) *The encylopedia Americana*, vol. xxi. Danbury.

HASTINGS, J. (ed.) (1900) *A dictionary of the Bible*. New York.

HAVERTY, M. (1867) *The history of Ireland*. New York.

HEALY, J.N. (1962) (Reprint 1979) *The second book of Irish ballads*. Cork.

HELY, J. (ed.) (1793) *Ogygia or a chronological account of Irish events*, vol. ii. Dublin.

HERBERT, D. (ed.) (1876) *The poetical works of Thomas Moore*. London.

HERITY, M. and EOGAN, E. (1977) *Ireland in prehistory*. London.

von HESSLING, T. (1859) *Die perlmuscheln und ihre perlen*. Leipzig.

The HIGHLAND SOCIETY OF SCOTLAND (1828) *Dictionarium Scoto–Celticum: a dictionary of the Gaelic language*. Edinburgh.

HOGAN, E. (1895) *The Irish Nennius from L. na huidre and homilies and legends from L. brecc*. Dublin.

HOLINSHED, R. (1577) *The historie of Irelande from the first inhabitation thereof, unto the yeare 1509: collected by Raphaell Holinshed, and continued till the yeare 1547 by Richard Stanyhurst*. London.

HOLMES, G. (1801) *Sketches of some of the southern counties of Ireland*. London.

HUNTER, D. (1957) *The diseases of occupations*. London.

JACKSON, J.W. (1917) *Shells as evidence of the migrations of early culture*. Manchester.

JAMES, F.G. (1995) *Lords of the Ascendancy*. Dublin.

JEFFARES, A.N. (1982) *Anglo-Irish literature*. New York.

JEFFRIES, D. (1751) *A treatise on diamonds and pearls*. London.

JOYCE, K. and ADDISON, S. (1992) *Pearls: ornament and obsession*. London.

JOYCE, P.W. (1875) *The origin and history of the Irish names of places*. Dublin.

— (1903a) *A social history of ancient Ireland*, vol. i. London.

— (1903b) *A social history of ancient Ireland*, vol. ii. London.

— (1906) *A smaller social history of ancient Ireland*. Dublin.

JOYNT, M. (arr.) (1939) *Contributions to a dictionary of the Irish language—M*. Dublin.

KANE, R. (1845) *The industrial resources of Ireland*. Dublin.

KENNEY, J. (1929) *The sources for the early history of Ireland*, vol. i. New York.

KERNEY, M. (1999) *Atlas of the land and freshwater Mollusca of Britain and Ireland*. Colchester.

KNOX, A. (1875) *A history of the County of Down*. Dublin.

KOVÁCS, É. and LOVAG, Z. (1988) *The Hungarian crown and other regalia*. Budapest.

KUNZ, G.F. (1913) (Reprint 1971) *The curious lore of precious stones*. New York.

— (1917) *Rings for the finger*. New York.

KUNZ, G.F. and STEVENSON, C.H. (1908) *The book of the pearl*. London.

LABARGE, M.W. (1982) *Medieval travellers*. London.

LACEY, R. (1973) *Sir Walter Ralegh*. London.

de LAVERGNE, L. (1855) *The rural economy of England, Scotland and Ireland*. London.

de LATOCNAYE (1917) *A Frenchman's walk through Ireland 1796–7*. Belfast.

LAWRENCE-HAMILTON, J. (1902) *Pearl and mother-of-pearl industries*. Brighton.

LESLEY, J. (1578) *De origine moribus et rebus gestis Scotorum*. Rouen.

LHUYD, E. (1707) *Archæologia Britannica*. Oxford.

LINN, R. (1908) *A history of Banbridge*. Banbridge.

LINNAEUS, C. (1811) *Lachesis Lapponica, or a tour in Lapland, now first published from the original manuscript journal of the celebrated Linnaeus.* London.

de LÍON, C. (n.d. *c.* 1968) *The vale of Avoca.* Dublin.

LONGFIELD, A.K. (1929) *Anglo-Irish trade in the sixteenth century.* London.

LOVELL, M.S. (1884) *The edible Mollusca of Great Britain and Ireland.* London.

LOVER, S. (1844) *Treasure trove.* London.

MacAIRT, S. (1951) *The annals of Inisfallen, MS Rawlinson, B.503.* Dublin.

— (ed.) (1977) *The annals of Inisfallen.* Dublin.

MACALISTER, R.A.S. (1925) *The present and future of archaeology in Ireland.* Dublin.

— (1949) *The archæology of Ireland.* London.

MACBAIN, A. (1896) *An etymological dictionary of the Gaelic language.* Inverness.

MacCARTHY, B. (ed.) (1893) *Annala Uladh: annals of Ulster,* vol. ii. Dublin.

MacCARTHY, J. (1996) *The last king: Donal IX MacCarthy Mór King of Desmond and the two Munsters.* Kanturk.

MacGEOGHEGAN, J. (1844) *The history of Ireland.* Dublin.

MACKENZIE, D.A. (1994a) *China and Japan.* London.

— (1994b) *India.* London.

MacLYSAGHT, E. (1939) (Reprint 1979) *Irish life in the seventeenth century.* Dublin.

MacMAHON, T. (ed.) (1846) *The casket of Irish pearls.* Dublin.

MAGNUS, Olaus, (1555) *Historia de gentibus.* Romae.

MAGUIRE, J.F. (1853) *The industrial movement in Ireland, as illustrated by the National Exhibition of 1852.* Cork.

MATHIAS, P. (1969) (Reprint 1983) *The first industrial nation: an economic history of Britain 1700–1914.* London.

MATLINS, A.L. (1996) *The pearl book: the definitive buying guide.* Woodstock.

MAXWELL, W.H. (1832) *Wild sports of the West.* London.

McEVOY, J. (1802) *Statistical survey of the County Tyrone.* Dublin.

McNEIVE, J. (n.d.) *Concise economic history of Ireland.* Dublin.

MEYER, K. (1910a) *Fianaigecht, a collection of hitherto inedited Irish poems and tales relating to Finn and his Fiana.* Dublin.

— (1911) *Selections from ancient Irish poetry.* New York.

MITCHELL, B.R. and DEANE, P. (1962) *Abstract of British historical statistics.* Cambridge.

MÖBIUS, C. (1846) *Die echten Perlen.* Hamburg.

MOMMSEN, T. (1898) *Monumenta Germaniae historia,* vol. iii. Berloni.

MOORE, D. (n.d. *c.* 1980) *Off-beat Ireland.* Dublin.

MOORE, T. (1837) *The history of Ireland,* vol. i. Paris.

— (1846) *The history of Ireland,* vol. iii. Paris.

MORRIS, J. (ed.) (1980) *Nennius: British history and Welsh annals.* London and Chichester.

MORRIS, R. (1869) *Complete works of Edmund Spenser.* London.

MULLIGAN, J.F. (1886) *A ramble through Dromore.* Banbridge.

MURRAY, P.J. (ed.) (1986) *The deer's cry: a treasury of Irish religious verse.* Dublin.

MURRAY, R. (1840) *Outlines of the history of the Catholic Church in Ireland.* London.

NORRIS, H. (1947) *Costume and fashion: the evolution of European dress through the earlier ages.* London.

O'BRIEN, D.M. (1991) *Beara: a journey through history.* Cork.

O'BRIEN, G. (1919) *The economic history of Ireland in the seventeenth century* (Dublin & London,).

— (1923) *Advertisements for Ireland, being a description of Ireland in the reign of James I contained in a manuscript in the library of Trinity College Dublin.* Dublin.

— (Reprint 1977) *The economic history of Ireland in the eighteenth century.* Philadelphia.

O'CONOR, C. (1814) *Rerum Hibernicarum scriptores veteres,* tom. i. Londini.

— (1825) *Rerum Hibernicarum scriptores,* tom. ii. Londini.

— (1826) *Rerum Hibernicarum scriptores,* tom. iv. Londini.

Ó CRÓINÍN, D. (1995) *Early medieval Ireland 400–1200.* London.

Ó CUÍV, B. (ed.) (1952) (Reprint 1977) *Parliament na mban.* Dublin.

O'CURRY, E. (1873) (Reprint 1996) *On the manners and customs of the ancient Irish,* vol. iii. Dublin.

Ó DANACHAIR, C. (1978) *A bibliography of Irish ethnology and folk tradition.* Dublin and Cork.

O'DONOVAN, J. (ed.) (1856a) *Annala rioghactha Eireann: annals of the kingdom of Ireland, by the Four Masters,* vol. i. Dublin.

— (ed.) (1856b) *Annala rioghachta Eireann: annals of the kingdom of Ireland, by the Four Masters,* vol. ii. Dublin.

— (ed.) (1856c) *Annala rioghachta Eireann: annals of the kingdom of Ireland, by the Four Masters,* vol. iii. Dublin.

— (ed.) (1856d) *Annala rioghactha Eireann: annals of the kingdom of Ireland, by the Four Masters,* vol. vi. Dublin.

O'FLAHERTY, R. (1684) (Edited from a manuscript by J. Hardiman 1846) *A chorographical description of west or H-Iar Connaught.* Dublin.

— (1685) *Ogygia: seu, rerum Hibernicarum chronologia.* Londini.

O'FLANAGAN, J.R. (1844) *The Blackwater in Munster.* London.

Ó GRÁDA, C. (1995) *Ireland: a new economic history, 1780–1939.* Oxford.

O'HANLON, J. (1875) *Lives of the Irish saints,* vol. i. Dublin.

O'HANLON, J. and O'LEARY, E. (1907) *History of the Queens County,* vol. i. Dublin.

O'HARA, G. (1986) *The encyclopaedia of fashion.* London.

Ó MÁILLE, T. (ed.) (1916) *Amhráin Chearbhalláin: the poems of Carolan.* London.

O'MEARA, J.J. (ed.) (1951) *The first version of the topography of Ireland by Giraldus Cambrensis.* Dundalk.

O'RAHILLY, T.F. (1946) *Early Irish history and mythology*. Dublin.

OTWAY, C. (1827) *Sketches in Ireland*. London.

PAYNE, J. (1793a) *Universal geography*, vol. i. Dublin.

— (1793b) *Universal geography*, vol. ii. Dublin.

— (1794) *Universal geography*, vol. iii. Dublin.

PENNANT, T. (1812) *British zoology*, vol. iv. London.

PERCIVAL, R. (1803) *An account of the island of Ceylon*. London.

PERRIN, R. (1977) *Jewels*. London.

PICKERING, D. (1995) *The dictionary of superstitions*. London.

PONTOPPIDAN, E. (1754) *Versuch einer natürlichen historie von Norwegen*, tom. ii. Kopenhagen.

PRAEGER, R.L. (1950) *Natural history of Ireland: a sketch of its flora and fauna*. London.

PRESTON, J., ROBERTS, D. and PORTIG, A. (2002) *Culturing freshwater pearl mussel Margaritifera margaritifera in Northern Ireland*. Edinburgh.

REPORT BY THE JURIES (1852) *Exhibition of the works of industry of all nations 1851*. London.

RIBEIRO, A. (1986) *Dress and morality*. London.

An ROINN OIDEACHAIS (1978) *Ainmneacha plandaí agus ainmhithe*. Baile Átha Cliath.

ROTHWELL, W., STONE, L.W. and REID, T.B.W. (eds.) (1992) *Anglo–Norman dictionary*. London.

ROYAL IRISH ACADEMY (1983) *Dictionary of the Irish language*. Dublin.

R.W.A. (1967) *Chambers's encyclopaedia*, vol. x. Oxford.

RYNNE, E. (ed.) (1987) *Figures from the past. Studies on figurative art in Christian Ireland in honour of Helen M. Roe*. Dublin.

SCARISBRICK, D. (1989) *Ancestral jewels*. London.

— (1994) *Jewellery in Britain 1066–1837*. Norwich.

SHIPLEY, A.E. (1908) *Pearls and parasites*. London.

SMITH, C. (1746) *The antient and present state of the County and City of Waterford*. Dublin.

— (1750) *The antient and present state of the County and City of Cork*. Dublin.

— (1756) *The antient and present state of the County of Kerry*. Dublin.

SMITH, S. (1854) *The works of the Rev. Sydney Smith*. London.

SMYTH, J. (1875) *On the industrial uses of the Upper Bann river*. London.

STANDING COMMITTEE OF THE CONVENTION ON THE CONSERVATION OF EUROPEAN WILDLIFE AND NATURAL HABITATS (1992) *Guidelines on the taking of the pearl mussel (Margaritifera margaritifera) and on pearl fishing*. Strasbourg.

STEINBERG, S.H. (1966) *Historical tables 58 BC–AD 1965*. London.

STEVENSON, J. (ed.) (1838) *Nennii Historia Britonum*. Londini.

STOKES, M. (1878) *Christian inscriptions in the Irish language*. Dublin.

STOKES, W. (1868) *The life and labours in art and archaeology of George Petrie,*

*LL.D., M.R.I.A.* London.

STOKES, W. (1890) *Lives of saints from the Book of Lismore.* Oxford.

STREETER, E.W. (1886) *Pearls and pearling life.* London.

SUETONIUS, G.T. (1692) *The lives of the twelve Caesars, the first Emperors of Rome. Now done into English by several hands.* London.

TABURIAUX, J. (1985) *Pearls: their origin, treatment and identification.* Ipswich.

THOMPSON, W. (1856) *The natural history of Ireland,* vol. iv. London.

THOMSON, D. and McGUSTY, E. (eds.) (1980) *The Irish journals of Elizabeth Smith 1840–1850.* Oxford.

TODD, J.H. (1848) *Leabhar Breathnach annso sis: the Irish version of the Historia Britonum of Nennius.* Dublin.

TOLLER, T.N. and CAMBELL, A. (1980) *An Anglo-Saxon dictionary: based on the manuscript collections of Joseph Bosworth.* Oxford.

TOWNSEND, D. (1904) *The life and letters of the great Earl of Cork.* London.

UA DUINNÍN, P. (1902) *Amhráin Eoghain Ruaidh Uí Shúilleabháin.* Baile Átha Cliath.

USSHER, J. (1632) *Veterum epistolarum Hibernicarum sylloge.* Dublinii.

VANCE, P. (1990) *Irish literature: a social history.* Oxford.

WAKEMAN, W.F. (1891) *Handbook of Irish antiquities.* Dublin.

WALSH, L. (1984) *Historic Limerick: the city and its treasures.* Dublin.

WARAEO, J. (1654) *De Hibernia & antiquitatibus ejus disquisitiones.* Londini.

WARD, F. (1995) *Pearls.* Bethesda.

WARE, J. (1705) *The antiquities and history of Ireland.* Dublin.

WATT, J. (1972) *The Church in medieval Ireland.* Dublin.

WEISE, C.H. (ed.) (1874) *C. Cornelii Taciti opera quod extant,* tom. ii. Lipsiae.

WELCH, R. (ed.) (1996) *The Oxford companion to Irish literature.* Oxford.

WELLS, S.M. and CHATFIELD, J.E. (1992) *Threatened non-marine molluscs of Europe.* Strasbourg.

WELLS, S.M., PYLE, R.M. and COLLINS, N.M. (1984) *The IUCN invertebrate red data book.* Gland.

WHATELY, R. (1832) *Introductory lectures on political economy.* London.

WHILDE, T. (1994) *The natural history of Connemara.* London.

WILCOX, R.T. (1970) *The dictionary of costume.* London.

WILDE, Lady (1890) *Ancient cures, charms, and usages of Ireland: contributions to Irish lore.* London.

WILLIAMS, N.L. (1988) *Sir Walter Raleigh.* London.

WINTON, J. (1975) *Sir Walter Ralegh.* London.

WOODWARD, F. (1994) *The Scottish pearl in its world context.* Edinburgh.

WRIGHT, T. (c. 1850) *The history of Ireland,* vol. i. London.

WULFF, W. (ed.) (1929) *Rosa Anglica sev rosa medicinae Johannis Anglici.* London.

## Articles (books, journals and magazines)

ALTABA, C.R. (1990) 'The last known population of the freshwater mussel

*Margaritifera auricularia* (Bivalvia, Unionoida): a conservation priority', *Biological Conservation* **52**, 271–86.

ALVAREZ, R.M. (1998) 'La industria del nácar de *Margaritifera auricularia* en Aragón y la gestión ambiental' *Temas de Antropología Aragonesa* **8**, 113–212.

A.M. (1892) 'Natural history notes: Irish pearls', *Journal of the Cork Historical and Archaeological Society* **1**, 210–11.

ANON. (1811) 'Abstract of foreign occurrences: Germany', *Gentleman's Magazine and Historical Chronicle* **81**, 373.

— (1834) 'Hardiman's Irish minstrelsy.—No. iv.' *Dublin University Magazine* **4**, 514–41.

— (1838) 'Report of the Committee of Antiquities, relative to an ancient tomb discovered in the Phoenix Park', *Proceedings of the Royal Irish Academy* **1**, 186–90.

— (1894) 'The pearl fishery in the north of Ireland', *Science Gossip*, December, 138.

— (1967/68) 'Donations to and purchases for the museum, 1967–68: No. 92–3: samples of Scottish river pearls by Mrs Q.E. Fraser-Mackenzie, Muir of Ord, Ross-shire; Mrs G. Gascoigne, Evanton, Ross-shire', *Proceedings of the Society of Antiquaries of Scotland* **100**, 201–05.

— (1971) 'Ulster pearls', *Ulster Annual*, 64–65.

— (1984) 'The sligger man', *Grassroots*, Oct/Nov, 12–13.

BARKER, J. (1862–65) 'Notes on some dissections of the fresh-water mussel (*Unio margaritifera*)', *Proceedings of the Natural History Society of Dublin* **4**, 111–14.

BAUER, G. (1986) 'The status of the freshwater pearl mussel *Margaritifera margaritifera* L. in the south of its European range', *Biological Conservation* **38**, 1–9.

— (1988) 'Threats to the freshwater pearl mussel *Margaritifera margaritifera* L. in central Europe', *Biological Conservation* **45**, 239–53.

— (1992) 'Variation in the life span and size of the freshwater pearl mussel', *Journal of Animal Ecology* **61**, 425–36.

BRASH, R.R. (1871) 'The precious metals and ancient mining in Ireland', *Journal of the Royal Historical and Archæological Association of Ireland* **1**, 509–34.

BROSNAN, M. (1985/86) 'Fishing for pearl in the King's River', *Journal of the West Wicklow Historical Society* **11**, 47.

BUCKLAND, F.T. (1864) 'A run through Connemara and Galway', *The Field* **24**, 10.

CHESNEY, H.C.G. (1996) 'Irish pearl mussels: going, going, gone?', in J.D. Reynolds (ed.), *The conservation of aquatic systems*, 142–50. Dublin.

CHESNEY, H.C.G., OLIVER, P.G. and DAVIS, G.M. (1993) '*Margaritifera durrovensis* Phillips, 1928: taxonomic status, ecology and conservation', *Journal of Conchology* **34**, 267–99.

CLARKE, A. (1989) 'The colonisation of Ulster and the rebellion of 1641

(1603–60)', in T. W. Moody and F. X. Martin (eds.), *The course of Irish history*, 189–203. Cork.

COLE, G.A.J. (1902) 'Irish minerals and building stones', in W.P. Coyne (ed.), *Ireland: industrial and agricultural*, 17–27. Dublin.

COLGAN, N. (1914) 'Field notes on the folk-lore of Irish plants and animals', *Irish Naturalist* 23, 53–64.

CRANBROOK, Earl of (1976) 'The commercial exploitation of the freshwater pearl mussel, *Margaritifera margaritifera* L. (Bivalvia: Margaritiferidae) in Great Britain', *Journal of Conchology* 29, 87–91.

CRAWFORD, W.H. (1975) 'Landlord–tenant relations in Ulster 1609–1820', *Irish Economic and Social History* 2, 5–21.

CURLE, J. (1931/32) 'An inventory of objects of Roman and provincial Roman origin found on sites in Scotland not definitely associated with Roman constructions', *Proceedings of the Society of Antiquaries of Scotland* 66, 277–397.

D.C. (1830) 'Some account of the British pearl fishery now existing on the Conway', *Lauden's Magazine of Natural History* 3, 132–34.

DALTON, J. (1828) 'Essay on the ancient history, religion, learning, arts, and government of Ireland', *Transactions of the Royal Irish Academy* 16, 3–379.

DAVIES, A.C. (1975) 'The first Irish industrial exhibition', *Irish Economic and Social History* 2, 46–59.

DEANE, C.D. (1965) 'Pearls from Ulster rivers were highly thought of in days gone by', *Ulster Commentary*, November, 6–7.

DICKENS, C. (1869) 'Scotch pearls', *All the Year Round*, January, 125–27.

DINELEY, T. (1862) 'Extracts from the Journal of Thomas Dineley giving some account of his visit to Ireland in the reign of Charles II' *Journal of the Kilkenny and South-East Ireland Archaeological Society* 4, 38–52.

DIXON, J. (1865) 'Observations: *Unio margaritiferus*', *Naturalist* 1, 81–82.

de DODD, M.J. (1945) 'The manor and fishery of Killorglin Co. Kerry', *Journal of the Galway Archaeological and Historical Society* 21, 140–73.

FERNANDES, F.C. and SEED, R. (1983) 'The incidence of pearls in populations of the blue mussel, *Mytilus edulis* L., from North Wales', *Journal of Molluscan studies* 49, 107–15.

FISHER, N. (1927) 'British pearls', *Irish Naturalists' Journal* 1, 233.

GARNER, R. (1873) 'On the formation of British pearls and their possible improvement', *Journal of the Linnean Society (Zoology)* 11, 426–28.

GASPAR, G., LAURENT, G. and de BAST, B. (1990) 'La situation, en Belgique, des populations d'invertebres de la Convention de Berne', in *Colloquy on the Berne Convention Invertebrates and Their Conservation*, 20–24. Strasbourg.

GILLMAN, W.H. (1859) 'On the time during which pearl divers remain under water', *Journal of the Royal Dublin Society* 2, 288–90.

GRAVES, J. (1869) 'Proceedings: treasure trove at Waterford', *Journal of the*

*Historical and Archaeological Association of Ireland* **1**, 241–43.

GREEN, M. (1985/86), 'Humphalflatrin, Gabber and Black Rig: the history of Scotland's freshwater pearls', *British Heritage* December/January, 28–35.

HART, H.C. (1884) 'Plants of some of the mountain ranges of Ireland', *Proceedings of the Royal Irish Academy* **4**, 211–51.

HAYMAN, S. (1856–57) 'The ecclesiastical antiquities of Youghal—No. III', *Journal of the Kilkenny and South-East Ireland Archaeological Society* **1**, 14–28.

HENDELBERG, J. (1960) 'The fresh-water pearl mussel, *Margaritifera margaritifera* (L.)', *Report of the Institute of Freshwater Research Drottingholm* **41**, 149–71.

HITCHCOCK, R. (1914) 'Dingle in the sixteenth century', *Kerry Archaeological Magazine* **2**, 203–11.

HOARE, H.F. (ed.) (1862) 'Particulars relative to Wexford and the Barony of Forth by Solomon Richards (1682)', *Journal of the Kilkenny and South-East Ireland Archaeological Society* **4**, 84–92.

HRUSKA, J. (1992) 'The freshwater pearl mussel in South Bohemia: evaluation of the effect of temperature on reproduction, growth and age structure of the population', *Archiv für Hydrobiologie* **126**, 181–91.

JACKSON, J. (1991) 'The geology and raw materials of the Bronze Age', in M. Ryan (ed.), *The illustrated archaeology of Ireland*, 73–75. Dublin.

JACKSON, J.W. (1913) 'On the presence of shell-fragments in prehistoric pottery', *Lancashire Naturalist* December, 321–22.

— (1925) 'The distribution of *Margaritana margaritifera* in the British Isles', *Journal of Conchology* **17**, 195–211.

KENNEDY, L. (1987) 'The rural economy, 1820–1914', in L. Kennedy and P. Ollerenshaw (eds.), *An economic history of Ulster, 1820–1940*, 62–108. Manchester.

KINAHAN, G.A. (1883) 'On the mode of occurrence and winning of gold in Ireland', *Scientific Proceedings of the Royal Dublin Society* **3**, 263–85.

KOBA, K. (1933) 'Habitat notes on the freshwater pearl-mussel, *Margaritana margaritifera* (Linné) in Hokkaidô', *Scientific Reports Tokyo Bunrika Daigaku* **1B**, 175–80.

KOCH, L. (1989) 'Pearls at what price', *Missouri Conservationist* **50**, 25–28.

LINN, R. (1910) 'Historical notes, parish of Seapatrick, Co. Down', *Journal of the Royal Society of Antiquaries of Ireland* **20**, 316–23.

LUCAS, A.T. (1969) 'Sea sand and shells as manure', in G. Jenkins (ed.), *Studies in folk life* 183–203. London.

LUCEY, J. (1993) 'The distribution of *Margaritifera margaritifera* (L.) in southern Irish rivers and streams', *Journal of conchology* **34**, 301–10.

— (1995) 'The distribution of *Anodonta cygnea* (L.) and *Anodonta anatina* (L.) (Mollusca: Bivalvia) in southern Irish rivers and streams with records from other areas', *Irish Naturalists' Journal* **25**, 1–8.

— (1998) 'Freshwater mussels eaten in Ireland', *Conchologists' Newsletter* **146**,

54–55.

— (2000) 'Mussel shells used as spoons in Ireland', *Ulster Folklife* **46**, 76–79.

MARKHAM, C.R. (1867) 'The Tinnevelly pearl fishery', *Journal of the Society of Arts* **15** March, 256–62.

MAYO (1899–1902) 'Furness, or Forenaghts Great', *Journal of the Kildare Archaeological Society* **3**, 57–60.

McCREA, D.F. (1973a) 'Pearl fishing in Ulster' *Ulster Tatler*, October, 10.

— (1973b) 'A hundred "good" pearls from the rivers of Ulster', *Ulster Commentary* **329** December, 13.

MEAGHER, C.H. (1928) 'Pearl fishing in Ireland: a vanished industry', *Ireland's Own* **51**, 385.

MEYER, K. (1910b) 'The Irish mirabilia in the Norse *Speculum regale*', *Ériu* **4**, 1–16.

MORIARTY, C. (1994) 'The pearl mussel', *Technology Ireland* **26**, 18–20.

MITCHELL, G.F. (1989) 'Prehistoric Ireland', in T.W. Moody and F.X. Martin (eds.), *The course of Irish history*, 30–42. Cork.

MURRAY, J. (1830) 'Pearls in the Conway', *Loudan's Magazine of Natural History* **3**, 451–52.

O'BEIRNE CROWE, J. (1870) 'Siabur-charpat con Culaind. From "Lebor na huidre" (fol. 37, *et seqq.*), a manuscript of the Royal Irish Academy', *Journal of the Historical and Archaeological Association of Ireland* **1**, 371–448.

OTHICK, J. (1987) 'The economic history of Ulster: a perspective', in L. Kennedy and P. Ollerenshaw (eds.) *An economic history of Ulster, 1820–1940*, 224–40. Manchester.

QUINN, O. (1939) 'Pearls in our rivers', *Irish Digest* **4**, 37–38.

PETRIE, G. (1838) 'An account of an ancient Irish reliquary, called the *Domnach-airgid*', *Transactions of the Royal Irish Academy* **18**, 14–24.

PREECE, R.C. (1988) 'A second interglacial record of *Margaritifera auricularia*', *Journal of Conchology* **33**, 50–51.

PRENDERGAST, F.J. (ed.) (1900) 'Ancient history of the kingdom of Kerry by Friar O'Sullivan, of Muckross Abbey', *Journal of the Cork Historical and Archaeological Society* **6**, 146–56.

RAUT, S.K. and BISWAS, A. (1989) 'Pearls in freshwater mussels *Lamellidens marginalis* in India', *Basteria* **53**, 105–09.

REDDING, R. (1693) 'A letter concerning pearl fishing in the north of Ireland, communicated by Dr. Lister', *Philosophical Transactions of the Royal Society* **18**, 659–64.

REEVES, T.J. (1971) 'Gold in Ireland', *Geological Survey of Ireland Bulletin* **2**, 73–85.

ROSS, H. (1992) 'The reproductive biology of the freshwater pearl mussel *Margaritifera margaritifera* (L.) in Co Donegal', *Irish Naturalists' Journal* **24**, 43–50.

R. W[elch] (1908) 'Lagan pearls', in R. Patterson (ed.), *Ulster nature notes*, 90.

Belfast.

R.Y. (1833) 'Donegal Steatite' *Dublin Penny Journal* 1, 388–89.

SANDIUS, C. (1674) 'Extract of two letters, written to the publisher from Hamborough by the learned Christophorus Sandius, concerning the origin of pearls', *Philosophical Transactions of the Royal Society* 7, 11.

SCHARFF, R.F. (1916) 'On the Irish names of invertebrate animals', *Irish Naturalist* 25, 140–52.

SHERIDAN, C. (1996) 'Mining our own business', *Technology Ireland* 27, 38–42.

SHIRLEY, E.P. (ed.) (1860) 'Extracts from the journal of Thomas Dineley, Esquire, giving some account of his visit to Ireland in the reign of Charles II'. *Journal of the South-East of Ireland Archaeological Society* 1, 143–46.

SIMMS, J.G. (1989) 'The Restoration and the Jacobite war', in T.W. Moody and F.X. Martin (eds.), *The course of Irish history*, 204–16. Cork.

STELFOX, A.W. (1911) 'A list of the land and freshwater mollusks of Ireland', *Proceedings of the Royal Irish Academy* 29B, 65–165.

STOKES, W. (1892) 'The Bodleian Dinnshenchas', *Folk-lore* 3, 467–516.

SYNNOTT, N. (1899–1902) 'Irish pearls', *Journal of the Kildare Archaeological Society* 3, 192–93.

TAYLOR, J.W. (1928) '*Margaritana margaritana* in County Clare', *Irish Naturalists' Journal* 2, 36.

TEAHAN, J. (1990) 'Silver and other metalwork', in J. Teahan (ed.), *Irish decorative arts 1550–1928*, 1-24. Dublin.

VALOVIRTA, I. (1990) 'Conservation of *Margaritifera margaritifera* in Finland', in *Colloquy on the Berne Convention invertebrates and their conservation*, 59–63. Strasbourg.

WÄCHTLER, K. (1986) 'Zur biologie der flussperlmuschel *Margaritifera margaritifera* (L.)', *Naturwissenchaften* 73, 225–33.

WARD, F. (1985) 'The Pearl', *National Geographic Magazine* 168, 192–223.

WATKINS, M.G. (1896) 'Scotch pearls and pearl hunting', *Gentleman's Magazine* 280, 626–29.

WATSON, D.A. (1982) 'Demand', in D. Greenwald (ed.), *Encyclopedia of economics*, 231–34. New York.

WEATHERUP, D.R.M. (1974) 'Pearl in fresh water mussel (*Margaritifera margaritifera*)', *Irish Naturalists' Journal* 18, 54.

WEIR, T. (1985) 'The Alyth pearl fisher', *Scots Magazine* 123, 292–97.

WENT, A.E.J. (1947) 'Notes on Irish pearls', *Irish Naturalists' Journal* 9, 41-45.

YOUNG, M.R. (1984) 'Scottish freshwater pearl fishing—a dying tradition', *Scottish Field Studies*, 25–32.

YOUNG, M. and WILLIAMS, J. (1983) 'The status and conservation of the freshwater pearl mussel *Margaritifera margaritifera* Linn. in Great Britain', *Biological Conservation* 25, 35–52.

## Articles (newspapers)

A.N.N. (1960) 'When Omagh's pearls were profitable', *News Letter*, 17 March, 3.

ANON. (1851a) 'Great Exhibition', *Tyrone Constitution*, 16 May, 1.

— (1851b) 'List of the Irish Exhibitors', *Daily Express (Dublin)*, 3 May, 4.

— (1863) 'The Scotch pearl fishery', *The Times*, 24 December, 11.

— (1892) 'Blackwater pearls', *Cork Constitution*, 23 October, 3.

— (1908) 'Pearl fishing in Ulster', *Daily Mail*, 28 July, 5.

— (1926) 'A glut of diamonds', *Irish Times*, 6 December, 6.

— (1928) 'Fresh water pearl find in a French river: purple hue tinged with gold', *Daily Mail*, 26 March, 4.

— (1965a) 'Ulster's pearls in new Hamlet', *News Letter*, 11 March, 3.

— (1965b) 'Go pearl fishing at Easter in Tyrone', *News Letter*, 17 April, 1.

CAMLIN, E.G. (1959) 'Necklace of Ulster-grown pearls', *Belfast Telegraph*, 3 September, 10.

LEAKE, J. (1996) 'Huge gold deposits found in Britain', *Sunday Times*, 11 August, 6.

LOUDAN, J. (1943) 'Because of the war Ulster's pearl fishers are busy again', *Belfast Telegraph*, 21 April, 2.

MacCONNELL, C. (1987) 'Pearl hunters plundering river riches', *Sunday Press*, 7 March, 4.

MORIARTY, G. (1995) 'Omagh Minerals given permission for a gold and silver mine', *Irish Times*, 27 May, 16.

MULLIN, T.E. (1947) 'Pearl fishing in Tyrone rivers', *Ulster Herald*, 13 September, 5, 8.

NEALE, G. (1991) 'Pearl fishing at risk as amateurs muscle in', *Sunday Telegraph*, 6 January (CD-ROM copy).

OSCAR II, (1977) 'The art of the "sligger men" is not lost in Omagh', *Ulster Herald*, 29 October, 5.

PILKINGTON, E. (1991) 'The lament of the last pearl fisher', *Guardian*, 30 March, 26.

QUIDNUNC, (1931) 'Irish pearls', *Irish Times*, 25 March, 4.

ROBB, C.J. (1939) 'Fishing for pearls in the Bann and Strule', *Irish News and Belfast Morning News*, 12 May, 6.

VINEY, M. (1995) 'Pearls before swine', *Irish Times (weekend)*, 30 December, 15.

## Manuscripts

*Belfast: Ulster Museum*

HYNDMAN, G.C. (1843–57) *Papers of G.C. Hyndman, Belfast conchologist, containing notes on oysters, pearls, conchology, lists of shells from Belfast Lough, Carlingford, Groomsport, Kish Bank, Co. Dublin, Larne, etc. dredging notes.* Hyndman MSS.

*Dublin: National Library*

DINGLEY, T. (1675–80) *Observations in a voyage through the Kingdom of Ireland.*

MS 392 (Microfilm: Pos. 7515).

MILNE, J.N. (1907) *A letter from James N. Milne (probably to G.F. Kunz of New York) describing pearl fishing on the Mourne and Strule river, Co. Tyrone.* MS 18233.

O'SULLIVAN BEARE, P. (*c.* 1630) *Vindicae Hiberniae or zoilomastix.* MS 2759 (Photostat of original at the Library of the University of Upsala, Coll. Sparwenfeldt)

WILLES, E. (1759–60 [62]) *Letters on Ireland from Lord Chief Baron Willes to the Earl of Warwick, Letters on Ireland.* MS 806.

### Dublin: Trinity College

ANON. (n.d.) *Advertisements for Ireland, relating to $y^e$ trade, manufactures and state of Ireland in $y^e$ reign of K. James $1^{st}$.* MS 842.

— (1683b) *Common place book of papers relating to the natural history of Ireland: a short description of ye County of Donnegall.* MS 883/1.

REDDING, R. (1688) *Sir Robert Redding's letter to Dr Lister concerning pearls found in the North of Ireland with some further queries relating to the same.* MS 888/2.

### Dublin: University College

MacDOMHAILL, P. (1937) *Pearl fishing in the Doirín once a lucrative occupation.* Department of Irish folklore, Main MSS collection 407.

### London: British Library

COPPING, J. (1740) *A letter concerning muscles that have pearls in them in a river near Coleraine.* Add. MS 4436.

COTTON, R. (n.d.) *Copy of letter from Gillebert of Limerick to Anselm Archbishop of Canterbury,* Cotton MS Claudius A. xi.

DUBLIN PHILOSOPHICAL SOCIETY, (1683–87) *Minutes and register of the Philosophical Society in Dublin, from 1683, to 1687, with copies of the papers read before them,* Add. MS 4811.

MICHAEL OF KILDARE, Friar, (n.d.) *The land of Cockaygne.* Harley MS 913.

NENNIUS (AD 831) *Historia Britonum.* Harley MS 3859.

## Unpublished theses

GEORGIOU, M. (1992) Beitraege zur oekologie der flussperlmuschel, *Margaritifera margaritifera* (Bivalvia: Margaritiferidae) im oberen waldviertel, Niederoesterreich. D.Phil. thesis, Universitaet Wien.

KROPF-GOMEZ, D.M. (1993) The potential of the freshwater clam (*Corbicula fluminea*) for the artificial production of pearls with special emphasis on techniques of pearl seed implantation. M.S. thesis, University of Texas at Arlington.

LUCEY, J. (1997) A history of pearls in Ireland. M.Phil. thesis, The Queen's University of Belfast.

MACKIE, T.G. (1992) The distribution and current status of *Margaritifera margaritifera* in the north of Ireland. M.Sc. thesis, The Queen's University of

Belfast.

MOORKENS, E.A. (1996) Studies on the biology and ecology of *Margaritifera* in Ireland. Ph.D thesis, University of Dublin.

PIKE, B. (1976) Gilbert of Limerick and the reform of the Church. M.Phil. thesis, University College Dublin.

ROSS, H.C.G. (1988) Aspects of the ecology of the freshwater pearl mussel *Margaritifera margaritifera* (L.) in NW Ireland. M.Sc. thesis, The Queen's University of Belfast.


## State papers

BURKE, B. (ed.) (1882) *British Departmental Correspondence 1683–1714*, vol. i. Dublin.

HAMILTON, H.C. (ed.) (1867) *Calender of the state papers relating to Ireland, of the reign of Elizabeth 1574–1585*. London.

— (ed.) (1885) *Calender of the state papers relating to Ireland, of the reign of Elizabeth, 1588, August–1592, September*. London.

HARDY, W.J. (ed.) (1903) *Calender of state papers, domestic series, of the reign of William and Mary, 1693. Preserved in the Public Record Office*. London.

MORRIN, J. (ed.) (1863) *Calender of the patent and close rolls of chancery in Ireland, of the reign of Charles the First*. London.

STATE PAPERS (Domestic Series) (1693) Public Record Office London, Petition Book 2, 9 October, 40. SP44/237.

SWEETMAN, H.S. (ed.) (1881) *Calendar of documents, relating to Ireland, 1293–1301*. Dublin.

# Index